Humor and the Eccentric Text in Puerto Rican Literature

New Directions in Puerto Rican Studies

Florida A&M University, Tallahassee
Florida Atlantic University, Boca Raton
Florida Gulf Coast University, Ft. Myers
Florida International University, Miami
Florida State University, Tallahassee
University of Central Florida, Orlando
University of Florida, Gainesville
University of North Florida, Jacksonville
University of South Florida, Tampa
University of West Florida, Pensacola

New Directions in Puerto Rican Studies
Edited by Félix V. Matos Rodríguez

This series focuses on the diasporic experience in the United States and on the economic, political, cultural, and social aspects of life on the island of Puerto Rico. Of particular interest are manuscripts about the interplay between Puerto Rican and Latin identities; racial identity and racism; art history; nationalism and identity; migration and transnationalism; politics in the United States; the militarization of Puerto Rico; sexuality and gender; culture studies; and environmental issues.

Vieques, the Navy, and Puerto Rican Politics, by Amílcar Antonio Barreto (2002)
The Phenomenon of Puerto Rican Voting, by Luis Raúl Cámara Fuertes (2004)
Race and Labor in the Hispanic Caribbean: The West Indian Immigrant Worker Experience in Puerto Rico, 1800–1850, by Jorge Luis Chinea (2005)
Humor and the Eccentric Text in Puerto Rican Literature, by Israel Reyes (2005)

Humor and the Eccentric Text in Puerto Rican Literature

Israel Reyes

University Press of Florida
Gainesville/Tallahassee/Tampa/Boca Raton
Pensacola/Orlando/Miami/Jacksonville/Ft. Myers

Copyright 2005 by Israel Reyes
Printed in the United States of America on recycled, acid-free paper
All rights reserved

10 09 08 07 06 05   6 5 4 3 2 1

A record of cataloging-in-publication information is available from the Library
of Congress.
ISBN 0-8130-2820-5

The University Press of Florida is the scholarly publishing agency for the State
University System of Florida, comprising Florida A&M University, Florida Atlantic
University, Florida Gulf Coast University, Florida International University, Florida State
University, University of Central Florida, University of Florida, University of North
Florida, University of South Florida, and University of West Florida.

University Press of Florida
15 Northwest 15th Street
Gainesville, FL 32611-2079
http://www.upf.com

To my eccentric Puerto Rican family

Contents

Foreword

Although it may seem like a simple task, writing the forewords for a series such as New Directions in Puerto Rican Studies is not always easy. The task is even more complicated when one is writing about a book in a field distant from one's own academic area of expertise. *Humor and the Eccentric Text in Puerto Rican Literature* by Israel Reyes adds another challenge: readers might expect the foreword to be funny!

After reading *Humor and the Eccentric Text in Puerto Rican Literature*, I was struck by how little has been written in Puerto Rico regarding humor. Apart from a few essays and monographs in the field of literary criticism and some social science classics on concepts such as *respeto* and *relajo*, humor has not attracted the kind of attention one would suspect in a culture that places such a high value on laughter and joking. The lack of research on humor is particularly puzzling in the field of literature, given the role that humor, parody, and satire play among contemporary Puerto Rican writers.

Humor and the Eccentric Text in Puerto Rican Literature looks at the works of Nemesio Canales, Luis Rafael Sánchez, Ana Lydia Vega, and Pedro Pietri to explore the ways in which Puerto Rican writers use humor to parody literary canons and social conventions. For Reyes, the humor found in the works of these four authors invokes solidarity with marginalized subjects in order to criticize social practices and representations. Humor is also a tool to deconstruct the solemn narratives of the nation and to destabilize the self-centered discussions on Puerto Rico's national identity.

One of the most attractive features of Reyes's book is its inclusion of both island and mainland Puerto Rican authors in its analysis. Literary critics tend to segregate Puerto Rican literature by geographic location, usually analyzing authors from Puerto Rico and those born/raised in the United States separately. Reyes includes the recently deceased playwright and poet Pedro Pietri among his subjects. Pietri exemplifies the Nuyorican literary culture of the 1960s and 1970s with its reliance on street language, code switching, and performance. Pietri's writing embraces the "eccentric" with its emphasis on what Reyes calls "a performance of absence" and its exploration of the key dilemmas of the Puerto Rican diaspora's process of identity formation.

Readers, particularly those familiar with Puerto Rican literary analysis, will find novel insights into the works of Ana Lydia Vega and Luis Rafael Sánchez in *Humor and the Eccentric Text in Puerto Rican Literature*. I found refreshing the inclusion in this book of Nemesio Canales, a writer generally forgotten in the Puerto Rican literary canon. Reyes highlights the often neglected fact that Canales had attended law school in the United States and thus had a connection with the Puerto Rican migratory experience to New York and the Northeast. Canales is an interesting figure, given the combination of his work in journalism, his participation in electoral politics as a socialist (elected to the local state legislature in 1908), and his support for feminist causes such as women's suffrage.

Finally, it remains to be seen whether fellow critics will accept Reyes's theoretical paradigm of "the eccentric" as a legitimate one from which to approach Puerto Rican literature. One wonders too if other scholars will begin to explore the use of humor in contemporary Puerto Rican society in a more systematic way. Reyes certainly makes a good case for both in this book. As ironic as it may seem, *Humor and the Eccentric Text in Puerto Rican Literature* is one book that must be taken seriously.

Félix V. Matos Rodríguez
Series Editor

Preface

Puerto Rican literature, while not as well known in the United States as the literatures of other Latin American nations, has a long and rich history and includes many outstanding texts. Yet this particular study of Puerto Rican literary humor will not attempt to catalogue that textual history, nor will it take a historical or genealogical approach to the texts that it does study. Although establishing historical context is an important part of any literary criticism, I intend to focus more acutely on the textual structures that function to elicit laughter from the reader. The texts by Nemesio Canales, Luis Rafael Sánchez, Ana Lydia Vega, and Pedro Pietri that I will discuss negotiate laughter with the reader, which does not mean that a reader will always find these texts funny. However, rather than proceed under a rubric of reader-response theory, I look to the texts themselves to see how they make use of all the protean forms of the comic and humor. Theories of the comic come from many cultural traditions and intellectual disciplines, and this theoretical diversity will help me to shed light on the many textualities of humor. In addition, an ever growing body of critical work on Puerto Rican literature and culture has given me the tools with which to contextualize my readings and analyses.

The writers whose texts I will discuss are by no means the only Puerto Rican writers who use humor in their literary works. The four writers I study do share a textual strategy that is not commonly found: their texts reflect on and critique their own textuality. This self-reflexivity constitutes a large part of their use of humor, which is, itself, a self-reflexive form of the comic. Yet humor is not the only comic form that these four writers use, and they often combine their humor with satire, irony, *guachafita*, *jaibería*, and the absurd. Because of this textual diversity, my own critical approaches must be equally diverse. I have looked to philosophy, psychoanalysis, literary criticism, and cultural studies in my attempt not only to understand the workings of humor but also to discern how these writers make use of humor as a literary intervention in the discourse on Puerto Rican national identity. In many ways, my critical approach attempts to accomplish what Michel de Certeau suggests in *The Practice of Everyday Life*: "an art of diversion, which is a return of the ethical, of pleasure and of invention within the scientific institution" (28). De Certeau focuses on cultural practitioners (we all practice our cultures) and their ways of "making do" within social and institutional constraints. Subjects who live as migrants in other cultures must often create for themselves "a space in which [they] can find *ways of using* the constraining order of the place or of the language" (30). Not only does de Certeau's notion of "making do" resonate with the quintessentially Puerto Rican *arte de bregar* (Díaz Quiñones 2000a), as I intend to show, but his call for a diversionary tactic in criticism sits well with my own resistance to limiting my reading to a single, all-encompassing theory. After all, "making do" with incongruity lies at the heart of humor and Puerto Rican national identity.

I would like to acknowledge those whose help has been invaluable to me in the writing of this book. First, my most heartfelt thanks go to my parents, Anastacio and Margarita, to my sisters, Lucy, María, and Haydee, and to my brother, Michael. The love and respect we share are without measure. I would also like to thank Adriana Méndez-Rodenas, my graduate advisor, and Diana Vélez, who served on my dissertation committee, for their guidance and faith in my early work. Much of the research on Nemesio Canales was completed with a grant from the Caribbean Resource Center at the Universidad de Puerto Rico, Río Piedras. My thanks go to director Emilio Pantojas-García and the Center's helpful staff. I am also indebted to Beatriz Pastor, Marsha Swislocki, Raúl Bueno-Chávez, Agnes Lugo Ortiz, and Silvia Spitta for their unwavering support as colleagues. My friend George Payán has shared with me his humor for as long as I can remember, so he deserves a mention here. Finally, my deepest gratitude goes to my partner, Kevin Spaulding, whose love and patience have helped me in ways I cannot enumerate.

Note on Translations and References

For ease of reading, I have placed the longer Spanish-language citations in the endnotes and have provided English translations in the body of the text. In cases of short citations, wordplays, puns, colloquialisms, or neologisms, I include both the Spanish original and the English translation in the body of the text. Most translations are my own, but when I use published translations I include the translator's name in the parenthetical reference in the body of the text; the original Spanish text and corresponding page numbers appear in the endnotes. For texts in languages other than Spanish, I rely solely on published English translations.

Introduction

When considering some of the recent critical bibliography on Puerto Rico and Puerto Rican literature, an incongruous pattern begins to emerge: Puerto Rico's national identity resides on a divided border (Flores 1993). Puerto Rico is a commuter nation (Torre et al. 1994), a nation on the move (Duany 2002). Puerto Ricans struggle to write their broken memory (Díaz Quiñones 1993) and read from the fragments of their history (García Calderón 1998). Puerto Rican literature is written in Spanish, English, and a Spanglish "disparatero" (Aparicio 1988), yet this literary diversity is part of a whole (Barradas 1998). Recent Puerto Rican writers have confronted the traditions of literary paternalism (Gelpí 1993) and continue to *virar el macho* (Cruz-Malavé 1993) by subverting the authoritarian discourses of cultural and hetero-normative legitimacy. These oppositional discourses sometimes move laterally as in a *jaibería* (García Passalacqua 1993), and Puerto Ricans have learned the *arte de bregar* (Díaz Quiñones 2000a) as a strategy for confronting and challenging colonialism. Yet in spite of the seriousness of national identity and Puerto Rico's commonwealth status, the Puerto Rican subject belongs to a comic "race" (Ríos Avila 2002), whose only identifiable feature is incongruity.

Puerto Rican writers have used the comic and humor in literature to engage, expose, and often subvert the many incongruities in Puerto Rico's national identity, its history as a colony of both Spain and the United States, and its continued commonwealth status under present-day conditions of globalization. Puerto Rican literary humor confronts the incompatibility between an Afro-Hispanic national identity and the Anglo-American presence on the island. Humor's textual and linguistic resources can negotiate the incongruity of how one Puerto Rican may speak Spanish inflected with English while another may speak English inflected with Spanish, and yet the two can understand each other. Humor in Puerto Rican literature simultaneously delineates and blurs the border between

Puerto Ricans *de acá* (from here) and *de allá* (from over there). Puerto Rican writers can elicit humorous pleasure from the multiple contradictions of national identity not as a means to trivialize, but as a means to overcome incongruity's pathos. The comic and humor do not turn a blind eye to Puerto Rico's political situation but can look at it from another side and offer a new clarity. The daily struggles of millions of Puerto Ricans who face economic exploitation, racism, political disenfranchisement, and social marginalization are no laughing matter. Yet Puerto Rican literary humor confronts many of those struggles by reaffirming an incongruous national identity through the power of laughter.

Not all laughter is the same. A joke invites you to laugh at someone else's expense; satire solicits your laughter in order to expose and condemn social ills; and parody draws out your laughter as it exposes the mechanisms of a shared cultural history. Yet when you laugh at your own circumstances and overcome pathos, that laughter is the triumph of humor. This humor is not an aggression against another, it is a destabilization of the subject, who becomes its own object of laughter. Humor has long been a way for the marginalized and the oppressed to withstand abuses of authority and the machinations of power, regardless of country of origin, class, race, gender, or sexuality. The writers whose work I will discuss in the following chapters adopt humor as a means of scrutinizing the incongruities in Puerto Rican national identity. As Enid Pagán González argues in "El humor y la sátira: Segunda mitad del siglo XX," Puerto Rican writers have been constrained to put national identity at the forefront of their literary discourse (221). Writers who use humor in these efforts have been able to elicit laughter in the face of the adversities of Puerto Rico's colonial situation and the diaspora, but they have also been able to draw attention to the very literary discourse with which they elicit that laughter. Humor is not incompatible with other, more aggressive species of the comic such as satire, caricature, parody, irony, or the absurd. Yet humor goes beyond ridicule, exaggeration, mimicry, negation, or nonsense and seeks an affirmation from those who laugh at life's cruelties. Humor allows these writers to suggest that national identity survives in spite of, and perhaps because of, the many incongruities of the Puerto Rican experience.

The Tragic and the Comic, the Insular and the Eccentric

In the serious business of nation building, many Latin American foundational fictions established a national identity in tragedy rather than comedy. Doris Sommer, in *Foundational Fictions: The National Romances of Latin America*, argues that novels like *María*, by Jorge Isaacs of Colombia, *Sab*, by Cuba's Gertrudis Gómez de Avellaneda, and *Amalia*, by the Argentinian José Mármol, imitated and improved on European sentimental tragedies, combining eroticism with patriotism so that tragic loss "open[ed] a space" for looking toward the future (46–47). Unlike its Latin American sister nations, Puerto Rico did not engage in a successful war of independence from Spain, and the printing press, which arrived on the island as late as 1806, was a strictly controlled tool of the Spanish colonial government (Rivera de Alvarez 1955, 25–27).[1] Early Puerto Rican literature differed from other national canons in that it lacked the tragic antecedents that usually appear before great works of comedy. This was due to the censorship that diverted attention away from serious issues and focused on trivial matters that posed no threat to colonial authority (Pagán González 1994, 221). These early writings helped to establish the national literature based on rural folk traditions of the comic. For example, Manuel A. Alonso's *El jíbaro* (1849) combined comic sketches, *leyendas*, editorial commentary, and humorous verse in a light style known as *festivo-satírico*. Alonso's *costumbrismo* used the comic in order to correct social customs through pleasure—"corregir las costumbres deleitando" (3). However, Alonso's *costumbrismo* does not use tragic loss to look toward the future in the way other Latin American foundational texts did. Instead, his use of the comic serves as a means to preserve *criollo* cultural traditions.

Nevertheless, the tragic mode has been a central component in the development of a Puerto Rican literary canon as well as in the literary discourse on national identity. Tragedy appeared in Eugenio María de Hostos's romantic novel *La peregrinación de Bayoán* (1863), in which Bayoán, Marién, and Guarionex represent allegorically Puerto Rico, Cuba, and Santo Domingo (Dominican Republic). Alejandro Tapia y Rivera also developed tragic melodrama in his antislavery play *La cuarterona* (1867), yet this work is set in Cuba, thus addressing the issue of slavery in Puerto Rico indirectly. Toward the turn of the century, Manuel Zeno Gandía cultivated and adapted the naturalist novel to depict Puerto Rico as a "sick" and stagnant society. Zeno Gandía's *La charca* (1894) employed the tragic mode to portray the waning cultural influence of coffee plantation society. Although this novel has been considered extremely pessimistic, Juan Flores writes (1993, 76) that it harkens to the period of liberal reforms of the 1860s, and that it "could be read as a testament to the Puerto Rico of that early outburst of national affirmation."

However, it would be misleading to suggest that the tragic mode in Puerto Rican literature perforce supplanted the comic, or that the comic has played a minor role in the literary discourse on national identity. Throughout the nineteenth and early twentieth centuries, newspapers represented an important literary venue for satire, particularly in the form of personal attacks against politicians and the social elite. The satirical press flourished at the turn of the century due to decreased censorship, and many humorists and caricaturists openly criticized figures of authority as well as their rivals in the press. José "Momo" Mercado, Luis Bonafoux y Quintero, and Luis Rodríguez Cabrero cultivated the aggressive humor of personal attack, which in some cases led to duels with those whose honor they impugned (Pedreira 1941, 243–44). Yet this type of comic literature has not received sufficient critical attention for its role in defining the Puerto Rican national character. Enid Pagán González argues that comedy and humor in Puerto Rico did not evolve evenly because political, social, and economic conditions obliged writers to produce a monothematic literature that articulated the struggle for a national identity above all other concerns (221). In other words, comedy, humor, and satire were not considered the appropriate means for literary discourse to take up the task of nation building. This endeavor required solemnity and introspection, as well as the cathartic force of tragedy that could instill a sense of urgency for change. Like the periodical medium in which it appeared, satirical journalism was considered ephemeral and unable to carry out the "serious" task of national identity formation.

When finding correlations between the prevalence of either comedy or tragedy and the sociopolitical realities that Puerto Rican literature addresses, it is important to remember that, whatever mode flourishes at a particular historical moment, literary comedy and tragedy develop in relation to each other rather than in isolation. Rubén Ríos Avila, in *La raza cómica del sujeto puertorriqueño*, suggests that the contemporary Puerto Rican literary canon constantly moves between the tragic and the comic modes. He compares two of the central figures in the Generación del Treinta,[2] Antonio Pedreira and Luis Palés Matos, as representatives of the opposing tendencies in Puerto Rican literature: the white, *criollista* solemnity and the black, Afro-Caribbean carnivalesque.[3] Pedreira's 1934 essay *Insularismo* invokes the Spanish heritage in a lament over Puerto Rico's debility as a nation, while Palés Matos's book of poems *Tuntún de pasa y grifería* (1937) celebrates Puerto Rico's vital African heritage. Pedreira's text aims for abstraction, while Palés Matos's delves into corporeality. One writes from the discursive space of the "house," or the interior of national consciousness, while the other dances and sings in the "street"—the phenomenological exterior (121–22). Ríos Avila argues that although these binary oppositions appear mutually exclusive and antagonistic, they actually develop as a polarity mediated by an internal necessity in both terms. In other words, they are two sides of the same coin: "no son sino las dos caras de la moneda de un mismo sujeto" (129).[4] Ríos Avila's analysis allows for a reconsideration of how the tragic and comic modes have developed together rather than separately, synchronically as well as diachronically, and, most important, how the discursive borders between the two are porous rather than impermeable.

In Ríos Avila's comparison, the tension that differentiates yet binds Pedreira's and Palés Matos's texts generates another set of opposing metaphors for Puerto Rican national identity: the insular versus the eccentric. Ríos Avila discusses how in Pedreira's *Insularismo* the central metaphor of the house contrasts with another metaphor: the ship adrift at sea ("nave al garete"). On the other hand, Palés Matos's poetics of the street incorporates the image of the tree, albeit a tree without roots. In these texts, the binary opposition between the insular (the stationary, the autochthonous, the purist) and the eccentric (the displaced, the foreign, the hybrid) acts as an internal contradiction. Many writers before and after Pedreira and Palés Matos have depicted Puerto Rico as either insular or eccentric. Zeno Gandía's *La charca* had already established the metaphor of the insular by using the titular figure of the stagnant pool to characterize the dying culture of Puerto Rico's coffee plantations. On the other hand, like Palés Matos's *Tuntún*, other texts before and since have depicted Puerto Rico eccentrically as open to the crosscurrents of cultural contact, its society constantly changing and its subjects continually on the move. Hostos's *La peregrinación de Bayoán* had developed this metaphor with the transatlantic peregrinations of its titular character, and Tapia's satiric novels *Póstumo el transmigrado* and *Póstumo envirginiado* portrayed a picaresque antihero who not only traveled across geographical borders but whose soul made the leap from one body to another.[5]

Often a writer may develop the metaphors of the insular and the eccentric individually in separate works, as in the case of René Marqués's plays *La carreta* (1951–52) and *Los soles truncos* (1958). The *jíbaro* family in *La carreta* is set adrift on the waves of migration that displaced tens of thousands of Puerto Ricans from the island to U.S. cities, but the aristocratic family in *Los soles truncos* cloisters itself along with its memories and ghosts in its dilapidated San Juan mansion as a way to shelter itself from the modernization that is taking place on the island. More recently, Luis Rafael Sánchez's "La guagua aérea" (1983) offers a comical *crónica* of the Puerto Ricans who travel between the island and the mainland on such a regular basis that they reside in the airspace between the here and there. Even the works of Nuyorican writers display an obsession with the opposing metaphors of immobility and movement. Pedro Pietri's play *The Masses Are Asses* (1984) imprisons its main characters in a bathroom/apartment, while Tato Laviera's collection of poetry *La Carreta Made a U-Turn* (1979) redirects the despair of the migrants in Marqués's play toward cultural self-affirmation. From the earliest texts in the Puerto Rican literary canon to the most recent literature of the diaspora, the tension between the insular and the eccentric reflects the ongoing debate over how to define national identity. Jorge Duany, in *The Puerto Rican Nation on the Move*, argues that the Puerto Rican nation defies the traditional standards of national formation. He writes that "Puerto Rico is a nation on the move" and the "political, geographic, and linguistic categories long taken as the essence of national identity . . . no longer capture the permeable and elastic boundaries of the Puerto Rican nation" (37).[6]

The tragic and the comic, the insular and the eccentric: the first pair of terms describes literary traditions as well as modes of discourse; the second pair describes textual architectures as well as patterns in Puerto Rican history. The chapters in this study will pay close attention to the ways Puerto Rican writers, for different reasons and to different effects, have adapted comic traditions and modes of discourse to write eccentric texts—works in which metaphorical tropes of displacement act as an intervention in the discourse on national identity, crossing the lines between cultures, languages, racial and class affiliations, genders and sexualities. An eccentric text represents Puerto Rican subjects on the move, not only migrating geographically, as many real-life Puerto Ricans have done and continue to do, but also traversing the border between self and other. Thus, it imagines a Puerto Rican identity that sustains several cultural and geographic centers simultaneously and a subjectivity that others itself, so that the voice of the other speaks as the self emerges in discourse. An eccentric text uses the self-reflexivity of humor to estrange Puerto Rican culture to itself, while incorporating more aggressive forms of the comic as an oppositional discourse. This comic heterogeneity in a literary text manages to undermine social, political, and cultural institutions as it scrutinizes the very authority of the writing subject. While metaphors of displacement are not exclusive to the comic mode, writers who do combine the comic with the eccentric contest the notion that Puerto Rican literature must imagine national identity solely within the discursive realms of the tragic and the insular. By engaging the comic, the eccentric text stands outside the center of traditional literary discourse on national identity and refuses to resolve its own incongruities, thus allowing Puerto Rican literature to remain an oppositional discourse while it sustains ambiguity and contradiction.

From the Comic to Literary Humor: Text, Incongruity, and Affect

The theoretical and critical literature on the comic and humor is vast and reaches across disciplines as diverse as philosophy, psychology, literary criticism, anthropology, ethnography, and biology. Different cultural and national traditions also contribute to the lexicon of humor theory with subtle variations in terminology. Yet some basic questions must be asked in order to understand the ways in which Puerto Rican writers have embraced the comic and humor in their reconstruction of national identity: How does the comic function to elicit pleasure? How does that pleasure manifest itself as laughter? Is the comic always communitarian and celebratory, or are there uses of the comic that contravene openness and multiplicity? Finally, what roles do the many complex forms of the comic play in the literary discourse on Puerto Rican national identity? Despite the near impossibility of summarizing this rich theoretical field without resorting to an encyclopedic work,[7] and in order to make humor theory accessible for the purposes of this literary study, I will consider at least one or all three of the following registers that occur in comic literature: text, incongruity, and affect. Studies that pay close attention to text examine the linguistic devices, the literary traditions or genres, and the poetic, dramatic, performative, or narrative structures that are associated with laughter. Theorists in philosophy and psychology have placed great emphasis on the role cognition plays in the perception of the comic and humor, particularly as part of an analysis of incongruity or cognitive shifts. Also in philosophy and psychology, but in the social sciences as well, theorists have explored the affective implications of humor—that is, how humor elicits an emotional response from a subject and functions to define social and communal relations through intersubjective discourses. At the affective register, the comic and humor can be sympathetic or subversive, a celebration or a condemnation, unifying or divisive.

By focusing on text, incongruity, and affect, this study embraces a broad spectrum of humor theories. Most humor theory has traditionally fallen into one of three categories: the Superiority Theory, the Relief/Release Theory, or the Incongruity Theory. In *The Philosophy of Laughter and Humor*, John Morreall collects important examples from all three categories of humor theory. Morreall identifies Plato, Aristotle, and Thomas Hobbes as exponents of the Superiority Theory, which argues that laughter manifests a subject's "feelings of superiority over other people" (5). This notion is often understood as the Hobbesian "sudden glory" that the laughing subject feels when he or she perceives some folly in an enemy. Morreall also includes in his anthology texts that support the Relief/Release Theory, as in Sigmund Freud's argument that the laughter of jokes manifests a release of stored-up psychical energy. The Relief/Release Theory draws heavily on the physiological reasons for laughter—that is, that laughter is beneficial to physical and psychical health. For Morreall and the other contemporary humor theorists included in *The Philosophy of Humor and Laughter*, these theories fail to explain all the instances of humor that result in laughter, for a subject can certainly find humor in a situation that involves neither the failure of others nor the release of pent-up energy. The Incongruity Theory, then, offers contemporary theorists the most insight into how a subject perceives an object or event and processes that perception as an amusing, rather than threatening or perplexing, incongruity. Morreall cites among the exponents of the Incongruity Theory nineteenth-century philosopher Arthur Schopenhauer, who argues: "The cause of laughter in every case is simply the sudden perception of the incongruity between a concept and the real objects which have been thought through it in some relation, and laughter itself is just the expression of this incongruity" (52). In other words, no matter what the nature of the object or event in question, and no matter what psychological or social implications are brought to bear, the underlying trigger for humorous laughter is the perception of a discrepancy, or a cognitive shift from one realm of signification to another.[8]

Within the scope of the present study, it becomes necessary to understand just how a literary text inscribes an incongruity that can elicit laughter. Furthermore, if one is to analyze the role that laughter plays in Puerto Rican national identity, one must reconsider the Superiority and Relief/Release Theories of humor, since these pay close attention to the subjective processes and social relations that allow for laughter within a communal setting. Therefore, I intend to examine the textual means for producing amusing incongruities and to discuss the possible affective registers these examples of the comic and humor generate. My own categories of text, incongruity, and affect reflect this focus on literature, yet many theorists from diverse disciplines and schools of thought map out to some degree this critical topography. For example, Freud's *Jokes and Their Relation to the Unconscious* undertakes a close analysis of a joke's linguistic and narrative devices (text), the role that the unconscious plays in destabilizing meaning (incongruity), and the psychological and social implications of these jokes (affect).

The comic, as opposed to the tragic, refers to all those uses of discourse or performance, or all those moments of perception, in which incongruity elicits, or results in, the pleasure associated with play and amusement. Max Eastman in *The Sense of Humor* argues, "The condition in which laughter most continually occurs is that of play" (11). For Eastman, play is instinctual, arising from the need for pleasure, but beyond a mere expression of joy, laughter manifests a triumph over "playful pain." In other words, the laughter of humor "is an act of welcoming a playful shock or disappointment—an act for which our nervous systems are arranged at birth as perfectly as they are arranged to greet with anger and pugnacious effort a more serious blockage of our wills" (14). Johan Huizinga, in *Homo Ludens: A Study of the Play-Element in Culture*, argues that laughter and the comic are associated with, but subsidiary to, play. He writes: "The category of the comic is closely connected with *folly* in the highest and lowest sense of that word. Play, however, is not foolish. It lies outside the antithesis of wisdom and folly" (6). Play establishes its own order outside "ordinary" life, but is bounded by limits of space and time (10). According to Huizinga, "play is a voluntary activity executed within certain fixed limits of time and place, according to rules freely accepted but absolutely binding, having its aim in itself and accompanied by a feeling of tension, joy and the consciousness that it is 'different' from 'ordinary life'" (28). However, the comic often functions within the realm of play to achieve highly political ends. The comic allows for a politics of pleasure in which laughter acts as a release from solemnity and as a provocation toward self-awareness.

I have been employing "the comic" the way most contemporary theorists use the term "humor," as does the philosopher John Morreall in the following description of humor as incongruity perceived within the realm of play and amusement: "A creature capable of humor, then, needs to have a system of mental representations, especially a system of class concepts. It also needs to be able to operate with its concepts in a non-practical, non-theoretical, in short *playful*, way, so that the violation of conceptual patterns won't evoke negative emotion or disorientation" (202). While I do not contest this use of "humor" to encompass a broad range of risible discourses, performances, and perceptions, and indeed its usage has become much more pervasive in almost every discipline, in the past many theorists made a clear distinction between the comic and humor. Humor—like satire, irony, parody, and the absurd—is a species of the comic, yet while other forms of the comic separate the laughing subject from the object of laughter, humor tends to bring them together. In fact, humor is distinct from other species of the comic because its subject and object are often one and the same. Henri Bergson makes this distinction in his classic text *Laughter: An Essay on the Meaning of the Comic,* in which he describes how the subject laughs at another person—the comic object—who takes a sudden fall, who displays a physical deformity that an able-bodied person can imitate, or who wears an ill-fitting article of clothing. Bergson argues that the subject perceives the comic in "a certain rigidity of body, mind and character" that hinders society's ability to "obtain from its members the greatest possible degree of elasticity and sociability. This rigidity is the comic, and laughter is its corrective" (24). For Bergson, the subject laughs at a perceived incongruity in others as long as the comic object remains unconscious of the incongruousness of his or her behavior or appearance. However, Bergson argues, "When a humorist laughs at himself, he is really acting a double part; the part who laughs is indeed conscious, but not the self who is laughed at" (132). We can see how Bergson's notion of the comic is more like Morreall's definition of humor, while humor, for Bergson, is a much more self-reflexive form of the comic. The writers that I discuss in the following chapters use different species of the comic to expose and often subvert incongruity, yet they also develop a self-reflexive form of humor as they scrutinize not only the incongruities in Puerto Rican national identity but also their own status as writers and agents of cultural production.

Sigmund Freud's distinction between the comic and humor also helps to shed light on how writers can perform a self-reflexive critique. In *Jokes and Their Relation to the Unconscious* Freud argues that in an instance of the comic a person laughs at someone else's misfortune, but in an instance of humor a person laughs at his or her own misfortune. Freud writes:

"Humour is the most easily satisfied among the species of the comic. It completes its course within a single person; another person's participation adds nothing new to it. I can keep to myself the enjoyment of the humorous pleasure that has arisen in me, without feeling obliged to communicate it" (284). Freud subscribes to the general theory that the comic results from a perception and rapid resolution of an incongruity. The comic emerges through comparison, and thus fulfills Morreall's contention that a "creature capable of humor" must be able to classify different mental representations. Yet, for Freud, humor is distinct from its comic cousin, the joke, in which the teller targets an object who does not share in the joke, and the listener laughs at that absent object. In this case, the listener of the joke must perceive the incongruity, perform the comparative operation, and come to a resolution, responding with laughter. One can see from this theory why some jokes fall flat: the listener fails to perceive the incongruity and does not arrive at a pleasurable resolution. In sum, both the perception of the comic and the successful decoding of a joke cause a person to laugh at an exterior object.

On the other hand, a subject who perceives humor finds the risible in him- or herself as an internalized object. Humor functions both ways, and in *Jokes* Freud argues that when a humorist does laugh at others, it is usually out of sympathy (289); that is, the subject projects the self onto external objects. Freud later refined his theories on humor according to the tripartite id-ego-superego psychological model. In his 1927 essay "Humour," Freud takes the position that when a subject produces humorous pleasure in himself, his ego insists on remaining unaffected by "the traumas of the external world; it shows, in fact, that such traumas are no more than occasions for it to gain pleasure" (162). Freud contends that the subject assumes the role of the grown-up in relation to himself and sees his own dilemmas as childish (163). Therefore, the humorist withdraws his "psychical accent" away from his ego and toward the superego, which serves as a parental, paternal voice within the subject's psyche (164). When a subject perceives another person humorously, he likewise takes on this parental role and reduces the other to the status of a child (163), yet unlike jokes and the comic, which are more aggressive and tendentious toward their objects, humor acts as a defense, whether for the self or the other with whom the self sympathizes. Humor shields the self and the other from pain, the way a parental figure protects a child. Freud writes: "It means: 'Look! here is the world, which seems so dangerous! It is nothing but a game for children—just worth making a jest about!'" (166). Freud implies that the person who takes a humorous attitude toward others enacts a kind of intersubjective ego identification, in which the subject and object share affect. Freud argues that humor "is a rare and precious gift, and many people are even without the capacity to enjoy humorous pleasure that is presented to them" (166). Indeed, it is a very common perception that people who take themselves too seriously lack a sense of humor, even if they display an exaggerated propensity for making jokes and finding the comic at the expense of others.

Unfortunately, because many theorists have held this type of self-reflexive, sympathetic humor in such high regard, some have ascribed elitist and ethnocentric qualifications to it. As we will see in more detail in the chapter on Nemesio Canales, for a long time humor was thought to belong exclusively to the well-bred races of the North, while those of lower-class origins and from southern climes lacked this more advanced quality of self-reflexivity and sympathy in their laughter. Much of this essentialist notion of humor developed as the etymology of the term shifted from its Latin origin, meaning a liquid substance, to the medieval medical theory of humors, in which a person's character was attributed to the overabundance of a particular bodily fluid: sanguine for blood, phlegmatic for phlegm, choleric or bilious for choler or bile, and melancholy for black bile (Wickberg 1998, 17). The medicine of humors also found expression in literature, particularly in the English "comedy of humours" from the sixteenth and seventeenth centuries. Ben Jonson's *Every Man Out of His Humour* depicted a character for every type of "humour," but those that feigned the outward trappings of an inappropriate "humour" were portrayed as "more than ridiculous" (qtd. in Wickberg, 22). Although humor eventually began to signify a mood or subjective frame of mind, the character traits associated with a humorous disposition took on national and racial connotations.

In 1911 Miguel de Unamuno, who rebaptized all humorists as *malhumoristas* for their overabundance of spleen, wrote: "In a humid and cold country, where arthritis and dyspepsia easily arise, that is where one finds the *malhumoristas*, and they are perforce wherever the sudden oscillations in temperature and pressure continually place the heart at risk" (109, 115).[9] Unamuno's naturalist explanation identifies England and the countries of Northern Europe as home to the splenetic, arthritic, and dyspeptic populations. Spain, with its warmer, temperate climate, induces intellectual lassitude and arouses the passions, so that a Spaniard is more likely to resort to crass ridicule—as in *burla*—than to the refined irony of the

French or the superior humor of the English. Yet Unamuno's self-reflexive novel *Niebla* reveals the irony in his own naturalist explanations of humorous tendencies. Unamuno appears to subscribe to an essentialist theory of "humours" only to subvert that theory in his own literary practice.

It is true that nations often claim particular species of the comic as part of their national character, and Spanish American and Hispanic Caribbean nations are no exceptions. Jorge Mañach's *Indagación del choteo* elucidates a culturally specific critique of the Cuban *choteo*, a type of subversive ridicule that lies at close quarters with the Puerto Rican *guachafita* (a term I will take up in more detail in my discussion of Luis Rafael Sánchez). According to Mañach, the *choteo* is incompatible with humor, for the *choteador* is an egoist who ridicules others, while the humorist expresses a deep human feeling ("hondo sentido humano") (74). Mañach's notion of the *choteo* subscribes to the kind of essentialism we saw in Unamuno; he even disallows that women possess a capacity for anything but "gracia" (mild wit) because this is a nonaggressive form of the comic, thus more in keeping with women's evasive natures (74–75). Nevertheless, Mañach's investigation into Cuban *choteo* provides a clear example of how the prevalence of one or another species of the comic in a cultural tradition reflects the kinds of social relations that obtain among the members of a national community. For Mañach, *choteo* coincides with the Cuban disdain for social hierarchies, but more than an immanent national character, *choteo* is the result of a particular collective experience—"una determinada experiencia colectiva" (84).

Mañach's description of Cuban *choteo* also resonates with Jorge Portilla's existentialist analysis of Mexican *relajo*. In "Fenomenología del relajo," Portilla describes the Mexican comic form as a derisive act performed publicly that negates the seriousness of a proposed social value. While seriousness invokes solidarity through affirmation, *relajo* sabotages the serious by inviting a solidarity of refusal. Portilla contends that *relajo's* negativity leads to a dead end, for it pursues an illusion of value: liberty as a simple "no." No action, in the existentialist sense, can come from *relajo* because it is an action ordered in disorder and an escape toward irresponsibility (83). Like Mañach with his distinction between *choteo* and humor, Portilla distinguishes *relajo* from humor as well. He writes: "Humor cancels out pathos, which is an attitude of desperation in the face of action. Pathos implicitly bears the affirmation 'there is nothing to be done'; it wishes to confirm a state of the world as insurmountable. Humor destroys this confirmation and returns its transitory character to the situation that pathos wished to make definitive" (85).[10] Portilla's definition of humor is very close to Freud's, and he equally places great value on it as a means for the subject to overcome trauma through self-reflection and, in some cases, self-mockery. Unlike Unamuno and Mañach, Portilla does not ascribe elitist or ethnocentric qualifications to humor. He finds that Mexicans of all stripes are as capable of producing and enjoying humor as anyone else. Humor allows a subject to overcome traumatic experiences and adverse circumstances, thus it is an attitude that a subject can choose or refuse to adopt in the face of adversity. Portilla writes: "Humor is an attitude of a stoical sort that demonstrates the fact that man's interiority, his very subjectivity, can never be overtaken or canceled out by the situation at hand, however adverse it might be; humor demonstrates that man can never be exhausted by his circumstances" (75).[11] It is in this way that the Puerto Rican writers I will discuss have confronted the traumatic events of their own history and the incongruities of their national identity. Despite their circumstances of displacement and disenfranchisement, Puerto Ricans survive as a nation through laughter and humor.

Puerto Rican Literary Humor and the Eccentric Text

The chapters that follow will discuss four twentieth-century Puerto Rican writers and the ways each one develops humor in an eccentric text. Like many other Puerto Rican writers, Nemesio R. Canales, Luis Rafael Sánchez, Ana Lydia Vega, and Pedro Pietri all address the incongruities of Puerto Rican national identity through the comic. What these four writers share that sets them apart from others is a humorous self-reflexivity that takes the writing subject as its object of laughter. This subjective displacement parallels the metaphors of dislocation that these writers incorporate into their texts. While focusing on four writers will no doubt overlook many important contributions to Puerto Rican literary humor, a major concern of this study will be an analysis of how these writers negotiate their agency in cultural production with the collective voice of national identity. Therefore, a discussion that focuses on the texts of a particular writer will be able to show how his or her work can be self-referential while maintaining an engagement with a notion of community.

The first chapter presents a cross-cultural analysis of the writings of Nemesio R. Canales (1878–1923), a humorist who practiced law, served as a legislator in Puerto Rico's early representative government under the

United States, and was one of the few men of his day to publicly advocate equal rights for women. Canales was also very active as a writer and editor in the island's periodical literature, publishing humorous essays, short stories, and one theatrical play in newspapers and *revistas* (literary magazines). One of Canales's best-known texts, *Paliques*, is a collection of his satirical and philosophical essays on life in Puerto Rico at the beginning of the twentieth century. Yet Canales inaugurates this series of humorous columns by taking himself as the principal comic object, portraying himself as both a Quasimodo and a Don Juan. This self-reflexivity allows Canales to establish a sympathetic bond with the reader while he vituperates against the political, economic, and cultural follies of his compatriots. Canales also targets the incipient colonial government of the United States and its intrusions into island life and politics. In many ways, Canales follows in the tradition of nineteenth-century Spanish satirists such as Ramón de Mesonero Romanos, Mariano José de Larra, and Leopoldo Alas "Clarín," but Canales also differs from these predecessors and from many of his contemporaries in that his satire is tempered with humor, which deauthorizes the writing subject and holds the figure of the writer to the same standard with which he comically objectifies others. This "weakened" subjectivity contravenes the social institutions that uphold a paternalistic "code of honor," which dictates an impervious and impenetrable masculinity as a gender ideal. It also diverges from the discourse on national identity that solidifies cultural, racial, and linguistic borders around the subject and the national community. I will discuss several of Canales's essays and one of his short stories, "Mi voluntad se ha muerto," which use humor to destabilize subjectivity while opening a space in literary discourse to unmask social customs, political institutions, and gender and sexual norms.

The second chapter focuses on the two novels of Luis Rafael Sánchez (1936–), and by doing so skips ahead several literary generations, bypassing particularly the Generación del Treinta and the Generación del Cuarenta y cinco. The predominant attitude among writers of those generations was to seek answers to the incongruities of national identity in the tragic mode. Yet this study's omission of a representative from those important writers does not imply that there was no use of the comic in Puerto Rican literature during the mid-twentieth century; Emilio S. Belaval, Manuel Méndez de Ballester, and even René Marqués, who produced some of the most influential dramatic and narrative tragedies in contemporary Puerto Rican literature, all made use of comic forms in their texts. However, what sets Luis Rafael Sánchez apart from these writers is the textual and subjective self-reflexivity of humor. His first novel, *La guaracha del Macho Camacho* (1976), and his second novel-length text, *La importancia de llamarse Daniel Santos: Fabulación* (1988), both break with conventional notions of the novel genre and elaborate Sánchez's trademark *poética de lo soez* (poetics of the vulgar), a heterglossic collage of voices from Puerto Rico's social margins that combines with the highly literary language of the neobaroque. Read together, *La guaracha* and *Daniel Santos* form a textual *jaibería* by moving between the opposing poles of guaracha and bolero, the insular and the eccentric, the collective and the individual. Furthermore, while *La guaracha* uses the carnival spirit of Puerto Rican *guachafita* to comically objectify its own narrative discourse, it is not until *Daniel Santos* that Sánchez turns a satiric lens on the figure of the writer himself. The narrator/implied author in *Daniel Santos* plays off the critical and popular success of Sánchez's *La guaracha* in a humorous critique of authorship and the cult of celebrity. This self-reflexivity allows the text to "queer" Puerto Rican national identity, demythologizing paternalism and machismo without delegitimizing the cultural icons of hypermasculinity that the disenfranchised in Puerto Rico and Latin America use as projections of an ego ideal.

The third chapter discusses the short stories and essays of Ana Lydia Vega (1946–), who has used humor as an effective means to break out of the limited space that national culture assigns to women's writing. She shows that women can appropriate ostensibly "unfeminine" genres such as the thriller, the detective story, and literary pornography. Her writing also parodies the genres that have been traditionally reserved for women, such as the romance novel and the children's fable. She combines a pan-Caribbean perspective with an affinity for the French language and culture to depict Puerto Rican women who have not only crossed the threshold of the domestic domain but have taken flight and left the island altogether as tourists in other countries. In such stories as "Puerto Príncipe abajo," "Pollito Chicken," and "Pasión de historia," Vega's female characters deploy what British scholar John Urry calls a "tourist gaze"—that is, they observe their cultural others from a space of economic and educational privilege. However, they also regard their own Puerto Rican culture as if it were foreign, and they see themselves as foreigners in their own land. Although they can create a space that is exterior to the culture within the purview of their tourist gaze, they are often the object of someone else's exploitative gaze, including that of the narrator and the reader. As tourists, they occupy a position of privileged consumption and heightened social mobility. Nevertheless, Vega shows that however "free" these cosmopolitan, middle-class Puerto Rican women have become in modern society, they are only taking an excursion from oppression. Because they are often the victims of colonial violence and objectification themselves, the women in her stories who travel abroad as tourists often identify with the objects of their tourist gazes. But Vega also shows that Puerto Rican women can choose to be blind to the history of colonialism that has increased their access to social mobility. They do so in order to disassociate themselves from the painful colonial history of Puerto Rico, the fragmented national identities that modernization has brought about, and the Afro-Caribbean reality that is often projected onto the "foreignness" of other nations. This misrecognition can be read from the ironic perspectives of the narrator and reader, who have their own complicity in objectifying these women as cultural tourists. Vega's self-reflexive irony, or humor, forces the reader to recognize his or her own cultural expectations and complicity in the construction of ironic distance. Consequently, Vega's ironic texts function humorously for the reader who visualizes the position from which he or she laughs at the comic depiction of others.

The fourth chapter considers the work of Pedro Pietri (1944–2004), who was born in Puerto Rico but, like many of his compatriots, migrated to the United States at an early age and wrote primarily in English. Pietri's poetic, dramatic, and narrative texts explore the Puerto Rican diasporic identity through a mixture of surrealism and the absurd. The Puerto Rican voices in his texts live in New York as if they were simultaneously existing somewhere else; they take "mind trips" or "trip out" on drugs and alcohol to travel there and leave the harsh urban reality behind. The self-reflexivity in Pietri's humor turns the city into a hostile agent that comically objectifies the Puerto Ricans who inhabit it, including the figure of the writer. Simultaneously, that same textual space in which comic objectification occurs opens a window to an affirmation of selfhood. Pietri's eccentric texts allow the migrant who yearns for the "lost" Puerto Rican homeland to relocate that utopian space in the imagination. Thus Pietri deconstructs the oppositions between here and there, reality and the imagination, the self and the other. The unstable sense of space in Pietri's texts reflects the incongruities of the diasporic experience, in which Puerto Ricans sustain several cultural, racial, and linguistic identities as part of a cohesive sense of community.

The eccentric text has reoriented the discourse on Puerto Rican national identity by having it intersect with those marginal identities that a paternalistic, patriarchal discourse excludes from the national community. According to the paternalist tradition, Puerto Rico is an inadequate nation because of its tragic flaws of miscegenation, a "matriarchal" social order, cultural infantilism, and the diaspora of its people across the North American continent.[12] For the Puerto Rican humorist, these "eccentricities" do not lie outside the nation. Humor and the eccentric text allow national identity to shift and overcome the incongruity of a nation without an independent state, as well as the paradox of a national community that traverses geopolitical borders without ever leaving home. In this way, humor and the eccentric text approach what Arcadio Díaz Quiñones (2000a) calls "el arte de bregar," that way of "making do" that is characteristically Puerto Rican. He writes: "The strategy of *bregar* consists of placing in relation that which previously appeared distant or antagonistic. It is a position from which one can act to settle very polarized conflicts without violence. In this sense, it connotes opening space in an uncertain cartography and facing up to decisions with a vision of the possible and desirable. It also implies—this is crucial—the recognition and acceptance of limits. . . . It is the art of the nontragic, without the fatalism or the weakness of *¡Ay bendito!*" (22).[13] Díaz Quiñones's description of the Puerto Rican *arte de bregar* resonates with the notion that humor, which allows the subject to overcome pathos, is a self-affirming survival strategy that operates, paradoxically, through the destabilization of selfhood. Puerto Rican literary humor is in *la brega* because it confronts incongruity with a sense of play and an expectation of pleasure, but also with a capacity for self-preservation and opposition. It "makes do" in the face of Puerto Rico's social, cultural, and political struggles by opening national identity to ambiguity, but always as a way to reaffirm those "eccentricities" through laughter, rather than to reject them out of apathy or fear. Finally, humor allows Puerto Rican subjects to place themselves in a nonviolent relation with those cultural "others" that often represent a threat to national identity. With a sense of humor, the Puerto Rican subject can *bregar*, or "make do," while confronting uncertainty and displacement without resorting to the dogmatism of norms or the intransigence of authenticity.

1

The Self-Mocking Satirist

Nemesio Canales and the Politics of Humor

Románticos somos . . . ¿Quién que Es, no es romántico?
Aquel que no sienta ni amor ni dolor,
aquel que no sepa de beso y de cántico,
que se ahorque de un pino: será lo mejor . . .

Rubén Darío, "La canción de los pinos"

Nemesio R. Canales begins one of his many self-reflexive essays by admitting: "Yo era un hombre muy feo y muy enamorado" [I was once a very ugly and very amorous man] (*Antología* 71). As a journalist, Canales was well known for his mordant political satire and astringent literary criticism, but as the citation above shows, he often used the rhetorical feint of writing as his own worst critic. Like his compatriots José "Momo" Mercado (1863–1911) and Luis Bonafoux Quintero (1855–1918), Canales cultivated the tradition of journalistic satire made popular in Spain by Ramón de Mesonero Romanos (1803–1882), Mariano José de Larra (1809–1837), and Leopoldo Alas "Clarín" (1852–1901). Like these other satirists, Canales found much to excoriate in his society, particularly Puerto Ricans' lack of interest in the arts, their politics of colonialist collaboration, and their regressive attitudes toward women. However, in contrast to the Spanish satirists, and especially in opposition to the vitriolic Bonafoux— whose type of satire Canales disdained as "la soez y brutal carcajada del bufón maldiciente e ignorante cuyo estólido oficio es el de hacer reír no importa cómo y no importa de qué" [the vulgar and brutal cackle of the foulmouthed and ignorant buffoon whose stupid purpose is to make one laugh no matter how and no matter at what] (*Antología* 85)—Canales did not portray himself as an observer who stood above the fray of social discord, nor did he exclude himself from satirical censure. Canales was always ready to lambaste his detractors in the press, but he frequently exploited his own weaknesses in order to expose a larger social issue.

Among those to which he admitted was a weakness for female beauty, and one would assume from the confession above that Canales was a lothario prone to objectifying women. However, the self-proclaimed admirer of Don Juan was one of Puerto Rico's staunchest proponents of women's emancipation and suffrage at a time when many Puerto Rican intellectuals still idealized women as their *ángeles del hogar*, Angels in the House. Canales displays an eccentric sensibility in his profeminist texts because his self-mockery flouts the code of honor and the inviolable male privilege that helped to define the Puerto Rican masculine ideal. As a member of the first generation of Puerto Rican writers to be educated in both Spain and the United States, his use of humor reflects the emerging rift in Puerto Rico's cultural landscape. Although Canales satirized the small-mindedness of his era much as earlier Spanish and Puerto Rican *humoristas* had done, his self-deprecating postures are more characteristic of a "sense of humor," a character trait often erroneously attributed exclusively to northern societies. Like Alejandro Tapia before him, Canales used satire to advocate women's rights and to condemn the code of honor, yet he articulated his profeminist politics through a humorous portrayal of his own shortcomings as a hopeless romantic.

Since the greater part of Canales's work originally appeared in newspapers and literary magazines, the ephemeral character of this form encouraged the notion that the author had never contributed a "serious" work to Puerto Rican literature.[1] In a biographical note that accompanied the 1935 edition of Canales's play, *El héroe galopante* (1923), Antonio de Jesús wrote:

> Nemesio R. Canales was an ill-fated genius. His personality would have scintillated in any field of our literature. His keen observation, his evident talent, and his facility of expression were clearly distinctive elements in his literary work with which we are familiar. But throughout his life he aimed at cultivating the philosophical humor that, although it won applause and popularity in his era, places him at a disadvantage compared to the other men of letters of our nation. (64)[2]

The 1930s, when de Jesús wrote this critical assessment, was the decade associated with the generation of intellectuals and writers who sought within solemnity and tragedy the keys to understanding the Puerto Rican national character (Flores 1993, 13–57). It was also the moment when intellectuals reinforced a Hispanicist paternalism with the intent of saving the nation from the forces of Anglo-American imperialism (Gelpí 1993, 15). In this cultural climate, the Generación del Treinta recognized Canales more for his humor and less for his incongruous antinationalist politics. He was a member of the Partido Unionista (Unionist Party), which supported the controversial Jones Act of 1917 that conferred U.S. citizenship on all Puerto Ricans. Canales was more concerned with political fairness than with political parties when he wrote: "Conste una vez más que soy partidario de la Independencia, de la Autonomía, del Estado, y hasta del demonio, con tal que signifique *un país emancipado bajo un gobierno inteligente y responsable*" [Let it be clear once again that I belong to the party of Independence, of Autonomy, of Statehood, even of the devil, if it signifies *an emancipated nation under an intelligent and responsible government*] (*Antología* 331). Furthermore, as is demonstrated in the essay "Nuestros jíbaros" (*Antología* 233–36), Canales refused to contribute to the literary mystification of a nationalist symbol of the rural peasant class, a cultural endeavor that the Generación del Treinta undertook with great fervor (Guerra 1998, 45–66). All of these "eccentricities" did place Canales at a disadvantage compared to the succeeding generation of writers who defined Puerto Rican national identity according to a rigidly delineated set of social codes, political ideologies, and cultural traditions.

In a more recent critical evaluation, Rogelio Escudero Valentín establishes in *Literatura y periodismo en la obra de Nemesio Canales* (1988) that throughout his career Canales gradually gave more focus to his political ideas, moving from a distrust of all the ideological isms of his day to a growing recognition of the importance of socialism in class struggle and in anti-imperialist movements. Escudero Valentín argues that Canales distanced himself from some of the iconoclastic ideas that appeared in his earlier writings, particularly those associated with the Fabian Society (71). A loosely organized group of bourgeois intellectuals that drew its name from Fabius Cunctator, Fabians like George Bernard Shaw and H. G. Wells advocated a socialist state, but they did not see its success as dependent on a working-class revolution, as orthodox Marxists did (91). As Canales moved away from Fabianism and toward more oppositional politics, his essays began to take on a more urgent tone. In 1917 he addressed the need for serious political commitment in the essay "Ya no nos reímos": "Pasó, pues, el período de la risa, que marcó siempre la infancia de toda idea. Ahora estamos en la etapa del ademán torvo y del puño cerrado. Buena señal. Esperemos, pues. El desenlace no ha de tardar mucho" [Gone, then, is the time of laughter, which always marked the infancy of every idea. Now we are in the stage of the fierce gesture and the clenched fist. A good sign. Let us wait, then. The outcome cannot be far behind] (*Antología* 165). This shift toward seriousness reveals the more radical and utopian tendencies of revolutionary socialism, an ideology Canales came to support fervently in his 1919 periodical *Cuasimodo* (Escudero Valentín, 151). However, Canales continued to develop aggressive satire and self-reflexive humor in his essays and short fiction. It is in these works that he offers a profeminist challenge to Puerto Rican paternalism as well as a parodic self-portrait of his own political evolution.

Humoristas, Humor, and the Code of Honor

Newspapers in the nineteenth century related more than current events; they were also a primary source for literature and literary criticism. Most identified with one political party or another, although censorship prevented many publications from launching serious attacks against the government. In some instances newspapers issued blank editions, as when the Spanish government censored an entire issue of *El Siglo* in 1834, or when the Puerto Rican censor did likewise to *El Buscapié* in 1880 (Navas Ruiz 1982, 284; Olivera 1987, 188). The more liberal publications saw it as their mission to expose injustices and denounce political corruption, as illustrated in these inaugural words by the founder of Puerto Rico's *El Buscapié*, Manuel Fernández Juncos: "Avivar y sostener en esta Antilla el amor a las artes; propagar la literatura nacional; publicar noticias útiles acerca del movimiento literario de Europa y América, propender al desarrollo de la instrucción pública; abogar por las reformas de las malas costumbres; 'Buscar el pie' a todo género de abusos—cualquiera que sea su causa o procedencia,—he aquí el objeto que proponemos" [To enliven and to support on this Antilles island a love of the arts; to propagate the national literature; to publish useful news regarding literary movements in Europe and America, to favor the development of public education; to advocate the reform of bad habits; to "get to the root" of all manner of abuses—whatever their cause or origin—here is the goal that we propose] (qtd. in Olivera, 189).

Newspapers like *El Buscapié* belonged to a genre known as *festivo-satírico* (witty-satirical) or *humorístico*. In these publications many satirists honed their wits on political targets, literary figures, and sometimes other journalists. When satirical attacks became too personal, journalists often challenged each other to duels, and Puerto Rican luminaries such as Luis Muñoz Rivera, Mariano Abril, and Manuel Zeno Gandía were not averse to defending their honor by such means (Pedreira 1941, 270). Some of the bravado remained confined to the printed page, as when Luis Bonafoux Quintero accused Leopoldo Alas of plagiarizing *Madame Bovary* for his novel *La Regenta*. Alas countered with a scathing essay, calling Bonafoux "escritor filipino o inca, o lo que sea (ultramarino lo es)" [Filipino or Inca writer, or whatever he is (he is certainly from overseas)] (4:218). For the most part, though, satirists veiled their attacks against political rivals and used pseudonyms to disguise their identities.

Periodical literature played an important role in the development of satire in Spain and the Spanish-speaking world, and although satirists were often called *humoristas*, the notion of a "sense of humor" was not widely used to describe the satirical content in Spanish-language newspapers, journals, and reviews. Spanish and Spanish American satirical journalism has its roots in *costumbrismo*, or the literature of manners, as in the essays of Ramón de Mesonero Romanos, who wrote for the *Revista Española* and *Diario de Madrid* under the pseudonym "El curioso parlante" (Navas Ruiz 193). Mesonero Romanos offered slice-of-life scenes of nineteenth-century Madrid; in one of his *Escenas y tipos matritenses* he claimed that their purpose was to attack the ridiculous aspects of the society in which he lived (121).

A more caustic satirist who influenced Canales was Manuel José de Larra, who wrote under the pseudonyms "Andrés Niporesas," "El pobrecito hablador," and, most famously, "Fígaro." Larra adapted the ideals of reason and liberty from the French Enlightenment in order to attack the stagnant political climate under the rule of Fernando VII and, later, to express his disillusionment with the liberal government of Mendizábal (Acevedo 1966, 187–88; Kirkpatrick 1989, 101). Writing for and contributing to a number of Spanish newspapers, Larra with his own brand of *costumbrismo* produced such essays as "El día de Difuntos de 1836," in which he laments the figurative death of the Spanish nation (580–86). Donning the pseudonymous mask of "Fígaro" allowed Larra to distance his identity from that of his satirical persona, but it also positioned that persona against the society it satirized.

In "De la sátira y los satíricos," Larra outlines the qualities necessary for a good satirist: "he should possess the highest perspicacity and penetration in order to see in their true light the things and men that surround him," and "personal circumstances must also constantly place him in an isolated and independent position, because otherwise, as soon as he becomes interested more in some things than in others, he cannot easily be a discreet observer and an impartial judge of them all" (467).[3] When Larra refers to the isolation and independence necessary for the satirist's ability to observe discreetly, he alludes not only to the pressures of censorship that often regulated and expurgated a journalist's politically subversive writings; his prescription for satirical objectivity also removes the satirist from the social sphere that he critiques. Susan Kirkpatrick, in *Las Románticas: Women Writers and Subjectivity in Spain, 1835–1850*, argues that Larra's objective distance comes to the surface of his text in the form of a painful feeling of isolation (100). Larra's romanticism situates the individual in a state of constant conflict with society. He exposes the ridiculous in others but takes his position as an aloof, inviolable satirist very seriously.

This satirical objectivity contrasts with a self-deprecating humor. The eminent Spanish scholar Julio Casares argues that humor does not regard society from a distance, and when the satirist stops to think that he is of the same ilk ("de la misma carne") as his victims, that he too could one day succumb to the very circumstances he ridicules, only then will he loosen the whip of his wit ("el látigo se le afloja") and see himself as the possible object of someone else's ridicule (45). Inevitably, Larra was unable to find the risible side to his own circumstances; in 1837, with a flagging career and a failed extramarital romance, he committed suicide. Although much in Larra's life and death must be left to conjecture, the essays in which he so virulently ridiculed the society around him rarely demonstrated any self-reflexive levity. Critic Ricardo Navas Ruiz writes:

> In politics and in life he became irritated . . . with those who blame their misfortunes on their unlucky star, and he proclaimed that everyone forges the destiny that he wants. . . . And knowing this, he could not or would not submit circumstance to his interests. At the most intimate level, he was perhaps weak, too idealistic for the task, torn between his sound rationalism and his romantic temperament. Larra is the kind of intelligent man, very gifted, whose will, in some way and for obscure reasons, fails him. (265)[4]

Larra's definition of satire pits the satirist against society yet does not consider the ridicule of the self as a viable means for social critique. For that sense of humor, we have to look to the satirical writings of Nemesio Canales, who emulated Larra but also differed from his predecessor in one important respect: Canales was often the subject and object of his own satirical censure.

Nemesio Canales's success as a satirical journalist in Puerto Rico began with a series of articles he wrote for the Ponce newspaper *El Día* from 1911 to 1914 (Romeu 1985, 111). Collected and published as *Paliques* in 1915, these essays were the first indication that Canales's self-deprecating humor distinguished him from his Puerto Rican compatriots and Spanish predecessors. From the very first essay, "La seriedad de mi tío," Canales writes with a tone of erudite self-mockery, ridiculing the very notion of literary origins by comparing the search to name his new column to the dissatisfaction he feels with his own name: "I didn't know that it was such a difficult thing to find a name but, since I have had to undergo the trials of Cain in order to search for a heading that would suit this section of the newspaper commissioned to me, I am even ready to forgive my father the hideous crime that he committed against me by naming me 'Nemesio'" (*Paliques* 7).[5]

Canales elaborates a comic metaphor in which his own duty to write this column is compared to the trials of Cain, the sinful and murderous son of humanity's first father. However, this metaphor leads to a metonymy if we consider that Canales's act of naming is but one in a series of paternalistic namings, in which original sin links father to son. Canales makes these allusions in order to demystify the act of naming and to desecrate the inauguration of his own discourse by ridiculing the Christian tradition of the father's right and duty to bestow a name on his progeny. Finally, his own name—not a pseudonym—becomes the object of ridicule, thus drawing a line of direct descent between himself and his satirical persona.[6]

He also takes a confrontational stance against seriousness when he goes on to say that if someone should think that making such a fuss about finding a name for a newspaper column is laughable and absurd, he would roar back ("yo le rujo") that if one were to eliminate everything laughable and absurd from life, there would surely be nothing left at all (7). He illustrates this point by recounting a childhood encounter he had with his uncle Bruno, the mayor of his hometown and a man known and feared by all the community for his stone-faced, implacable seriousness. His uncle takes him aside one day and sits him down as if to impose on him a sermon or lecture. However, Uncle Bruno merely asks if his tiepin shows from behind his beard. Uncle Bruno advises the young Canales not to be fooled by his serious demeanor, for very often he is merely contemplating the shine of his shoes or wondering whether his tie is straight. The stern uncle adds that he would willingly take time to play with his nephew if it were not for the stares they would elicit in the public square.

Canales develops the comic incongruity between the uncle's reputation and his private thoughts in order to show how playfulness and seriousness are socially determined types of behavior that are often misleadingly portrayed as manifestations of an essential selfhood. This separation between playfulness and seriousness reflects a social order in which individuals have personality traits that are more or less acceptable in relation to their stations in life and according to their perceived public personae. Children may express playfulness publicly in their games, while politicians and patriarchs must refrain from such overt displays of frivolity. This radical frontier between the worlds of play and work coincides with a distinction between private and public displays of personality, as well as with a hierarchical differentiation between those citizens who must sustain seriousness in order to enforce social order and those subjects whose lack of seriousness requires constant discipline. Yet Canales's anecdote about Uncle Bruno demonstrates that a sense of humor allows play to infiltrate the realm of the serious. Uncle Bruno enjoys his humorous perceptions privately, confirming Freud's contention that one can do so "without feeling obliged to communicate it."

Canales's deconstruction of the split between playfulness and seriousness implies a cognitive and psychical operation, which resonates with Freud's assertion in *Jokes* (284) that "humour is a means of obtaining pleasure in spite of the distressing affects that interfere with it; it acts as a substitute for the generation of these affects, it puts itself in their place." In other words, humor allows one to laugh through pain, and a sense of humor assigns that capacity more to a psychical process than to one's inherent personality. This notion of humor contends that one must cultivate and control the ability to divert personal injury away from feelings of indignation or anger toward pleasure. Yet while Canales localizes humor in himself by directing laughter at his physical traits and his ugly name, this self-reflexive sense of humor is also a performance for a Puerto Rican reader. According to Freud, the "unconcerned person"—in this case the reader—finds comic pleasure in Canales's self-deprecating discourse not because the text's implied author merits ridicule, but because he overcomes his pathos (284–86). By engaging Canales's textual display of frivolity and self-reflexive humor, the reader's pity is inhibited and becomes "unutilizable," allowing the reader to laugh with Canales rather than at him (286).

Canales's humorous text thus undermines more than his literary persona; it also destabilizes the "humor-free zone" of Puerto Rican society.

Canales's anecdote also reflects what Daniel Wickberg in *The Senses of Humor: Self and Laughter in Modern America* calls "the cult of the sense of humor" in North America that prevailed during the turn of the last century (186). Wickberg explains that attitudes in the United States toward work and play were dramatically altered as time and space were increasingly regimentated in a rapidly growing industrial economy. Wickberg argues that humor should not be understood as a universal concept, for the idea that a person can have a sense of humor is quite recent. He traces the discourses that have defined a subject as having personality traits to mid-Victorian industrialized and colonialist society. The modern separation of humor from the serious came about in the nineteenth century as "an attempt to preserve a 'humor-free zone' of meaning and experience in the face of the localization of the sense of humor in the self" (171–72). Play was seen as more than just a respite from daily cares, it was a safety valve that "allowed the serious person to achieve an equilibrium through the venting of energy, thus preventing a dangerous concentration that would undermine the serious action and goals which produced that concentrated pressure" (178–79). Laughter was seen as a way to function well in society and to achieve psychological balance and control. Wickberg details how the benefits of play, amusement, and laughter were extolled from the pulpit and confirmed in medical discourse, not only for workers in factories but for professional men such as lawyers, legislators, and physicians (180).

In "La seriedad de mi tío," humor acts as an intervention in the world of the serious, but also as a weapon with which to undermine the privilege of those who sustain the guise of moral superiority. Uncle Bruno tells the young Canales that he should laugh at and pity those afflicted with seriousness, for seriousness and respectability are worse than any vice (9). Henceforth, Canales admits, whenever he sees a haughty person who wears the mask of seriousness and respectability, he feels the desire to confront him with this imprecation: "My friend, I understand the immense burden of your tedium, and I sympathize with your pain, but I see no other recourse for you but suicide. If you do not have the courage to emancipate yourself from the yoke of your respectability by performing, in the sight of everyone, a few leaps and somersaults in order to cure yourself of that terrible spiritual paralysis from which you suffer, you will understand that I do you a service by recommending either poison or the noose" (*Paliques* 9–10).[7]

Canales not only advocates public displays of play but feels compelled to intervene in the world of respectability and threaten violence to those who persist in taking themselves too seriously. Respectability is a moral as well as a social code, imbued with the discourses of class, racial, and gender superiority. We learn from Canales's essay that humor can destabilize seriousness in order to loosen the subject from the constraints of social control, and that humor is a critical knowledge of self, for it distances the subject from the moral and social imperatives that valorize respectability.

In this way, Canales's humor contravenes the Spanish code of honor, which allows a male subject to attack those around him but imposes a rigid discourse of respectability around the masculine identity. This code was operative in the Puerto Rican satirical journalism of his day, as evidenced by the numerous feuds that resulted in duels (Pedreira 1941, 270). According to this tradition, the code of honor prevents the Spaniard—and, by extension, those who adhere to the code—from appreciating humor, as Wenceslao Fernández Flórez argues in *El humor en la literatura española*:

> We [Spaniards] do not understand humor, and we should even say sincerely that it bothers us, that it disquiets us, that we fear, even just seeing it pass by our side, that it will stain or diminish our own seriousness, which we love dearly and which we take great pains to guard, because it seems to us that to lose something of it is like losing something of our honor. Often, indeed, when we want to affirm that someone has lost his decency, we say he has lost his seriousness. (18)[8]

An appreciation of humor, as Fernández Flórez understands it, requires one to shed the defensive armor of egoism. Thus, the humorist must be able to find the ridiculous in himself, even as he unmasks and ridicules the foibles of those around him. Because the Spanish code of honor compels men to be on guard at all times against the injurious actions of others, humor would appear as a sign of weakness and emasculation. Evaristo Acevedo in *Teoría e interpretación del humor español* writes that in Spain the tradition of ridicule (*burla*), where one laughs at others but not at oneself, prevails as the norm: "No admitimos que nadie se ría de nosotros, pero nos pasamos el día riéndonos de los demás" [We do not allow anyone to laugh at us, yet we spend the day laughing at others] (63).[9]

Canales's display of self-reflexive humor breaks from the constraints of seriousness by attacking the moral and social codes of respectability.

Canales's humor destabilizes the subject that adheres to the code of honor, which deploys respectability as a defense around the masculine self. Yet this destabilizing humor does not constitute an emasculating discourse. Instead, the text presents these codes as comic objects for the reader by underscoring their incongruity. Canales's essay, through the figure of Uncle Bruno, reveals seriousness and respectability to be mere masks rather than essential parts of a person's character. In this way, Canales's humor implements a satirical function, much like Manuel Alonso's *El jíbaro*, whose stated purpose was to correct social customs through pleasure—"corregir las costumbres deleitando" (3). Yet while Alonso's satirical *costumbrismo* sought to save *criollo* social customs from being forgotten or falling into desuetude, Canales's satirical humor contravenes tradition and challenges social norms. Though a member of the *criollo* class, Canales adopts and adapts the *criollo* tradition of satirical journalism to advocate for cultural, social, and political change.

In 1896 Canales, like other upper-class Puerto Rican men of the nineteenth century, traveled to Spain for his university education.[10] Many of his older compatriots—Alejandro Tapia y Rivera, Manuel Alonso, Luis Bonafoux Quintero, Eugenio María de Hostos—had also left the island to obtain their degrees in medicine or law, since there were no possibilities to pursue an education in these professions in Puerto Rico. After only two years at the University of Zaragoza, Canales was forced by the Spanish-American War of 1898 to return to Puerto Rico and his family's mountain home in Jayuya. Canales spent a year in Puerto Rico learning English before his father sent him to complete his studies at the University of Baltimore School of Law (now part of the University of Maryland). Canales graduated with honors in 1902, returned to the island, and moved to Ponce to begin his career in law and, eventually, his career as a journalist (*Obras completas* 84–85). Canales went on to contribute to many Puerto Rican newspapers and cultural reviews, including *El Día*, *La Conciencia Libre*, *Juan Bobo*, and his own publication, *Cuasimodo*, which he published while traveling through South America. Throughout his career in journalism, Canales used his skills as a satirist to criticize vigorously the U.S. colonial occupation in Puerto Rico, and his experiences in North America subtly appeared in his writings as part of a self-deprecating sense of humor.

By graduating from a U.S. institution, Canales joined a new class of elite Puerto Ricans that he mockingly calls "los graduados americanos" (*Paliques* 148). Because the center of political and economic power had shifted from Spain to the United States, those Puerto Rican professionals with ties to the North American mainland insinuated themselves into advantageous positions in Puerto Rican government. In an essay titled "The Portorrican Association of American Graduates," Canales describes a group of young professionals, graduates of U.S. institutions, who have organized for the purpose of promoting self-government under North American rule. Canales employs a good dose of irony to ask: "¿Puede haber nada más patriótico que eso del *self-government* bajo una bandera gloriosa?" [Can there be anything more patriotic than *self-government* under a glorious flag?] (146). However, Canales does not stand at a distance and censure the group from the margins; he attacks the group's goals by making himself the object of ridicule:

> I was in San Juan, I was among my congenial and patriotic, graduated and associated companions; and hearing them I began to drool with delight—the delight of seeing the issue of the nation finally placed in competent hands, in a lawyer's hands—and from drooling I went to clapping and to shouting hurrah, and I threw my hat up seven times, and all aquiver I was ready, convinced and emotionally moved, to fall into the arms of the Portorrican Association of American Graduates. (147)[11]

Canales caricatures himself as a political neophyte, easily swayed by camaraderie and emotional appeals. He employs several linguistic devices in his ironic praise of the American graduates and their political cause, including a superfluity of adjectives ("simpáticos"; "patrióticos"; "graduados"; "asociados") and alliteration ("el pleito de la patria puesto"; "pasé al palmoteo"; "todo trémulo"; "convencido y conmovido").[12] However, the most humorous aspect of the passage obtains from the self-mocking portrayal of his own support for the group. The vivid image of physical buffoonery, ending with a semihysterical swoon, serves to satirize how easily one can be duped into adopting ill-conceived political ideologies solely on the basis of adhering to class and professional loyalties.

Canales continues this anecdote with the introduction of another character, a newspaper boy, and because Canales professes "una maldita afición a leer" [a cursed love of reading], he buys an edition of *El Heraldo* only to read a sharp critique of the Portorrican Association (147). Canales cites a rival publication as the outside source of satirical censure, which acts as a counterpoint to his feigned emotional volatility. Thus he achieves an objective satire within a subjective framework that is highly self-conscious. Canales the narrator maintains the wide-eyed posture of political naïveté throughout the essay and hopes that *El Heraldo*'s criticism will not incite the "lower classes" to ridicule the Portorrican Association:

> And the worst thing is that this nation has deep down in its blood the love of raillery, and any day, following the pernicious example of *El Heraldo*, anyone may get the idea, a bootblack, for example, to scream at us with sarcasm and even with polish, some annoying comment such as the following:
>
> "Hey you, mister: Since when in these here parts d'you need to have a 'Merican degree to stand up for a political i-deel?" (148)[13]

Once again, Canales transposes his satirical critique of the Portorrican Association onto a third party, this time a figment of his own class paranoia. The accusation that Puerto Ricans by nature love raillery and ridicule serves to implicate the narrator of this piece, whose caricature of lower-class diction underscores the social chasm that separates the educated from the illiterate. Although it would appear that Canales stands accused by his own self-parody, he demonstrates that a self-deprecating sense of humor can function as part of a politically motivated satire. This conflation of subject and object resonates with Henri Bergson's description of a humorist: "When the humorist laughs at himself, he is really acting a double part; the self who laughs is indeed conscious, but not the self who is laughed at" (132n). Canales laughs at his politically naïve, socially privileged self by adopting the voice of a politically astute working-class persona. This satirical other reveals that the narrator's U.S. degree and profession as a lawyer actually blind him to political realities of which even the illiterate are aware. Through this doubling of the self he brings into question the class privilege that gives him access to a U.S. education. By ridiculing himself, he reveals the incongruity of Puerto Ricans who believe that, by studying abroad, they will be better able to govern at home. The voice of the bootblack makes the presumably superior *criollo* appear inferior by unmasking his lack of self-awareness.

The self-reflexive humor in many of Canales's satirical essays focuses on the journalistic persona of "Nemesio Canales," which, unlike other satirists of his day who wrote under a variety of pseudonyms, bridges the gap between *costumbrismo* and humor. This act of self-naming allows Canales to situate the journalist in the society that he observes and critiques, thus exposing the journalistic persona to the same critical eye. By doing so, the text breaches the privilege of anonymity that, according to the code of honor, allows the satirist to laugh at everyone but himself. However, in Canales's short story "Mi voluntad se ha muerto," his humor approaches the question of self-reflexivity in a different way. The story conveys Canales's long-standing advocacy for women's emancipation and the tenets of free love, yet ironically it also elaborates a self-mocking subtext that reveals the incongruity of female sexual autonomy as imagined by male sexual desire. Humorous doubling allows Canales to counterpoise a feminist perspective against the male gender bias of his first-person narrator. The story achieves this doubling by exposing its own textuality and implicating literature as both the agent of seduction and the object of desire. Canales combines this metatextual humor with an eccentric sensibility; that is, the text deploys the metaphors of displacement in order to depict a clash of cultures that destabilizes gender norms. While the affective fallout of such a destabilization is melancholy for the first-person narrator, the reader collaborates with the implied author, Canales, to regard ideological incongruity as a source of laughter.

Curbing a Romantic Tongue

From his earliest essays published in *Paliques*, Canales represents himself as a defender of women's emancipation and suffrage, even as he idealizes romantically the feminine mystique. In the essay "El voto femenino" Canales relates how he orchestrated his nomination as a delegate to the House of Representatives, and he emphasizes the fact that, in the Puerto Rico of his era, "it is no secret to anyone here—or anywhere—[that] it is not our fellow citizens who nominate you, but you who *has his fellow citizens make the nomination* for you" (187).[14] By means of this posture in which Canales states the obvious, he uses humor to accomplish two things: to criticize the political system that tries to hide its electoral machinations, and to manifest that his integration in this system is an act of will. Yet he also claims that as a politician he faced a choice: either do nothing and leave things as they were, which is the respectable and traditional mission for a delegate, or foolishly attempt to correct abuses and remedy injustices (188). He uses ironic antiphrasis—saying the opposite of what he means—to ostensibly discredit himself as naïve and dim-witted, but Canales began this essay by congratulating himself ("darme un bombo") because he bravely, or foolishly, proposed the bill "For the Legal Emancipation of Women," which read: "Every right, whatever its disposition or nature, conceded by the laws in effect in Puerto Rico to the male citizens of legal age, will be understood as conceded to women as well, and regulated in its practice and application in the same manner and conditions as if dealing with men" (*Obras completas* 87–88).[15] The wording of this bill reveals that Canales's thinking in regard to women's emancipation was unequivocal, but the ironic tone of his essay adopts the perspective of his political opponents who ridiculed his position. Consequently, those opposed to women's emancipation fall in the camp of the respectable and traditional politicians who uphold the status quo, while Canales aligns himself with those who foolishly advocate change. Once again a humorous doubling, this time functioning through ironic antiphrasis, allows Canales to redirect self-mockery toward his real targets: male chauvinism and the political system that enforces it as law.

Canales's bill was soundly defeated after an impassioned refutation by José de Diego, well known in Puerto Rican politics for his flashes of oratorical brilliance ("períodos relampagueantes").[16] Although Canales does not reproduce de Diego's words in "El voto femenino," critic Servando Montaña Peláez, in *Nemesio Canales: Lenguaje y situación*, cites a passage from de Diego's speech that implores Canales to abandon his bill:

> . . . Let the author of this Bill leave the woman to the plenteous and dulcet empire that Nature has formed for her and God has conceded to her; do not strip her of her crown, her throne, and her scepter in the home; do not remove her from the love and calm of the family to the hatred and passions of virile struggles; do not remove her from the beatific serenity of the home to the often infernal din of political vexations.
>
> . . . Woman! Saintly Puerto Rican woman! You do not have the right to vote, like men, but you have the right to make men vote by the irresistible force of your weakness, your beauty, and your love: from your sacred womb will the future generations be born, and in your saintly bosom will they learn to love the nation and to fight and perhaps die for the triumph of its ideals! (102)[17]

According to de Diego, a woman's power and influence lie paradoxically in her weakness and silence, and her body's reproductive capacity is her greatest asset. De Diego's discourse reflects a conservative Spanish romanticism and its characterization of woman as the *ángel del hogar*. This idealized woman, free from passion but full of love, supposedly limits her affairs to the domestic and reproductive spheres for the benefit of the nation (Kirkpatrick 56–58).

Even though Canales does not quote de Diego's discourse in "El voto femenino," his readers would have been familiar with de Diego's style of oratory. Canales parodies de Diego's depiction of the "saintly" Puerto Rican woman by presenting his own ironic romantic gallantry to the "noble" Puerto Rican woman in order to show just how condescending such professions of worship really are. He presents this critique by caricaturing his own libidinous impulses, and this self-mockery combines with parody to expose the incongruity of idealizing women as a means of denying them their emancipation. He addresses this humorous critique to another well-known politician, Luis Muñoz Rivera, who came out in favor of women's suffrage only after the failure of Canales's bill, but avoided mentioning any affinity with said legislative venture at the time of its proposal. Canales writes:

> Señor Muñoz Rivera: this small man with his round, irregular, and tedious face, born in Jayuya, whom you undoubtedly remember and admire in silence for his past campaign in favor of the Puerto Rican woman, greets you on this luminous day to shout out his enthusiastic support and sincere admiration for your beautiful proposals in benefit of the noble cause of the noble Puerto Rican woman (whose tiny and graceful feet, very well scrubbed, I should never tire of kissing). (*Paliques* 189–90)[18]

Canales employs self-mockery to expose Muñoz Rivera's lukewarm support for women's rights, yet he also incorporates irony in his professed adoration of women as a means to refute de Diego's romantic conservatism. While Canales's gallantry appears to contradict his progressive feminist politics, the humorous doubling adopts the language and ideology of his political opponents in order to argue against them and denounce their hypocrisy.

Canales abhorred the overblown rhetorical style that predominated in Puerto Rican journalism, and his parody of de Diego's oratory demonstrates his rejection of a literature that aspires to grammatical correctness, euphony, and lyrical beauty but remains ideologically superficial. Canales criticized the cult of *casticismo* in literature because it favored outmoded rhetoric over ideas that challenged the status quo (*Antología* 349–50). For this reason, he named his 1919 literary magazine *Cuasimodo* after Victor Hugo's hunchback, who, while physically ugly, carried the possibility for beauty and nobility in his heart.[19] Escudero Valentín, in *Literatura y periodismo en la obra de Nemesio Canales*, writes that Canales chose this name to reflect on the ugliness of reality rather than produce a literature that turns away from reality's ugliness in order to become beautiful merely in appearance ("una mera belleza de tocador") (134). Yet even as Canales rejects superficial beauty in literature, he constantly professes his adoration of beautiful women, and when he does so his language approaches the superficiality he so deplored.

When Canales writes of himself as "un hombre muy feo y muy enamorado," he morphs from Hugo's Quasimodo into Don Juan Tenorio, José Zorrilla's legendary serial seducer. On the one hand, Canales admits to his own ugliness. In "El voto femenino" he even takes on some of Quasimodo's characteristics when he describes himself as a man with a "round, irregular, and tedious face." He also advocates stripping literature of its rhetorical ornamentation to see the ugliness of the ideas that such "purist" language masks. On the other hand, he proclaims himself a fervent devotee of Don Juan, the ultimate lover of beauty. He writes: "My cruel fate condemned me to be ugly, and I have been ugly beyond all hope, but I had in my blood a tiny drop of the glorious blood of that glorious ancestor [Don Juan], and I have followed in his footsteps, the resounding footsteps, the epic footsteps of the immense Don Juan, pursuing in every woman's mouth a new emotion and in every new emotion a furtive glimpse of the divine, ineffable mystery of life" (*Antología* 71).[20]

As the ugly Quasimodo, Canales acts as a defender of women and women's rights. His feminism made him an outcast among his more traditional compatriots, with their code of honor that relegated women to a subservient position. However, as Don Juan Tenorio, Canales idealizes women and objectifies them sexually. His *donjuanismo* also puts him in conflict with bourgeois morality and the code of honor's regulation of female sexuality. Canales admits that his less than agreeable appearance hindered his career as a true Don Juan, but his fervent desires for women never abated. Canales developed many of his feminist ideas in his essays, yet in others he provides evidence for his self-proclaimed *donjuanismo*. How does Canales reconcile the incongruity between his feminist stance supporting women's emancipation and his lascivious desire for women? Canales uses humorous doubling to expose the contradictions in his attitudes toward women. In his short story "Mi voluntad se ha muerto," Canales offers a pseudoautobiographical satire of this incongruity by adopting a woman's voice, which addresses the male subject and redirects the discourse of seduction back to its source.

Canales was not the only Puerto Rican writer of his era who straddled ostensibly opposing ideologies. Luisa Capetillo, who also fought for the emancipation of women—but from the worker's perspective—tempered her ardent socialist anarchism with a good measure of spiritualism. Consistent with anarchism, she advocated a cooperative society that did not rely on organized government (Capetillo 1992, 98). At the same time, the confraternity that she proposed as the motive force behind this utopian society was also the bond that would unite the diversity of existences ("la diversidad de existencias"), in which she proclaimed herself a firm believer (99). Capetillo, much like other feminists who took inspiration from romantic writers such as George Sand, did not completely renounce the idealism of the previous era, mostly because it had been romanticism that fomented the political and social revolutions of Europe and the Americas in the eighteenth and nineteenth centuries (Valle Ferrer 1990, 39–58).

Canales, too, often proclaims himself a hopeless romantic, writing in the essay "Romántico": "there is no recourse for this miserable sinner but to feel romantic to my very core this evening" (*Paliques* 154).[21] To escape from the political intrigues of U.S. colonialism and island politics, Canales turns to the type of romanticism that idealizes nature over society. He invokes his "romanticismo innato" to avoid the pedestrian issues of the day and focus on nature's beauty. Along with this poetic invocation, Canales anthropomorphizes nature and casts the natural elements as a woman who offers him furtive kisses: "furtivas caricias de labios amados que tímidamente me rozan la frente" (56). Canales is not shy about revealing his romantic tendencies and his sexual desire for women. In a poem titled "En tu oído" [In your ear], he resorts once again to romantic imagery and the language of seduction:

> I would like to press, in the rough-hewn
> Chalice of my rhyme, juices of madness,
> That would burn your satin flesh
> With the impure fire that tortures me.
>
> Let my phrases cut like a dagger
> And tear the veils from your chastity . . .
> Let my verses blaze with the fury of a torch
> Calling forth raptures of a crazed witches' sabbath
>   (*Antología* 78)[22]

These inflammatory words are very similar to those of the libidinous character in José Zorrilla's play *Don Juan Tenorio*, who seduces the chaste and naïve Doña Inés with a letter filled with sparks ("chispa"), a bonfire ("hoguera"), and a volcano ("volcán") (151–52). Canales's poem suggests that a woman is capable of burning with sexual passion, but it does not portray any hint of her capacity to love in a chaste, angelic way, as the more conservative romanticism would have imagined.[23]

Yet Canales's later writings begin to display an estrangement from his romantic idealization of women and, furthermore, an incipient seriousness in his socialist politics. In his 1916 essay "Nuestras mujeres," Canales vituperates against the poetic custom of taking women "por simples muñecas, por juguetes de puro artificio donde sólo hay exterioridad" [for simple dolls, for toys of pure artifice in which there is only exterior appearance] (*Antología* 155). Considering the romanticized passages we have seen above, this argument may be Canales's mea culpa, but the real purpose of the essay is to address Puerto Rican women and ask: "How can one explain the deathly apathy that keeps you tranquil, impassive, silent as statues in the midst of the grandiose din of the momentous fray, to which today's women are committed in order to save their souls and assure their future?" (156).[24] Canales addresses women as a man sympathetic to their cause, but his questions betray a somewhat condescending tone, as if women were unwilling to speak for themselves out of sheer apathy. What Canales does not acknowledge is that by 1916 Luisa Capetillo had already published four feminist books, had traveled to New York, to Ybor City and Tampa, Florida, and to Havana, where she was arrested for wearing men's clothing and was deported for spreading anarchist ideas (Ramos 1992, 66). Capetillo was a pioneer, and very few women in Puerto Rico followed in her footsteps at the time, so the accusatory and frustrated tone that Canales takes with Puerto Rican women is not entirely without justification. Yet his essay shows that he speaks for women without recognizing their own voice.

In 1917 in the magazine *Idearium* Canales published an essay in which, for the first time, he communicates the urgency of his feminist ideas by taking on the voice of a woman. In "Nuestras mujeres y la cuestión feminista" two interlocutors, one male, the other female, debate the validity of women's emancipation and suffrage. After exhausting all of his sophisms, the man asks: "Pero . . . ¿y la poesía?, ¿y la tradición?, ¿y el culto caballeresco a la mujer . . . ?" [But . . . what about poetry? what about tradition? what about the chivalrous worship of women . . . ?] (*Antología* 168). The woman responds:

Do not continue, by God, do not continue. I have tolerated everything from you for the sake of discussion, but this last bit is too much and

I will not tolerate it. To spout poetry about women, the physical beauty and morals of women, . . . to confess yourself still an advocate of the deceitful and degrading romantic tradition that makes of woman a plaything, an instrument for man's recreation . . . Oh, I will not tolerate another word from you. Charlatan or blind man, I can expect nothing from you. Out of my way, for time flies and the task at hand is urgent and in my blood there are flames of impatience and courage and faith. (168–69)[25]

Canales explicates his ideas in the form of a dialogue, giving the woman a voice of her own so that she can directly confront the man who subjects her to the "degrading romantic tradition." The woman in this dialogue, instead of being the object of poetic fancy, is the impassioned fighter who dedicates herself to the "task" of her own emancipation. Canales's rhetoric articulates the urgency of a feminist politics much more radical than the legislative reformism he proposed in 1909. Now it is the woman who has her own voice and who takes the initiative. While Canales's earlier poem attempted to ignite the flames of sexual passion in his object of desire, the woman he represents here burns with a political passion as she pushes the man aside in order to follow her own path. Canales reorchestrates this debate between male and female in his later short story "Mi voluntad se ha muerto." In this text, the woman's voice belongs to a female character who undermines the male's romantic tendencies by turning the language of seduction on its head through irony.

There are many elements in this story that invite speculation as to whether it is based on Canales's own experiences. The main character and first-person narrator, Miguel, is a Venezuelan medical student who has just graduated from an East Coast university, as Canales did with his law degree from Baltimore. Both Miguel and Canales originate from the mountainous regions of their respective homelands, and both have younger sisters named Paula. Another clue that indicates to the reader the pseudoautobiographical nature of this story is its title: "Mi voluntad se ha muerto" is a line from Manuel Machado's poem "Adelfos," which paints a melancholy self-portrait of its author. The citation of this poem frames the text, appearing at the beginning and the end, and acts at both the diegetic and extradiegetic levels as a means of questioning subjectivity.[26] José Ignacio Badenes, in "The Poetic Text as Dandy: Reading the Poetry of Manuel Machado," describes "Adelfos" as a testament to the kind of self-creation and self-aestheticizing characteristic of the dandy. Badenes writes:

"In 'Adelfos,' like in a typical verbal self-portrait, the poetic voice discourses about itself as if it were another self. This discourse is provoked by the self-portrait's fundamental question: 'Who am I?'" (408).

While it functions to inspire Miguel's reminiscence at the diegetic level, the citation also performs an extradiegetic reflection on Canales's career as journalist, his ideological evolution, and the incongruity of his feminist *donjuanismo*. Just as Canales mocked his own journalistic persona to satirize larger social issues, he uses humor in "Mi voluntad se ha muerto" to comment on writing and his status as a politically engaged writer. Unless the reader follows Canales's journalistic career, this story appears as the bittersweet musings of a fictional character. However, the story, like the poem that frames it, is a "verbal self-portrait" in which Canales discourses about his authorial self "as if it were another self."

The reader first encounters this fictional self, Miguel, as he walks down Fifth Avenue in Manhattan. Like a Baudelairean flâneur, Miguel traverses the urban space of modernity "una molécula de la gran marejada humana" [like a molecule in the great sea of humanity] (*Antología* 404). The avenue down which Miguel walks also marks the text's attention to exteriority and the open space in which the subject loses his singularity, becoming indistinguishable from the masses surrounding him. As a Venezuelan, however, Miguel's presence in New York initiates an eccentric sensibility, in which the culture and society of North America are seen through Latin American eyes. Miguel, anxious to return to his family's hacienda in Venezuela, is preparing to say farewell to Manhattan when he runs into his compatriot Narciso Díaz, a middle-aged businessman and friend of the family who has come unexpectedly to New York. Their excitement on meeting leads them to display their Latino otherness in full view of the New York passersby: "And I flew more than ran to the other side of the street, where you can already imagine the Latin commotion we kicked up with our salutations and questions and replies" (404).[27] Miguel and Narciso, like many other Latin Americans in New York at the beginning of the twentieth century, negotiate the urban space to make visible their Latino identities.[28]

Narciso informs Miguel that he has traveled to New York to commit the Seven Deadly Sins and recruits Miguel as a cohort in this decadent campaign (405). Miguel reluctantly postpones his return to Venezuela, and the two go from party to party in the cosmopolitan nightlife of 1920s New York.[29] Miguel quickly tires of the urban bustle and persuades his friend to continue their adventures in the Catskill Mountains, a resort area in upstate New York very popular with the bourgeoisie of the period. It is here that we see Miguel's romantic tendencies manifest themselves. Upon entering the nearby woods, book in hand, the young man unleashes a grandiloquent ode to a tree: "Oh tree, how ineffable your company! How calmly you transfigure yourself in the silence, almost appearing to have a soul that you offer up" (409).[30] The book that Miguel carries with him acts as the medium through which he communicates with nature; we see that his repose in this *locus amoenus* is mediated by literature. In this way Canales achieves a *mise en abyme* effect in which the representation of nature that the reader perceives is also a "reading" on Miguel's part. This irony, which the reader becomes aware of but Miguel ignores, directs the text toward a parody of the bombastic language of romantic poetry, which infuses representations of nature with sentimentality. Canales used the same language in his essay "Romántico" from *Paliques*, in which he allows himself to succumb to the soothing nocturnal atmosphere, but only because he does not want to think of the political intrigues that plague his mind (154–56). In this instance of romanticism, Canales's journalistic persona has sought solace in nature in order to escape the noise of modernity and societal artifice, yet in Miguel's case the scene is mediated by literature and reading, thus demonstrating how nature is already a "written" text.

Reading serves another important function in the story when Miguel enters the hotel library and finds a mislaid copy of Tolstoy's *The Fruits of Culture*. The owner of the book, Lucy, and her friend Raquel return to retrieve it, and encounter Miguel. Once again literature acts as the intermediary between Miguel and what will quickly become the objects of his desire. Miguel immediately takes the opportunity to strike up a conversation, and finds each of the two American girls fascinating in her own way. Raquel is blond, pretty, and "de cierta delgadez de busto y amplitud de caderas que sorprendían y encantaban" [of a certain smallness of breast and fullness of hips that surprised and delighted]. Lucy, on the other hand, is "bajita, morenucha, de líneas redondas, de una cara ni bonita ni fea" [short, rather dark, with rounded features, with a face neither pretty nor ugly] (*Antología* 410–11). In addition to their physical differences, Raquel is the daughter of a wealthy attorney, while Lucy is a poor but independent schoolteacher. The blonde is animated and loquacious, but the brunette is serious and pensive. These marked differences in appearance and character suggest that Raquel incarnates the romantic image of woman that Canales cultivated in his poetry and in *Paliques*, and Lucy is more like the strong, rational, and emancipated woman from his later essays. At first Miguel takes special notice of Raquel's physical attributes, but as the level of their conversation becomes more profound, he forgets about her and gives all of his attention to Lucy and her extraordinary intelligence.

Lucy proves herself quite capable of undermining men with her progressive ideas, her sharp, critical perspective, and the aggressiveness of her rhetorical ironies. When Miguel tries to take a tone of superiority with her in their discussion of Tolstoy, she trips him up with a simple smile and silences him with an earnest dissertation on the satirical portrayal of spiritualism in *The Fruits of Culture*.[31] The citation of Tolstoy's play offers a metatextual commentary on the text in which it appears. This comedy involves a young woman of the Russian servant class who outwits her aristocratic superiors by manipulating their spiritualist beliefs. She does so to ensure her marriage to a male servant from the same household, as well as to coerce her employer to sign a deed of land over to the resident peasants. By having this text act as the intermediary between Miguel and the American women, Canales already foreshadows the outcome of his own story. Just as the clever servant girl in *The Fruits of Culture* manipulates others with spiritualist fakery, showing them what they eagerly want to believe, so too will Lucy and Raquel dupe Miguel by using his own desires against him. Miguel desires Lucy for her intelligence and facility with language, but he also desires Raquel for her physical beauty and demure demeanor. Just like Canales with his feminist *donjuanismo*, Miguel hypocritically wants to see the plain Lucy as beautiful while desiring Raquel for her more superficial qualities.

We see an example of Lucy's wit in another scene. A debate takes place on the hotel terrace, and several guests begin to discuss women's emancipation, which offers Canales the opportunity to restage his confrontation with the opponents of women's rights. Miguel attempts to intercede with his stance in favor of suffrage, but a young doctor of philosophy and letters from Johns Hopkins University thwarts his tenuous arguments and captures the audience with his eloquence (419). This scene reenacts the political defeat that Canales suffered at the hands of José de Diego, but in the literary version it is a woman's wit and wisdom that rescue the clumsy male apologist for feminism. Lucy enters the discussion and crushes the presumptuous orator from Johns Hopkins "Con un fuego graneado de preguntas, suavemente moduladas, pero cargadas de ironía" [with a rapid-fire volley of questions, smoothly modulated, but charged with irony] (419). Thus Canales revises his previous political failure, but he gives the last word to a female character so that the voice of a woman may intervene in a male-dominated discursive space. Canales speaks through Lucy, even though this character turns her sharp wits against Miguel, his fictional alter ego. At the diegetic level, Lucy acts as a foil to Miguel and the other male characters, but at the extradiegetic level this female character is another of Canales's alter egos—a literary persona that the author uses to undermine his own authority through self-mockery. What Lucy mocks is not Canales but his writings and his career as a writer, in which contradictory ideas exist simultaneously without any clear resolution.

Literature acts repeatedly as an intermediary between Miguel and Lucy. In yet another scene the two find themselves in the woods, where the impetuous Miguel declares his affections. Miguel falls under a rhapsodic spell as Lucy reads from one of Oscar Wilde's books. Instead of trying to kiss Lucy, he takes the book from her hands and begins to kiss its cover. This action implies that Miguel has not overcome his fixation on physical beauty, and instead of offering himself body and soul to Lucy, he chooses to mediate his affections through literature—that is, the book. The scene also suggests that, by kissing the book, Miguel transforms the agent of seduction into the object of desire. He desires not so much Lucy as her language. Lucy, who maintains her composure, suggests that perhaps they should just remain friends, but Miguel continues to burn with a romanticized passion. He says: "Lucy, yo también he tenido muchas novias, pero nunca una amiga . . . ¡La amiga! Lucy, Lucy, ríete; ¡Pero tengo ganas de llorar!" [Lucy, I too have had many lovers, but never a woman friend. . . . The friend! Lucy, Lucy, go ahead and laugh. But I want to cry!] (418). To which she responds: "Sí, ¿verdad? Yo también. De llorar, como cuando se nace" [Yes, isn't it true? I do too. To cry, as when one is born] (418). This double entendre, very much in the spirit of Oscar Wilde, goes undetected by Miguel, who interprets it to mean that Lucy feels as if she has been reborn in love, but its other meaning is that Lucy considers Miguel a newborn babe: fresh, ingenuous, and easily swayed by emotion. Lucy's witticism recalls Canales's portrayal of himself as a political neophyte who succumbs to semihysterical emotional displays in favor of ill-conceived ideas. The levels of humorous doubling here multiply as one set of literary personae mirrors another. Lucy's character acts as the voice of the other, just as the bootblack—a figment of Canales's class paranoia—spoke back to the authorial persona in the essay on the Portorrican Association of American Graduates. Lucy also acts as the bridge in the shifts between the diegetic and the extradiegetic levels in the text. And as one of Canales's alter egos, her mediation demonstrates the difficulty of distinguishing the writer from the writing. In other words, the writer is both agent and object of his writing, particularly when using humorous doubling to speak of the self as if it were another self. In this case, there are multiple selves through which the writer speaks, but which also speak back to the source of writing. Through Lucy, Canales redresses the romanticism of his earlier texts and thus achieves a metatextual form of humor.

Eventually Lucy's skepticism of Miguel proves correct. Much in the spirit of Canales's self-proclaimed *donjuanismo*, Miguel is unable to limit his desire to one woman, and as soon as he finds himself alone in the woods with Raquel, he allows himself to be transported by the nocturnal ambience and the girl's physical beauty. He begins to shower her with long, fervent kisses, but this time on the lips. Raquel pulls Miguel back into romanticism, and his desire manifests itself as the kiss. Yet just like Lucy's character, Raquel recalls one of Canales's literary personae: the hopeless romantic who finds solace and sensuality in nature. Raquel kisses Miguel the way the tropical breeze of Puerto Rico kissed the implied author in the essay "Romántico." It is important to recall that Miguel's desire to travel to the Catskill Mountains was to assuage his true desire: to return to his mountain home and his family in Venezuela. Raquel represents that desire for the land and that yearning for home, and Miguel reaches out to fulfill those desires through her. Yet this seduction can take place only in Lucy's absence, since her liberal politics, wit, free way of speaking, and access to world literature represent a desire for cosmopolitanism and the urban center. The incongruity between the women also reflects that tension between the insular and the eccentric; that is, when the Puerto Rican subject confronts its cultural other. As in the essay critiquing the Portorrican Association of American Graduates, Lucy represents those values of the metropolis that Canales ridiculed as insufficient to address the political situation in Puerto Rico. At the extradiegetic level, Canales uses this love triangle to underscore the conflicting ideologies of his previous texts. The reader sees in Miguel's desire for both Lucy and Raquel a reflection of Canales's feminist *donjuanismo*.

As in Canales's writings, Miguel alternates between submitting to a woman's voice and desiring to seduce her. Yet Canales elicits the reader's laughter at this incongruity, and he transforms the love triangle into a comic situation. Just as Miguel begins to kiss Raquel, he is surprised by Lucy's voice behind him, saying, "Caramba, niños, dejen algo para mí" [Goodness, kids, leave some for me] (422). Miguel clumsily tries to explain himself, but Lucy calms him and tells him that she would like very much for the three of them to get together, and that she had been waiting for the right moment in which it would happen spontaneously. She stands next to Raquel and invites Miguel to kiss them both: "Come, Raquel . . . Like so, close together. Now . . . do us the favor, sir, of kissing us with a single kiss" (423).[32] This audacious proposition of a ménage à trois is an obligatory fantasy in contemporary pornography, but does it mean that Lucy, the intellectual schoolteacher, has been the seducer all along? How does her proposition undermine the seductive power of a young Don Juan like Miguel?

Canales anticipates the reader's skepticism because he has the stupefied Miguel ask Lucy if her libidinous offer is not just another cruel refinement of her irony (423). Lucy adopts a serious posture and answers, "But . . . what is this! Don't you understand? . . . And you, Raquel, do you think me ironical as well?" (423).[33] Raquel replies, "Lucy, my Lucy; now I admire you more than ever!" (424).[34] This response is purposely ambiguous since Raquel does not directly answer the question that Lucy has put to her. Does Raquel admire Lucy's willingness to share Miguel or her ability to undermine Miguel's serial seduction? Raquel answers Lucy's ironical question with irony of her own. Canales shows that his male character is not sufficiently clever to get the joke that the two girls are having at his expense, while he encourages the reader to hear the irony in Lucy's and Raquel's exchange in order to perceive Miguel's naïveté. Miguel is stupefied by the two women standing together, and the reader sees in his reaction a Don Juan trounced by his own discourse of seduction.

It is important to recall that one of Canales's other "selves" appears in his writings as the Puerto Rican heir to Don Juan Tenorio, whose own use of language was both seductive and seditious.[35] In an essay titled "Don Quijote y don Juan Tenorio," Canales declares that, as a writer, he would rather be a Cervantes than a Tirso de Molina or a José Zorrilla but, as a character, he would much rather be a Don Juan Tenorio than a Don Quijote. For Canales, Don Quijote only idealized one woman, but he did not truly love her. On the other hand, Don Juan did not exhaust his desire for women by limiting himself to idealizing them. Canales writes: "while

Don Quijote, I repeat, imagined love instead of feeling it, and he made use of it as if it were a toy or a pretense for imitating with a thousand feigned laments, sighs, litanies, and hallelujahs of platonic love the amorous anguish of the knights errant, Don Juan continued savoring, in living and overflowing amphoras of love, exquisite honeys, without ever slaking the immense thirst of his burning soul" (*Paliques* 203).[36]

Canales prefers the kind of love that the figure of Don Juan offers to women because it goes beyond idealizing them as abstractions and dares to engage them as corporeal beings capable of sexual pleasure. Yet as a serial seducer, Don Juan also objectifies women through limitless desire. For Canales, Don Juan's incurable yearning for beauty ("ansias incurables de belleza") is man's natural state, but marriage, with its promise of fidelity to one woman, is an artificial societal construction ("artificialismo del actual mecanismo social") (205). Once a man submits to this societal construction, he might as well confess to his self-imposed castration ("confesarse humillado que es casi un eunuco") (205). When Canales holds up the figure of Don Juan as the epitome of the lover, he advocates an ethics of free love in which love is not a means to an end but is the agent and the object of a discourse that reiterates itself as a ceaseless series of seductions. Shoshana Felman, in her analysis of Molière's version of the Don Juan myth (1983), argues that "seductive discourse exploits the capacity of language to reflect itself" and "exploits in parallel fashion the self-referentiality of the interlocutor's narcissistic desire." In other words, "the seducer holds out to women the narcissistic mirror of their own desire of themselves" (31).

However, Lucy turns that seduction on its head by confronting Don Juan—that is, Miguel—with his own desire. In other words, her proposition shocks the male seducer with his own narcissism and desire of himself. The Don Juan who seduces as a way to reveal to women their self-love has his self-love revealed to him. Once again, the text employs a metatextual humor that reflects Canales's own *donjuanismo* back on itself. But unlike the narcissism of seduction, humor holds up to the subject a mirror cracked. As Lucy and Raquel reflect Miguel's desire of himself back at him, he perceives the incongruity of Lucy and Raquel and what they represent: literature and nature; mind and body; active and passive; the center and the periphery. Unlike the seduction's narcissistic mirror, Lucy's proposition acts like the self-reflexivity of humor, which allows the subject to perceive itself as a fragmented self that has been fractured with otherness.

Lucy's proposition upsets Miguel so much that he runs hastily from the woods, gathers his friend Narciso (whose name should provide yet another clue to the self-reflexive humor of this story), and flees back to the city. The instant he arrives, he regrets his departure and returns to the Catskills in search of the two girls.

He convinces himself of his newfound consciousness along the way with a soliloquy: "Behind the fortress walls of the ancestral brutality that makes of love a sacrifice—barbarous if it is sincere and hypocritical if it is false—of one spirit to another, I did not see right away that it was my blind vanity that rose up before the very idea that my Lucy did not act, like all other women, jealous and miserly with the exclusive property of my heart" (426).[37] Miguel employs the metaphor of a warlike struggle between the tradition of marriage and free love. These two combatants acquire the characteristics of a feudal landlord—"behind the fortress walls of the ancestral brutality"—and of a socialist, who fights against "exclusive property." Canales shows how easily Miguel appropriates the political language of the moment to justify his ill-conceived actions. At the extradiegetic level, Canales suggests that the political discourse of socialism—which characterized his later writings—cannot entirely erase the romanticism that appeared earlier in his career. The two isms exist simultaneously in the space of the author's works, whose outlines take shape under the retrospective lens of self-criticism.

Nevertheless, the character Miguel lacks the ironic perspective with which to scrutinize his own volatile ideas. In the end, Miguel's belated rationalizations serve him little since, when he arrives at the hotel in the Catskills, Lucy and Raquel have disappeared without a trace. Miguel returns to Venezuela and, ten years later, he still laments the loss of the miracle ("el milagro") that he thought he had seen in the two American girls. The final irony is that the character maintains his romanticism, but what obsesses him in middle age is the lost love that is never to return. His heart tells him, in words that parody those of Edgar Allan Poe: "Nunca más volverán ni Lucy ni Raquel . . . Nunca más . . . nunca más" [Nevermore will they return, neither Lucy nor Raquel . . . Nevermore . . . nevermore] (427). With this denouement, Canales allegorizes his own alienation from romanticism and his espousal of socialist ideas, but the nostalgic contemplation of these ideological conflicts offers a humorous self-portrait of the writer as a young man. Many critics have accused Canales of being an incurable invalid of spirit (Rivera de Alvarez 232), but his self-flagellation serves as a critique of the notion of ideological evolution, for it is only in retrospect, and when one aestheticizes the self, that an evolutionary narrative can take shape. His depiction of a woman's wit and wisdom satirizes the Hispanic paternalism mired in romanticism, but the metatextual humor of "Mi voluntad se ha muerto" shows Canales's reluctance to fully abandon that romanticism.

Women's rights was just one of many social issues Canales addressed in his humorous essays, although all of his short fiction and his play, *El héroe galopante*, focus more directly on depictions of women coming into a liberating self-awareness and actively undermining the authority of men. Canales invested a serious political commitment in his humorous writings, as his treatment of women's issues clearly demonstrates. Canales's travels across the Americas, his prolific journalism, and his political activity proved he was a man of action, not a melancholic nonconformist. Canales's humor set him apart from many of his contemporaries who sought to validate Puerto Rican national identity according to a paternalistic tradition, which propagated the inviolability of male subjectivity and idealized a social order based on male privilege. Yet Canales's texts did not greatly influence a similar humorous self-scrutiny among the writers of succeeding generations, particularly those of the Generación del Treinta and the Generación del Cuarenta y cinco. Writers such as Antonio Pedreira, Tomás Blanco, Enrique Laguerre, René Marqués, José Luis González, and Pedro Juan Soto did attempt to answer the question "Who are we?" (¿Qué y cómo somos?).[38] With a few exceptions, the writers and intellectuals who addressed the question of Puerto Rican identity conveyed their pessimism through the tragic mode and the insular vision. Even writers like Luis Palés Matos, Manuel Menéndez Ballester, and Emilio S. Belaval, who explored the issue of Puerto Rican identity through the comic mode, did not use a self-reflexive humor to explore the limits of their own authorial image the way Nemesio Canales did in so many of his texts. In other words, while the issue of Puerto Rican identity generated a rich, complex literary tradition, rarely has the literary medium itself, along with its practitioners, come under an equally intense scrutiny.

Canales was a humorist almost to a fault, but his self-mockery served to expose so many of Puerto Rican society's incongruities and hypocrisies. In 1923, on a steamship bound for New York, Canales was ready to undertake a new journalistic enterprise, but he died before making it to his destination (*Obras completas* 104). His body was returned to Puerto Rico, where a series of events were hastily arranged in his honor, and his play, *El héroe galopante,* was staged for the first time as a posthumous tribute. In 1915 Canales wrote somewhat prophetically:

> I ask on my knees of this, my beloved and stingy country (the stingiest in the world), that it meditate well over what I have done and over what I have yet to do as an artist and a thinker, and if it has the idea that tomorrow it will lavish me with superlatives and glorify my pen, that it not commit, that it not commit, holy and blessed God, the stupid cruelty of sitting around waiting patiently for me to die from exhaustion or misery, to then come forth drooling all over itself with tenderness before my dead body and calling itself my admirer and friend! (*Antología* 125)[39]

Even though Canales reflects on his own death, he uses this morbid diatribe as a humorous critique against the narrow-mindedness of the Puerto Rican literary canon and its refusal to recognize living writers who do not necessarily conform to nationalist ideologies. Canales's sense of humor is very similar to what Mexican philosopher Jorge Portilla would describe almost thirty years after Canales's death: "The humorist indicates with his attitude the fact that we cannot write off our responsibility, that is, our liberty, simply because life is hard; he shows that man is called, always of his free will, for tasks whose demands cannot be deferred, even though life is a 'sea of misfortunes'" (81).[40] The ability to laugh at his own lot in the face of adversity made Canales one of Puerto Rico's best humorists; his self-awareness never degenerated into solipsism, and his social critiques always formed part of his quest for political and social change.

Humor and *Jaibería* in the Novels of Luis Rafael Sánchez

"The truths of metaphysics are the truths of masks."

Oscar Wilde, "The Truth of Masks"

For Puerto Rican writers who have elaborated an insular vision in their texts, engaging in a literary affirmation of national identity often relies on the notion of a stable, autochthonous tradition that finds its fullest expression on the island. Yet these efforts to situate Puerto Rican national identity exclusively on the island do not fully take into account the destabilizing effects of migration and the diaspora. In Luis Rafael Sánchez's "La guagua aérea," Puerto Ricans employ the *arte de bregar* in order to make do despite the constant comings and goings between the island and the mainland. Sánchez's short narrative describes the exuberant pandemonium that takes place on one of the regular flights between San Juan and New York. For many Puerto Ricans, the trip between the island and the mainland has become such a regular affair that boarding a plane is equivalent to getting on a bus, and living in two places has been so normalized that many of these frequent flyers travel without luggage, since they have a home at either end of the trajectory. During the particular flight that Sánchez describes, a pair of crabs—"jueyes"—escape from a passenger's bag and scramble across the cabin floor, causing the *gringa* flight attendant to scream as if she has just seen a terrorist or hijacker. At first the passengers panic, but when they see the cause of the commotion, the plane erupts in laughter, which "seems at the point of depressurizing the cabin and offsetting the angle-of-attack of the flying bus" (Laguna-Díaz 2002, 632).[1] Through laughter, the passengers release their tensions and disrupt the regimented order of the airplane. They share stories, food, and rum, but most of all they share a sense of community in opposition to their official status as "passengers." The narrator becomes aware that these passengers have made a home for themselves in the very airspace in which they travel. The Puerto Rican nation is no longer confined to the island's borders; it has spread out across the North American landscape and remains in constant motion. Like the crabs whose escape enlivens the airplane's atmosphere, Puerto Ricans' migration—once a source of despair and anguish—has brought new life to the multiple spaces where *el arte de bregar* continually transforms the landscape.

That crablike movement, or *jaibería*, has also become an alternate strategy for Puerto Ricans who survive under the adverse conditions of colonialism and the diaspora. Moving from side to side in their politics, language, and cultural practices, Puerto Ricans avoid being pinned down and defined by institutional discourses. Francisco Manrique Cabrera, in *Historia de la literatura puertorriqueña*, describes *jaibería* as a shrewd simulation meant to throw off anyone who confronts you directly ("simulación taimada para despistar a quien se acerque") (62). While this evasive maneuver has connotations of cowardice and weakness, more recent cultural critics such as Juan Manuel García Passalacqua have reaffirmed *jaibería* as a viable means of surviving in conditions of dependency and marginalization. García Passalacqua writes in *Dignidad y Jaibería* that the popular saying "Hay que ser jaiba para sobrevivir" ("You have to be slippery to survive") does not carry any pejorative connotations; rather, it is an affirmation of a worldview from the perspective of popular culture (59–60). Similarly, in their introductory essay to *Puerto Rican Jam: Essays on Culture and Politics,* Frances Negrón-Muntaner, Ramón Grosfoguel, and Chloé S. Georas also support the notion of *jaibería* as an alternative to oppositional discourses on national identity. They write: "Within the Puerto Rican usage, *jaibería* refers to collective practices of nonconfrontation and evasion . . . , of taking dominant discourse literally in order to subvert it for one's purpose, of doing whatever one sees fit not as a head-on collision ('winning' is impossible) but a bit under the table, that is, through other means" (30–31).

What makes *jaibería* such a compelling literary strategy for Puerto Rican writers is that, as subjects who live in incongruity, who move from side to side between languages and from one discursive extreme to another, Puerto Rican writers must often poach from power the means with which to articulate their multifaceted national identity. *Jaibería* becomes an empowering means of carving out a space in discourse through movement and flexibility.

Luis Rafael Sánchez performs a textual *jaibería* in his two innovative novels, *La guaracha del Macho Camacho* and *La importancia de llamarse Daniel Santos*. These texts elaborate what Sánchez calls a "poética de lo soez" (poetics of the vulgar), in which he combines a number of high cultural references and literary parodies with the highly immodest, eroticized language and imagery particular to the Puerto Rican popular classes. In both texts Sánchez attempts to represent a collage of marginal voices, imitating various "sociolects" of Latin American and Caribbean Spanish.[2] However, in *Daniel Santos* these voices serve as a means for the narrator to name himself as Luis Rafael Sánchez, the critically acclaimed author of the earlier *La guaracha del Macho Camacho*. Unlike *La guaracha*'s tendency to occlude the position of its satirical narrator, *Daniel Santos* offers an intricately coded exposé of Sánchez's authorial status in Puerto Rican literature. While an unseen narrator satirizes Puerto Rican characters in *La guaracha*, Sánchez has the marginal voices of Latin America in *Daniel Santos* speak of and for him, thus inscribing his authorial name with a politics of resistance. While *La guaracha* never directly names its omniscient narrator, *Daniel Santos* incessantly invokes Luis Rafael Sánchez as the name of its author. In fact, the author appears as himself in the text, making himself visible on the page to the reader. Although the other characters that interact with him diegetically—that is, within the world of the narrative—often challenge his authority, Sánchez reminds the reader that these characters are also "masks" through which he voices his particular view of the Americas, thus undermining any demands for realism while negotiating a political commitment with the marginal subjects he represents. In this way Sánchez, like Canales, uses self-reflexive humor to expose the incongruity of the author, who is both an agent and object of his own writing.

As an eccentric text, *Daniel Santos* presents its author/narrator as the protagonist in a mock-heroic quest for traces of Puerto Rican culture throughout the Americas. This eccentric sensibility contrasts sharply with the insular focus of *La guaracha*, which uses the metaphor of the traffic jam to characterize Puerto Rico as a society immobilized by capitalism and colonialism.[3] Sánchez also parallels the tension between the insular and the eccentric with a musical dialectic between the guaracha and the bolero, two musical forms whose cadences he inscribes into the structures of the two texts. The shifts between masking and revealing, insular and eccentric, and guaracha and bolero form a textual *jaibería*, the Puerto Rican tactic of political engagement that moves forward by moving sideways. By combining the evasive maneuvers of textual *jaibería* with the oppositional politics of the *poética de lo soez, Daniel Santos* challenges the critical inquisitiveness of the reader while attempting to recuperate an authorial agency. Sánchez uses humor to expose parts of his authorial persona to the reader's gaze, yet his narrative self alternates among several subject positions, adopting perspectives in the first, second, and third persons, thus evading the imperatives of historical or testimonial accuracy. Furthermore, the text presents its biographical subject—the totemic figure of the bolero singer Daniel Santos—as a conspicuous absence, since the details of his life are recounted neither by the characters nor by the narrator. For all those who speak his name, including Sánchez, Daniel Santos becomes one of many masks that the marginal subjects of Puerto Rico and Latin America wear in their attempts to represent themselves. Each subject's fascination with him reveals how numerous perspectives condition the singer's status as a collective myth. Consequently, reading *Daniel Santos* in conjunction with *La guaracha* as a narrative cycle revises the function of Sánchez's *poética de lo soez* as an oppositional discourse, for Sánchez makes himself a target of his characters' deprecatory remarks and becomes the site of authority that they contest. The underlying incongruity that Sánchez's humor exposes is the impossibility of narrating a collective voice without the mediating presence of an author. Through self-reflexive humor, Sánchez makes his authorial persona a comic object in order to inscribe a politically engaged *jaibería* in his narrative discourse.

The Musical Ties That Bind: Guaracha, Bolero, and Textual Spinning

One way that Sánchez establishes continuity between his two very different texts is by integrating into their narrative structures the qualities of Puerto Rican popular music. This allows *La guaracha* and *Daniel Santos* to be read as a cycle between two musical strains, something Frances Aparicio does in her essay "Entre la guaracha y el bolero: Un ciclo de intertextos musicales en la nueva narrativa puertorriqueña." Aparicio demonstrates how recent Puerto Rican narrative has incorporated different forms of popular music as metaphoric isotopes; that is, as tropes of intertextuality that confer semantic parity between two texts, one musical and the other narrative.[4] In the case of Sánchez's works, his first novel incorporates the openness and centrifugal quality of the guaracha, while *Daniel Santos*'s narrative simulates the phallocentric, centripetal force of the bolero. Aparicio draws her comparison from a passage in which Sánchez declares: "The guaracha opens the body, authorizes displacement, shows in diligent wigglings the most desirable parts, the spaces to moisten. The stretches to pulp. The bolero closes the body, prohibits displacement, reduces rotation to the gestation of a living death" (*Daniel Santos* 104).[5]

The relationship Sánchez establishes between the musical forms, as he describes them in this passage, and the narrative structure of his texts is parallel to the tension between the insular and the eccentric.[6] On the one hand, the guaracha's fast, African-based rhythms and its sexually suggestive lyrics open the body up to pleasure, to disorienting velocity and sweat, as in the rapid, sensual movements of the dance that accompanies the guaracha's rhythms. This is the type of comic upheaval that Sánchez inscribes into the vertiginous prose of *La guaracha*. The novel's title describes the smash-hit single "La vida es una cosa fenomenal" by the fictitious Macho Camacho, and the pulsating rhythm of this song penetrates every public and private space of the Puerto Rican society that the novel depicts. All the characters encounter, willingly or unwillingly, la guaracha's infectious beat. And all react, favorably or unfavorably, to its frenetic and hypnotic imperative to dance.

However, the novel's satirical portrayal of Puerto Rican society isolates the characters from one another in a stifling world of immobility and insularity. *La guaracha* offers a synchronic slice of Puerto Rican life, depicting what characters from different levels of society do on a Wednesday afternoon at five o'clock, a fact that the narrator repeats over and over again: "A las cinco de la tarde, a las cinco en punto de la tarde y son las cinco en todos los relojes" (*La guaracha* 35) [At five o'clock in the afternoon, at five o'clock sharp in the afternoon, and it's five on all the clocks (Rabassa 22)].[7] One of the devices this complex novel employs is a series of simultaneously occurring events, all taking place in different locations, each involving one of the six main characters.[8] Although all the characters are associated with one another, either through family ties or sexual relations or as neighbors, they remain physically and emotionally distanced from one another for the better part of the novel. The characters are also isolated in their respective textual spaces—except in the case of La Madre and Doña Chon, who appear together—since the individual narrative sections focus exclusively on the inactivity of each character. Yet all are waiting either for someone else to arrive or for their present circumstances to change, as if each were starring in a personal version of *Waiting for Godot*. Their immobility reflects the insular vision that influenced the work of so many Puerto Rican writers after Pedreira's essay *Insularismo*. Juan Gelpí, in *Literatura y paternalismo en Puerto Rico*, writes that *La guaracha* shares with *Insularismo* a totalizing conception of literature and a desire to represent Puerto Rican society in a globalizing way (28). Gelpí shows how Sánchez's novel parodies the insular vision by incorporating many of its most recurring tropes, particularly infantilization, the sick body, and the transient nation—"la nave al garete" (31–37).

Paradoxically, while the object of *La guaracha*'s satirical critique is Puerto Rico's stifling insularity and its political stagnation, the music that suffuses its narrative discourse is the unfettered, playful, and highly erotic guaracha. The music and its subversive power coincide with the notion of Puerto Rican *guachafita*, a form of the comic very similar to *relajo* and the carnivalesque. Luce López Baralt, in "*La guaracha del Macho Camacho*, saga nacional de la «guachafita» puertorriqueña," reads the *guachafita* as La Madre's obsessive compulsion to dance, enjoy life, and avoid taking anything seriously (115).[9] This *guachafita* is very similar to Jorge Portilla's definition of *relajo*, which he defines as a suspension of seriousness before a value that has been proposed in public discourse (25). López Baralt argues that the *guachafita* undermines any form of social order through *relajo* (relaxing or loosening of moral codes). The *guachafita* deflates the seriousness of everything and everyone as a self-defense mechanism, since the most fervent practitioners of the *guachafita*, like La Madre, who cannot keep still when she hears Macho Camacho's song, represent the most exploited and marginal members of society. This is somewhat similar to Mikhail Bakhtin's notion of the carnival spirit, which shares with Sánchez's literary *guachafita* a subversive laughter, but for Bakhtin (1965, 11) carnival laughter is part of a ritual of rebirth and regeneration. The *guachafita* in Sánchez's novel ends in a tragic death, and the laughter it generates is revealed to be a hollow form of commercialist escapism.

López Baralt also argues that not only does the *guachafita* permeate every sector of society that the novel depicts, but its infectious *relajo* undermines the very language of the text and the satirical perspective of the narrator as well. She contends that the difference between the satires of Quevedo or Cervantes, for example, and Sánchez's practice of literary *guachafita* is that while the former postulate a narrative perspective exempt from satirical censure, Sánchez's novel ridicules its own linguistic performance, thus implicating the narrator and his text as part of the *guachafita*. López Baralt objects to the novel's self-parody, particularly its many burlesque intertextual references in which Sánchez seems to implicate his own literary practice. She writes: "Luis Rafael Sánchez appears to make fun of something unquestionably serious: his own literary enterprise" (119).[10] López Baralt critiques this all-pervasive, subversive laughter and suggests that a satirist should stand at a distance from the object of his ridicule. Yet what López Baralt does not take into account is that Sánchez's literary *guachafita* serves as a form of self-reflexive humor that overcomes the pathos of the insular vision.

In *La guaracha del Macho Camacho* the frenetic, festive guaracha music functions at cross-purposes with the insular, tragic narrative that culminates in the senseless death of El Nene, la Madre's retarded son. While the *guachafita* of La Madre represents an escapist attempt to ignore her desperate circumstances, the novel's humor offers readers a way to confront and overcome the pathos of Puerto Rico's insular vision. One could argue that the literary *guachafita* functions ironically against the tragic narrative, but Arthur Schopenhauer in *The World as Will and Idea* contends that, while irony disguises a joke behind seriousness, humor is "seriousness concealed behind a joke," and that "every poetical or artistic presentation of a comical, or indeed even a farcical scene, through which a serious thought yet glimmers as its concealed background, is a production of humor" (Morreall 1987, 62–63). So when the novel repeatedly declares that "Life Is a Phenomenal Thing" ("La vida es una cosa fenomenal"), it is being ironic and humorous, for the ludicrous statement masks the serious social, political, and cultural malaise that has made the Puerto Rican nation stagnate and has led to its insular vision—its *tapón*. Arcadio Díaz Quiñones writes that, despite all the festive dancing represented in the novel, there is something unnamable underneath. In a clear reference to Michel Foucault, Díaz Quiñones argues (2000b, 36–54) that *La guaracha del Macho Camacho*, like Luis Palés Matos's *Tuntún de pasa y grifería*, undermines the kind of patriotism that tries to discipline and punish those who raise the curtain ("el «telón isleño»") and expose the phantoms of Puerto Rico's internal racism or its colonial subordination. Therefore, if Sánchez's "literary enterprise" becomes infected with the very *guachafita* it satirizes, it does so to underscore the serious role that literature plays in the discourse on national identity. In order to overcome the insular vision's pathos, the novel must reject the premise that it is exempt from its own satirical gaze and subversive laughter. That rejection takes the form of a self-reflexive humor, which makes the Puerto Rican literary canon one of its many comic objects.

Despite the text's self-reflexive humor, *La guaracha* does not aim its satirical lens at its narrator, who addresses the reader and invites him or her to laugh at the cast of characters he presents for their pleasure. The novel opens with a direct interpellation of the reader and immediately places him or her in the role of a voyeur: "If you turn around now, a cautious turn, a cautious look, you'll see her sitting and waiting, calmness or the shadow of calmness passing through her. . . . You'll see her sitting and waiting on a sofa: her arms open . . ." (Rabassa 5).[11] The narrator repeatedly acts like an impresario who comments on the characters, sometimes addressing them from offstage. This narrative voice alternates with that of a radio deejay, who addresses the reader as if he or she were a radio listener. Efraín Barradas, in *Para leer en puertorriqueño: Acercamiento a la obra de Luis Rafael Sánchez*, explores the issue of *La guaracha*'s narrative voices when he asks, "¿Quién canta *La guaracha* . . . ?" [Who sings *La guaracha* . . . ?] (103). He points to three extradiegetic elements that stand apart from the main narrative. The first two, preceding the main narrative, are an epigraphic citation of the song's lyrics and an "Advertencia," or prologue, that reproduces within its own microstructure the macrocosmic structure of the novel. The third element is an appendix that transcribes the lyrics to Macho Camacho's song "La vida es una cosa fenomenal." Barradas argues that the narrator who presents these extradiegetic texts is the same as the voice that addresses the reader and the characters throughout the rest of the novel, but should not be confused with the voice of the radio deejay that repeatedly interrupts the narrative with a bombardment of inane panegyrics to the novel's theme song. This announcer ("locutor"), whose voice emerges between the separate scenes, does not speak from within any of them, which leads Barradas to conclude that this announcer is a completely separate narrator, whose passages help to reinforce the impression of textual autonomy created by the epigraph, the "Advertencia," and the song lyrics at the end of the novel (116). The academic tone of these extradiegetic texts confers a false verisimilitude to the novel. Thus Sánchez blurs the lines between what lies inside and outside his text without completely decentering the authority of a satirical narrator, who judges from afar, unseen by the characters while directing the reader's gaze. Although *La guaracha* approaches a self-reflexive humor by making its own textuality a comic object, the ostensibly centrifugal guaracha has served to draw the text toward a closure that exempts and excludes the satirical narrator from censure.

Sánchez brings this narrative perspective under scrutiny in *La importancia de llamarse Daniel Santos*, which not only reveals the narrator to be the famous Puerto Rican author Luis Rafael Sánchez but casts him as a character and makes him the object of his characters' derisive laughter.

Sánchez inscribes this hybrid text with the music of the bolero, with its slow, romantic cadence and lyrics of seduction, lost love, and regret. These boleros chronicle both the sexual conquests and the narcissistic pain of the macho, who withdraws from the world in self-abjection after seducing and losing the object of his desire. A bolero can also mark the macho's scorn for a faithless woman. As Sánchez suggests in his description of the bolero, this music draws in upon itself, either as a solipsistic lamentation, a scornful indignation, or a seductive call to sexual union. The bolero is the quintessential expression of Latin American sentimentality and solemnity, but, like the guaracha in Sánchez's first novel, the bolero in *Daniel Santos* functions at cross-purposes with the narrative. The bolero represents movement toward a center, but *Daniel Santos* depicts an eccentric movement outward with the quasi-testimonial travel narrative of a narrator/author who chronicles his journeys inside and outside of Puerto Rico. He visits the seedy underbelly of various Latin American cities, where he interviews a number of characters who recall their experiences with the "Inquieto Anacobero," Daniel Santos.

In this way *Daniel Santos* eccentrically picks up where *La guaracha*'s insular vision left off, with a Puerto Rican narrator exploring the self-affirming possibilities that cultural mobility can provide. Rather than depict this mobility as a desperate attempt to break from insularity and docility, Sánchez recuperates the idylls of music and literature in order to reorient Puerto Rican national identity toward a broader cultural horizon. Yet the most noticeable difference between the texts is that in *Daniel Santos* humorous self-reflexivity takes the figure of the author as one of its main comic objects. Adopting the persona of a *cronista*, Sánchez takes great pains to name himself in the narrative as he offers fictionalized interviews that he has ostensibly gathered from various corners of the Americas, but which are really products of his own imagination. This hybrid *fabulación* takes the reader to the places where the dispossessed members of Latin American and Caribbean communities remember the rowdy nights of music, liquor, and sexual exploits that accompanied Daniel Santos wherever he went. The text ends deep in the heart of Puerto Rico, with the narrator contemplating his own persona as a famous author. Sánchez re-creates the literary idyll of the *locus amoenus* in order to revel in his own romantic nostalgia and the narcissistic celebration of his authorial voice. The anonymous narrator of *La guaracha* is unmasked in *Daniel Santos*, redirecting laughter from satirical depictions of others to a humorous critique of the authorial persona.

The Name Game, and What's Wilde Got to Do with It?

La importancia de llamarse Daniel Santos's title clearly refers the reader to Oscar Wilde's comedy *The Importance of Being Earnest*. The pun in the title of Wilde's satirical farce plays on the fetishized name of the eponymous character and the Victorian aristocracy's seriousness in all matters trivial. The name is the thing in this play, so much so that Gwendolen and Cecily, the young female characters, will not allow themselves to marry any man who does not bear the name Ernest. The quest for this name leads to all manner of deception and "Bunburying" until finally, thanks to the intervention of Lady Bracknell, John Worthing discovers his true identity and name to always have been Ernest, even though his personal character has been deceitful and trivial, the very opposite of earnestness.

What does this epigrammatic play about the ins and outs of English social propriety and aristocratic legitimacy have to do with Sánchez's narrative exploration of Puerto Rican popular culture? The switch from "being earnest" to "llamarse Daniel Santos" (to be named Daniel Santos) gives us our first clue in the textual game that Sánchez initiates with the title of his book. In Spanish, Wilde's play has been translated as *La importancia de llamarse Ernesto*, in which the pun between "Ernest" and "earnest" is lost, so that the Spanish translation of the title refers exclusively to the character's name.[12] Yet Sánchez's invocation of the English play produces a new linguistic game that capitalizes on the ambiguity of the verb *llamarse*.

For which subjects is it important to name themselves Daniel Santos? The use of the reflexive in the infinitive allows the verb to refer to several subjects at once. The first, and most obvious, is Daniel Santos, since the meaning of the title can be understood as the importance of the singer calling himself by his own name. Yet this does not exclude a reading in which *llamarse* can refer to the third-person indefinite, as in the importance of calling *oneself* Daniel Santos. Another possibility is that *llamarse* can refer to the second-person singular formal, *usted*, or the second-person plural, *ustedes*, in Latin American usage. Finally, the verb can imply the third-person plural, as in *ellos* and *ellas*. We can summarize the possible meanings of the title in the following way:

La importancia de llamarse [él] Daniel Santos
La importancia de llamarse [uno] Daniel Santos
La importancia de llamarse [usted/ustedes] Daniel Santos
La importancia de llamarse [ellos/ellas] Daniel Santos

Sánchez's title translates the ironic ontological implications of Wilde's "being earnest" to refer to the representational performativity of Daniel Santos calling himself, one calling oneself, you calling yourself/yourselves, or they calling themselves Daniel Santos; the subject named in the title is variable and interchangeable, yet it goes by the same name. Sánchez draws from Wilde's original irony (those who call themselves Ernest are the least earnest characters in the play) to propose that immanent Being gives way to the indeterminate and contingent performance of naming.

The "Being" in "being earnest/Ernest" carries the stamp of an essentialism, one that allows for social (and sexual) mobility only through heredity and privilege; yet its ironic usage exposes the hypocrisy of "the shallow mask of manners," as Cecily puts it in her vitriolic exchange of affected pleasantries with Gwendolen (364). Consequently, we can read Sánchez's title, *La importancia de llamarse Daniel Santos*, as consistent with extant Spanish translations of Wilde's play, but we can also interpret the use of *llamarse* as a corrective translation of "Being," since Sánchez proposes that taking on Daniel Santos's name is a performative act of self-legitimization, regardless of the particular subject that can be included in the indefinite capaciousness of the singer's name. Sánchez may have written over the essentialist implications of Wilde's title, but he does so by inscribing the mythic status of Daniel Santos, who is not so much a father figure as he is a Puerto Rican Don Juan—the quintessential Bunburyist, or *burlador*. It is in this macho singer's name that Sánchez undertakes a narrative quest in search of his own Latin American family.

Sánchez invokes the title of Wilde's play not only to comment on the relation between Being and performance; this citation also draws attention to the way a displacement of identities often accompanies a geographic dislocation. Frances Aparicio, in *Listening to Salsa: Latin Popular Music and Puerto Rican Cultures*, makes a similar argument when she compares Wilde's play to Sánchez's narrative. She writes: "*La importancia de llamarse Daniel Santos* also finds a major subtext in Oscar Wilde's *The Importance of Being Earnest*, a dramatic work that similarly explores the ambivalence of identity, the possibilities of double identities, and the mask that destabilizes the concept of a unitary, coherent identity" (140). In Wilde's play, the characters take on different names and identities in order to facilitate their excursions between town and country. Sánchez's *fabulación*, on the other hand, parodies a heroic journey from one urban context to another, although the narrator's travels do end in a pastoral setting. The narrator's identity and the structure of the narrative change according to the geographic locations that the text portrays. In each of the text's separate sections, the narrator serves a different function and the narrative performs a parody of a different literary genre. However, the narrator's travels across the Americas do not go from point A to point B; there are many deviations in this narrative itinerary, as well as many intertextual citations that take place along the way.

El "relajo con orden": Narrative Humor as Controlled Chaos

By beginning *Daniel Santos* with a prologue, "Presentación: El método del discurso" [Presentation: The method of the discourse], Sánchez once again parodically inscribes in his text one of the stylistic elements associated with the narrative traditions of the baroque. Any reader of Golden Age narrative will be familiar with the numerous prologues and "advertencias" that precede the main text. In the first part of *Don Quijote* (1605), for example, the texts that the reader first encounters are not written by Cervantes at all, but by Juan Gallo de Andrada, Francisco Murcia de la Llana, and the king's representative Juan de Amezqueta. These are standard legal certifications that testify to the novel's imprimatur and the author's rights of publication. Following these, Cervantes dedicates his novel to his patron, the duke of Béjar. Only after all these preliminary texts does Cervantes directly address the reader in the prologue. In the second part of the novel, published in 1615, there are six preliminary texts that precede the main narrative, and these not only certify the authenticity of the work and the author's legal rights, they also attest to and approve of the moral imperatives that the novel upholds. After a new dedication, this time to the count of Lemos, Cervantes once again addresses the reader in order to clarify that this novel is the authentic second part to the one published in 1605, since in the interim an unknown author with the pseudonym of Avellaneda published a spurious sequel to the original text. Cervantes lays great stress on the legitimate authorship of his *Don Quijote*, thus reclaiming its characters and the fictional world they inhabit as products of his own creative labor.

Given the twentieth-century context in which Sánchez writes, much of the legal and institutional recognition of his authorship is condensed on the copyright page, and there are no pre-texts that attest to the work's moral and ethical value. Nevertheless, Sánchez readily employs the prologue device in *Daniel Santos* as a way to address the reader and blur the lines between the "real" world and the textual world. The prologue gives the reader several clues on how to approach the chapters that follow, as well as reproduces the structure of the text as a whole, since the prologue is divided into smaller sections that correspond to those of the larger text. Its title, "El método del discurso," is an inverted, parodic reference to René Descartes' *Discurso del método*[13] (*Discours de la méthode* or *Discourse on the Method*). This essay, in which Descartes makes the famous truth claim "I think, therefore I am," relates how the author arrives at his scientific method of reasoning by first rejecting the lessons of his tutors, then learning all he can by traveling and "studying in the book of the world," and, finally, looking inward to learn from himself: "In this I succeeded much better, it would seem to me, than if I had never been away, either from my country or from my books" (25). *Discours de la méthode* was originally published anonymously in 1637, but Descartes' publisher eventually coerced him into claiming authorship in order to obtain the king of France's permission for publication. Despite the confessional self-scrutiny that Descartes elaborates in this text, in the philosopher's letters and later writings he claims that he sought anonymity in the publication of his works "in the role of an artist 'hidden behind the picture in order to hear what one will say about it.' . . . Regarding 'the world' as 'a theater,' '. . . larvatus prodeo . . .' ('I appear as one who is masked')" (155). Descartes also had much to fear from the Inquisition, and claiming authorship was a risk he eventually took, even though he left the essay unfinished so that its rational explorations would not contradict the Church's authority (141–52). With this intertextual usage of Descartes' essay, Sánchez suggests that he, too, is very aware of the risks he takes when claiming authorship, for it opens the writing subject to the reader's scrutiny and judgment. Sánchez's prologue confronts the legal, institutional, and critical discourses that authorize his authorship, but when he plays the artist "hidden behind the picture," it is with a clear indication that it is in his name that he regards the world as a theater, and that it is he who appears as the one who is masked.

Thus, the reader of Sánchez's work can expect a parody of the confessional mode from the author, who hides his identity behind the literary masks he offers in his texts. Unlike Descartes, though, Sánchez embarks on a ludic exploration of textual performance rather than a scientific defense of rational Being. He describes the method of his discourse as one in which he first had to travel across the real-life Americas in search of the legend of Daniel Santos, but says the text he authors and on which his name appears is a product of his own imagination:

Later, alone and wary, perfecting my neurosis of dissatisfaction, I interviewed the phantasms of my own making, I forged letters from faraway addresses, I faked textual copies of apocryphal conversations in order to nurture myself with speculation. Then I orchestrated dialogues of a credible affectation and I falsified the accents of the bitter America, the barefoot America, the America in Spanish that idolizes the personage in whom his person culminates. (*Daniel Santos* 4–5)[14]

Sánchez's narrative is not a search for truth through reason, but a mixture of fact and fiction, chronicle and confession, at which the author arrives by means of a series of textual masquerades. Should the reader scrutinize the narrative to tease out the "truth" from the phantasms that populate Sanchez's text? Which one, if any, of the characters speaks in the author's "true" voice? They all do, even those that are obviously burlesque caricatures of well-known literary figures, as well as those that might be based on actual persons. In consonance with Mikhail Bakhtin's theory of heteroglossia, Sánchez's prologue draws attention to the role of the author who controls this multivoiced narrative.[15] In *The Dialogic Imagination* Bakhtin describes how an author speaks through his characters, and how, in the comic novel in particular, those voices emerge simultaneously as if in a dialogue. Bakhtin writes:

Heteroglossia, once incorporated into the novel (whatever the forms for its incorporation), is *another's speech in another's language*, serving to express authorial intentions but in a refracted way. Such speech constitutes a special type of *double-voiced discourse*. It serves two speakers at the same time and expresses simultaneously two different intentions: the direct intention of the character who is speaking, and the refracted intention of the author. . . . Double-voiced discourse is always internally dialogized. Examples of this would be comic, ironic or parodic discourse, the refracting discourse of a narrator, refracting discourse in the language of a character and finally the discourse of a whole incorporated genre—all these discourses are double-voiced and internally dialogized. (324)

Sánchez's use of parody and his outright declaration as the voice behind the voices of his characters capitalizes on this notion of heteroglossia, going so far as to offer at the end of the novel a list of all the literary figures he imitates. Thereby, Sánchez extends the reach of self-reflexive humor to not only foreground the textuality of his novel but also unmask the authorial persona behind the characters and the various intertexts that his novel integrates. Sánchez prepares his readers for a game of textual hide-and-seek, whose object is to obfuscate the distinctions between reality and fiction, not so much as a denial of truth, but rather as a search for Wilde's "truths of masks" (1078).

In "Primera parte: Las palomas del milagro" [Part one: The miraculous doves],[16] the narrator/author searches in different cities for Daniel Santos's reputation as a Don Juan. He takes on the role of an interviewer who gathers testimonials from the denizens of San Juan, Panama City, Havana, Caracas, Lima, Mexico City, Cali, Santo Domingo, New York, Guayaquil, and Managua. Lest we forget to read the fictive quality of the voices that Sánchez orchestrates throughout his text, he reminds us that just as these testimonial "subjects" invent stories to sustain themselves—"Inventan para vivir y viven para inventar"—the narrator is the authorial subject who is behind their inventions:

> But, I invent them all. Like a god who, on yellow, ruled pages, gives birth to his human creations. I correct their sermons—a god who, with a No. 2 pencil, denies an entry visa to a comma, an inoperable word, the burdensome preposition. I listen to their confiding postures—a god who reads aloud the postures and poses of their existences as I shape them. I take ownership of stops and starts, the flood of words that build at the sole mention of Daniel Santos's name—a god who presses the print key if the writing on the screen of the Japanese Silver Reed seems effective, worthy of disclosure, able to incite pleasure. Reader, hear these phantasms open their hearts! (13)[17]

This grandiloquent self-deification is charged with irony, since it also reveals the mundane tools of the author's craft: a legal pad, a No. 2 pencil, and a Japanese word processor. The narrator's divinity as an omnipotent author is revealed as a product of Sánchez's creative human labor as a writer. Sánchez suggests that authorship does not confer authenticity and truth to his text, but that the writer's artistic endeavor gives the authorial subject a voice. Sánchez reminds the reader to hear the testimonies of his characters as a narrative performance, and that the reader can take pleasure in their discourse as products of an imagination that has access to the literary means of production. The characters are the "masks" that Sánchez fashions from language and wears throughout the textual performance that engages the reader.

Despite the authorial control that Sánchez declares for himself, he casts himself as a character in his novel who is open to the suspicion, disrespect, and even ridicule of his fictional interviewees. Unlike the extradiegetic narrators of *La guaracha*, who remained on the periphery of the novel's action, the self-named author of *Daniel Santos* occupies several levels of the narrative. At the extradiegetic level, the author/narrator presents the text to the reader from outside the narrative, as in the prologue. Yet as the interviewer who interacts with his characters, Sánchez is an intradiegetic interlocutor to whom the characters tell their stories. Sánchez also tells his own story by recounting his itinerary across the Americas, placing this first-person narrator at the autodiegetic level.[18] These shifts blur the line between the inside and the outside of the text, between fiction and reality. Sánchez challenges the reader's expectations by claiming authorial autonomy from his text, yet his entry into his narrative world ironically reveals his authorial persona to be an effect of textuality. The heteroglossia of *Daniel Santos* allows the author to speak through his characters, but as the characters speak back to the author, Sánchez shows that the agents of discourse are also subjects constituted in language.

One such character appears when Sánchez stages an encounter in Manhattan between himself and a Nuyorican, Guango Orta. Guango addresses Sánchez somewhat familiarly, calling him "Wico" Sánchez. Sánchez uses this character as a mouthpiece for his own notions of humor as an oppositional discourse. Guango launches into a tirade against the sadness that characterizes white culture, and since whites are no fools, they have invented a profundity to their sadness, and have inflated it with a sense of the tragic (60). Guango proudly extols black, mulatto, and Caribbean cultures, whose "bullanga" is explosive, loud, and laughing, and whose intellectual turns exhibit vitality, rhythm, and a subversive skepticism (60). Guango is so impressed with his own discursive performance he cries out, "¡Gózate cómo me expreso, Wico Sánchez!" [Get a load of the way I express myself, Wico Sánchez!] (60). His discursive performance acts as a parodic echo of Sánchez's own literary enterprise—his *poética de lo soez*. Throughout his literary career, from his early work in theater to his influential collection of short stories *En cuerpo de camisa* (1969), Sánchez has sustained a commitment to the celebration of Afro-Caribbean *mulatería* and *mestizaje*, in clear opposition to the Hispanophile paternalism of the Puerto Rican literary canon. Sánchez employs the device of the literary double to parody himself, revealing through Guango his long-standing literary enterprise of racial and cultural self-affirmation.

However, Sánchez's New York alter ego is quick to turn on his island counterpart, threatening to usurp the author's fame should he one day write his own literary work. Guango takes every opportunity to punch holes in Sánchez's literary achievements, vehemently expressing his dislike for the author's theater, referring to negative critiques of his work and even to rumors about Sánchez's sexuality: "Aunque se sotovocee que eres, seguramente, un *homo ludens* porque eres, inseguramente, un *homo closet*." [Though it is whispered that you are, surely, a *homo ludens* because you are, unsurely, a *closet homo*] (63). Guango alludes to the accusation that the literary style of the playful, trickster author—a literary *burlador*—is an indication that he is gay. Roberto González Echevarría tells of a similar accusation laid against Severo Sarduy, the Cuban author who, along with Alejo Carpentier, José Lezama Lima, and Guillermo Cabrera Infante, wrote innovative Latin American novels in the ludic style of the neobaroque.[19] One example of this negative reaction appeared in Roberto Fernández Retamar's *Calibán: Apuntes sobre la cultura en nuestra América*. Fernández Retamar labels Sarduy's critical endeavors in the journal *Nuevo Mundo* "el mariposeo neobarthesiano" (75).[20] Fernández Retamar's criticism constitutes a homophobic epithet, since "mariposa" is a commonly used term for pansy or faggot. Clearly, one of the risks that a Latin American writer takes when writing outside the narrowly defined parameters of nationalist traditions is that critics will launch ad hominem attacks, equating ludic literary style with degenerate or perverse personal morals.

Rather than distance himself from the neobaroque in order to dispel rumors of his own sexual orientation, Sánchez acknowledges his debt to Sarduy with a parody. In *Daniel Santos* Sánchez offers his own version of a dialogue among three Cuban transvestites that appeared as part of the "Dolores Rondón" section of Sarduy's novel *De donde son los cantantes*. Indeed, a piece of dialogue from Sarduy's novel—"Relajo. Orden. Palabras llenas" (158)—is lifted, as one of Sánchez's transvestites repeats a similar phrase, "¡Que el relajo sea con orden!" (21–25). Sánchez also lists Sarduy as one of his "saqueos," the writers whose works he has pillaged (210). So although Guango tries to "out" Sánchez as a homosexual, Sánchez uses this character's accusations to "out" the criticism that a *homo ludens* is equivalent to a "closet homo." Sánchez unmasks such critiques as blatant attempts to dismiss the neobaroque as a degenerate, effeminate art form. Sánchez's ludic narrative style operates in politically radical ways that contest racial and colonial oppression from within Caribbean and Latin

American traditions. Like the phrase one of his transvestite characters lifts from Sarduy, Sánchez combines his ludic narrative style with a political engagement to form a "relajo con orden."

This tactic is part of Sánchez's *poética de lo soez*, which he associates with the radical literatures of opposition that contest notions of linguistic purity and moral propriety. In an interview with Julio Ortega, he states:

> My theory of the vulgar, which I have elaborated according to my upbringing and my experiences as an adolescent, is not easy to distill because it is full of social and artistic implications. Nevertheless, I could tell you that I have always understood the vulgar as a provoca-tion, that I believe the vulgar finds its expressive dynamic in a par-ticular social milieu and in particular historical circumstances. From Valle Inclán to Edward Albee, from *La lozana andaluza* to the novels of Henry Miller, the literary vulgar has tried to function as moral demolition. That theory allows me to journey back to my origins, my country, and my social class. (*La guagua aérea* 92–93)[21]

Sánchez's *poética de lo soez* incorporates the ludic textuality of the neo-baroque with the language of the marginal classes, thus organizing his literary games around an oppositional discourse. His "relajo con orden" counters Fernández Retamar's objection to neobaroque poetics, for it dem-onstrates that a highly playful literature can be politically engaged and culturally affirming. In *Daniel Santos* Sánchez employs his *poética de lo soez* to valorize the poor of color and of indigenous heritage who survive at the most abject margins in the urban centers of the Americas. He does not flinch when he shows how, on the one hand, these marginal subjects en-dure violence and oppression, yet, on the other, reproduce it in the culture of machismo, embodied in the figure of Daniel Santos. Sánchez elevates certain elements of mass culture and popular music while rejecting those that he sees as affected, flashy imports from hegemonic centers. Through-out the narrative, Sánchez paints a dichromatic picture of the West's rela-tion to Latin America: the political and economic elite versus the disen-franchised poor; the serious culture of the Western canon versus the playful, bohemian culture from the margins; and the white (European, North American) versus the dark (black, indigenous, mulatto, mestizo). Sánchez allies his literary enterprise with the most marginal classes of Latin America, or "el mierda" ("the crap"), and against the dominant classes from Latin America, the United States, and Europe, or "la crema" ("the cream"). Sánchez's "relajo con orden" oscillates between opening the text to a wide readership and gathering itself centripetally around a particular set of cultural values. Although he appropriates ideas and poetics from high literary sources, his prose sustains an oral readability, making the text simultaneously challenging and accessible.

It is because of this politically engaged literary enterprise that Guango admits he still admires Sánchez despite all the negative rumors. Speaking through Guango, Sánchez delivers a panegyric to himself that reaffirms his authorial status in Puerto Rico and Latin America. Once again, humor masks a serious critique, for Sánchez's self-mockery rebuffs the criticisms that attribute to him moral and ethical flaws in order to discredit his literary enterprise. This humor overcomes the pathos of those negative criticisms, and Sánchez asserts the relevance of his literary practice in spite of the accusations against his personal life. The self-mockery that masks self-assertion serves to defuse ridicule and its negative affect. Sánchez's text displays what Freud describes as humor's unique ability to counteract negative affect. In "Humour" Freud writes:

> Like wit and the comic, humour has something liberating about it; but it has also something of grandeur and elevation, which is lacking in the other two ways of deriving pleasure from intellectual activity. The grandeur in it clearly lies in the triumph of narcissism, the victorious assertion of the ego's invulnerability. The ego refuses to be distressed by the provocations of reality, to let itself to be compelled to suffer.... Humour is not resigned; it is rebellious. It signifies not only the triumph of the ego but also of the pleasure principle, which is able here to assert itself against the unkindness of the real circumstances. (162–63)

Sánchez's humor does more than just assert his own ego; by manipulating narrative heteroglossia Sánchez also allows the marginal subjects of the Caribbean and Latin America to speak of themselves and display their own narcissism. These voices are rebellious and contest even the authority of the author who channels them into his text. Sánchez makes very clear in his text that humor functions as a negotiation between self and other, between the author and the reader.

Once again, Sánchez uses Guango to perform his theory of authorship. Before this character takes his leave from "Wico" Sánchez, he declares, "If tonight I finish reading the Foucault that's keeping me busy, tomorrow I'll treat myself in La Taza de Oro to a plate of gandinga" (63).[22] Employing his *poética de lo soez*, Sánchez combines a reference to Puerto Rican comfort food with an indirect citation of Foucault, whose notion of the "author-function" separates the writer from the authorial persona and from the narrator. In "What Is an Author?" Foucault writes:

> It is well known that in a novel narrated in the first person, neither the first person pronoun, the present indicative tense, nor, for that matter, its signs of localization refer directly to the writer, either to the time he wrote, or to the specific act of writing; rather, they stand for a "second self" whose similarity to the author is never fixed and undergoes considerable alteration within the course of a single book. It would be as false to seek the author in relation to the actual writer as to the fictional narrator; the "author-function" arises out of their scission—in the distance of the two. (129)[23]

Sánchez's humor contests these radical divisions and demonstrates that the lines between these different egos are blurred and unstable. Foucault's "author-function" cannot account for the kind of self-reflexive humor that Sánchez performs in his narrative masquerade; neither does Foucault's term explain the self-naming that Sánchez's text develops as an intervention in the discourse on national identity. Sánchez's heteroglossic text uses humor to blur the lines between the subject who writes and the one who is written as an effect of textuality. Humor not only allows for a triumph of the ego but, within the heteroglossic textuality of the novel, it also fosters an interplay of egos, so that one cannot tell who is really speaking in any given utterance or at any diegetic level. Humor (con)fuses the borders between narrative interiority and exteriority, and as part of a Puerto Rican *poética de lo soez*, the constant shifts between diegetic levels performs a textual *jaibería* that, nevertheless, negotiates a "serious" political statement through the humorous modes of discourse.[24]

Ironically, the vehicle for this textual *jaibería* and humorous interplay of egos are Daniel Santos's boleros, a musical form that lies within the realm of the tragic rather than the comic. Bolero also separates the self from the other, representing the lover either as an unattainable object of desire or as an object of scorn. This seems incompatible with the way humor blurs the line between the subject and the object, particularly in a heteroglossic narrative where the other speaks through the self and vice versa. Sánchez negotiates the bolero and humor by situating them on the common ground of pleasure. In other words, just as the bolero represents a pleasurable catharsis for the marginal Latin American subject, narrative

humor offers the reader a playful entry into the discourse of the other—
that is, Sánchez's own eccentric text.

Bolero's Bliss and Narrative Aperture:
Giving the Reader the Last Word

In *Fenomenología del bolero*, Rafael Castillo Zapata writes that the bolero, like other forms of sentimental mass culture in Latin America, offers the marginal, proletarian subjects of the Caribbean and Latin America a respite from the demands of modern industrialized life. Castillo Zapata argues that the bolero sings of love and its vicissitudes: desire, eroticism, jealousy, loss, scorn, and survival. The subject, usually male, sees himself reflected in the bolero's lyrics and declares ownership: "Ese bolero es mío" [That's my song] (37). Much like Greek tragedy, the bolero opens a space for catharsis, and in that space the subject is comforted and spiritually healed so that he can carry on with his battles of love ("se siente confortado y recuperado anímicamente para seguir sosteniendo sus batallas de amor" (38–39). In some boleros the lover idealizes his object of desire, in others he sings of the impossibility of attaining that object. However, when love goes wrong, when the lover is spurned, he makes use of irony to annihilate the other. This irony is a double-edged sword, and the lover risks losing himself as he destroys the other. How, Castillo Zapata asks, can the lover kill the other that lives in him, that was his life and that continues to be his life, without at the same time killing what survives as the part of him that is most alive? (106)[25] The bolero's sentimentality allows the subject to overcome pathos, but through the cathartic pleasure of tragedy. The subject who sees himself reflected in the bolero, who claims its dramatization of pain and betrayal as his own, will be moved by both pity and fear in the most classic manner of Aristotle's *Poetics*: "pity is aroused by unmerited misfortune, fear by the misfortune of a man like ourselves" (XIII.2).

When Sánchez incorporates the lyrics of Daniel Santos's boleros in his humorous narrative, he breaks all the Aristotelian rules of genre and literary propriety. Moreover, those lyrics serve not as a means of annihilating the other but of allowing the other to speak. As José Quiroga suggests in *Tropics of Desire*, boleros enact an erasure and exist in a "space of contradiction, which is what gives them their erotic tension: the voice always wants to annihilate Voice itself" (152). This concurs with Frances Aparicio's argument in *Listening to Salsa*: the catharsis of bolero allows the male subject to appropriate female sentimentality, but as a way of silencing the woman (133–34).[26] The male's bolero performance seduces the female other by holding up a mirror to her own narcissism, as Shoshana Felman suggests in her analysis of Molière's Don Juan (31). Consequently, the male who adopts feminine sentimentality seduces by reflecting back to the woman her self-love, but he does not necessarily reveal his own narcissistic desire. The man who uses the bolero as a seduction ostensibly opens himself to the woman, yet as the object of his desire the woman only sees a mask of vulnerability. When the man loses his object of desire, he exacts revenge for having "opened" himself. He uses the bolero to "kill" the other and to close himself off from alterity.[27] Yet in Sánchez's narrative the bolero marks the space of writing where the self is authored through the discourse of the other. This aperture violates the bolero's masculinist imperative, which demands that the male close himself off from the outside world and shield himself from the gaze of the other.

Sánchez's reformulation of the bolero subverts the heteronormative paradigm of the "open" female and the "closed" male. He does this in two ways: first, he queers the macho image of Daniel Santos through homoerotic desire; second, he resituates bolero's bliss—its cathartic pleasure—within the realm of the comic. In particular, Sánchez stages an encounter in which the bolero serves as the soundtrack for an erotic comedy. As discussed previously, Sánchez parodies a scene from Severo Sarduy's *De donde son los cantantes*. In this scene Sánchez transcribes the heady conversation of three aging drag performers as they wax nostalgic about Daniel Santos's arrival in Havana in the forties. The dialogue starts with Cisne Negro declaring, "¡Que el relajo sea con orden!" [Let there be order in this abandon!] (21), but the other two, Blanche Du Bois and Gina Velia Raquel, continually interrupt her with such campy references as "Ay Cisne Negro, no seas tan damisela tornadiza de una novela de Caridad Bravo Adams" [Oh, Black Swan, don't be such a fickle damsel from a Caridad Bravo Adams novel] (22). Although one of the transvestites, Cisne Negro, rhapsodizes about the Puerto Rican singer, she recognizes that Daniel Santos was never within reach of the nefarious sin ("pecado nefando") of homosexual intercourse (24). Throughout the scene, the Three Cuban Graces address their interviewer, who laughs uncontrollably as he transcribes their conversation. Sánchez queers Daniel Santos's mythic status as a Latin American macho by portraying an instance of same-sex desire directed at him, even if it is a frustrated longing from afar. Yet these transvestites are literary inventions that appear on paper; at one point, one of the Cuban Graces calls Cisne Negro a "loca traspapelada" [mislaid- and miscast-paper queen]. In other words, her same-sex desire for Daniel Santos is a textual desire, and as one of Sánchez's characters Cisne Negro functions heterglossically to voice the author's own demystification of masculinity. That demystification is the "serious" statement that the novel's humor negotiates with the reader.

Sánchez carefully explores that demystification in the section titled "Vivir en varón" [Living as a man], an essay that dispenses with characters and addresses the reader directly. Sánchez invites the reader to witness his attempt to disarm or disassemble ("desarmar") the myth of Daniel Santos. His tone is often that of a street crier or *pregonero*, and in the ensuing textual performance he takes apart the theories and descriptions of myth offered by Joseph Campbell and Sigmund Freud in order to argue that the figure of a popular hero like Daniel Santos acts as a communal dream, one toward which the individual subject aspires (74–75).[28] Sánchez rejects the Freudian notion of repression, for he sustains that the marginal subject imitates what he or she perceives to be the hero's most seductive traits, thus performing in the light of day what psychoanalysis says is repressed in the realm of dreams (74). Sánchez does not essentialize machismo; in fact, he clearly states that machos of all races from Latin America must first learn the many postures and attitudes ("Los mil y un tics") that comprise a performance of the macho gender role: "Que ser varón obliga parecerlo primero" [To be a man you have to look like one first] (125).[29] In *Listening to Salsa*, Frances Aparicio offers an insightful reading of this chapter and its homoerotic implications. She writes:

> It is a critique of the macho physique, of hard bodies, of the male body as performance and of machismo as performative act. The ambiguity of this performance is linguistically constructed in the anaphoric patterns of the phrase *parecer varón* (to look like a male), an utterance that signifies both machismo as performance and an articulation of homosexuality as a histrionic act. The description also revels in the pleasure of the narrator's gaze as he meticulously describes the body parts of this *varón*, gazing down the male body like a gradual, eroticizing striptease that concludes with a gastronomical discourse on the *güevo* (testicles). (140–41)

By choosing Daniel Santos as the icon onto which he projects his textual desires, Sánchez homoeroticizes the macho and glorifies an ideology and power of phallic proportions—"Ideología y poder del güevo" (127). The text opens up the masculine mystique in ways that destabilize the macho's unicity, and the textual homoeroticism reflects the narrator's own narcissism back to its source. Thereby, Sánchez restages Daniel Santos's boleros to perform as self-reflexive humor in a heteroglossic narrative.

The second way in which Sánchez restages bolero's bliss—as the soundtrack for erotic comedy—occurs in the final leg of the narrator's eccentric journey. Sánchez returns to Puerto Rico after his tour of the slums and seedy nightspots of the Americas, taking refuge in El Verde Forest Park—a small tract of Puerto Rican rainforest preserved from the encroaching urbanization around it. Like Canales's character Miguel in "Mi voluntad se ha muerto," Sánchez repeats the romantic cliché of secluding himself in nature with a book. Predictably, Sánchez soon succumbs to a highly stylized reverie, but his flight into poetic fancy is cut short by the invasion of a group of teenagers—"Invasores del planeta tierra" [Invaders from planet Earth] (198). Although he cannot see them at first, the narrator imagines their activities from the sounds he hears nearby. He listens as they whistle, cry out, and play a disco version of Beethoven's Fifth Symphony from a portable radio. He watches as one pair breaks from the group and comes into his undetected view. The narrator (supposedly) wishes to leave, but any movement on his part would reveal him to the newcomers: "One remains on the solitary rock, immobilized, sheltered in the academic fiction of critical distance" (201).[30] In this usage of the third person impersonal, Sánchez simultaneously refers to his textual self—the diegetic narrator in the scene—and to the reader, who watches from the safety of his or her own critical distance, which is just as much a fiction as is the narrator's. Intent curiosity soon swells to enthralled voyeurism as the narrator describes the youths in glowing terms, particularly the young man, whose impressive erection, rippling chest, and sculpted shoulders make him a splendid male specimen, born for loving ("Animal macho espléndido, criado para amar que se diría") (202).

In a very complex triangulation of perspectives, Sánchez portrays the young man as the object of the girl's appreciative gaze, the narrator's watchful eye, and the reader's critical scrutiny. Although he also describes the young woman in equally favorable terms, he reserves the most graphic depictions for the male body, and it is the young man on whom three separate gazes converge.[31] The male's body becomes the erotic object of two diegetic gazes: the woman's is licit since she participates in the sexual act, but the other gaze—that of the male narrator—is illicit since he is an uninvited voyeur. Even though the narrator is invisible to the characters, as he was in *La guaracha*, he is visible to the reader as a diegetic spectator. As he looks at the young man, his homoerotic gaze performs a narrative verisimilitude that casts the reader as a fellow (that is, male) voyeur, but Sánchez also opens the possibility for the reader to see the male body through the woman's eyes, since the narrator shows her as a spectator. In this way Sánchez uses language and imagery to seduce the reader into eroticizing the male body from both male and female perspectives.[32] Sánchez combines an ambivalent representation of masculinity with a celebratory articulation of a romanticized universal Spirit, as Frances Aparicio in *Listening to Salsa* argues in her analysis of this scene: "The glorifying reaffirmation of free sensuality, pleasure, and eroticism—coded in the mountains where *cimarrones* (maroons) found liberty on the margins of the city—becomes a sort of erotic utopia outside the boundaries of social etiquette, sexual mores, and rules" (141).

Indeed, Sánchez has demonstrated throughout his text that the mythic status of Daniel Santos derives its universality from multiple projections of erotic desire: both hetero- and homosexual. When Sánchez brings his *fabulación* to a close, he opts for a comedic ending in which spiritual and sexual union takes place in the natural world, accompanied by Daniel Santos singing one of his most famous boleros, "Amor." After the edenic lovers fulfill their desires for one another and reach their sexual climax, all the teenagers regroup as Daniel Santos's mellifluous voice flows from the portable radio. They dance uninhibitedly while the narrator feels himself overwhelmed and conjoined to their tribalistic sensual display. Even the warring forces of nature, in the form of concurrent rain showers and sunshine, act as witnesses to the spectacle at hand ("el testimonio del aguacero y el sol") (206). Sánchez's utopia is not projected into a future world in which Puerto Ricans overcome their social struggles; rather, the struggle between opposing forces is the unifying impulse that offers Puerto Ricans from different generations, races, classes, and sexual orientations a discourse on national identity as well as a oneness with a broader Latin American community. Although Sánchez began his narrative journey in *Daniel Santos* with the voices of characters who could address their interlocutor, he ends the *fabulación* with a narrative comedy in which he observes his characters from afar. This allows him to reveal his text as a masquerade, in which the author speaks through these other voices but not for them, while at the same time allowing the characters to reveal clues about the author. In other words, Sánchez bares himself by having other voices bear witness to the object of his textual desire: Daniel Santos. Sánchez imagines this spiritual union through the totemic figure of the Puerto Rican singer, onto which he projects his desire to be heard as an authorial voice from the margins. At the same time, his eccentric text disperses the point from which that voice emerges across a wide stretch of the American landscape.

Because Sánchez proposes a more open form of narrative humor in his *fabulación*, the text anticipates the "masks" that the reader will impose on the persona of the author. The last words in *Daniel Santos* command: "Lector, ahora diga usted" [Reader, now it's your turn to speak] (212). Only through a humorous perspective can Sánchez issue such a solicitation; with it he fuses his pleasure as author with that of the reader. Freud writes in "Humour" that "the humorous attitude—whatever it may consist in—can be directed either towards the subject's own self or towards other people; it is to be assumed that it brings a yield of pleasure to the person who adopts it, and a similar yield of pleasure falls to the share of the non-participating onlooker" (161). Similar to what Freud suggests here, Sánchez's text implies that the reader is no different from the author/narrator who takes pleasure in witnessing the comedic coupling on the forest floor. In other words, through humor Sánchez opens the text so that the reader can participate with his or her own voice. This narrative aperture decenters the reader's position as a static observer. Just as Sánchez's narrative embarks on a quest across the broad geographic expanse of the Americas only to end deep in the heart of Puerto Rico, his textual *jaibería* uses humor to move from the eccentric to the insular, from the comic to the tragic, and from self to other. His narrative will find new expression in the reader's voice, just as Daniel Santos's boleros will continue to be sung by the future generations of Puerto Rico and the Americas. His humor opens a porous space in discourse that confounds the rigid codes of autochthony and linguistic purity. Humor and *jaibería* blur the lines between the self who writes and the self who is written, so that authorial agency remains a viable means of intervening in literary discourse even if it is just one of many narrative masks that negotiate meaning and truth.

Ana Lydia Vega's Tourist Gaze
and the Eye of Irony

The ironic figure of speech has still another property that characterizes
all irony, a certain superiority deriving from its not wanting to be understood immediately, even though it wants to be understood. . . . it travels
around, so to speak, in an exclusive incognito and looks down pitying
from this high position on ordinary, prosaic talk.

Søren Kierkegaard, *The Concept of Irony*

Writers who employ irony in their texts take a considerable risk. A reader
might not perceive irony where it has been encoded and interpret the
ironic statement at face value. Irony places readers into two categories:
those who "get it" and those who do not. Those who can perceive an alternate meaning behind an ironic statement immediately join an exclusive
group of "superior" readers, whose knowledge and/or skill separates them
from the "inferior" reader who cannot grasp statements with double
meanings. Kierkegaard alludes to this superiority complex when he describes irony as an elusive figure of speech that resists being mastered the
way "ordinary, prosaic talk" offers itself with no resistance to interpretation. Ironic statements create distance between themselves and readers and
invite only a select few to participate in the unfolding of meaning. Yet an
even bigger risk for the writer who makes use of irony is that the "true"
meaning behind the ironic statement can be just as slippery, just as hard to
master, as the "surface" text. Furthermore, the "surface" text that the
"true" meaning is supposed to negate has a tendency to infiltrate its presumably superior other. In other words, irony performs its refusal of the
other by articulating the other's language. The ironic text risks a self-nega-
tion when the other's discourse infiltrates meaning.

Ana Lydia Vega is a Puerto Rican writer who takes many risks when she
employs irony in her short stories and essays. In a 1994 interview she told
Elizabeth Hernández and Consuelo López Springfield: "I think that con-

temporary Puerto Rican women's writing also has a wider ironic distance. People like that because it responds to our era, a time when no one believes in ideologies anymore. Irony, thus, is a necessary posture" (818). Vega would seem to refer here to the postmodern era as postulated by Jean-François Lyotard in *The Postmodern Condition,* in which Western subjects have lost faith in the master narratives that have shaped our history. Yet Vega's statement also refers specifically to Puerto Rican literature and society since the mid-twentieth century, an era in which the prevailing notions of national identity have come under scrutiny via the critical interventions of gender, sexuality, race, class, and the diaspora. Vega's fiction offers a strong feminist critique and subversion of machismo, and her stories expose the racism and class conflicts that plague contemporary Puerto Rican society. Vega articulates her critiques using multiple levels of irony, both as ironic statements and as tropic figures. These ironies undermine the oppressive ideologies of their targets by taking their logic to its most absurd extremes, but in order to do so these ironies must speak the language of oppression. Vega's use of irony not only risks enforcing a hierarchy of readership, it also risks reproducing the violence of the other in its own refusal of oppression.

However, there is a type of irony that approaches the self-reflexivity of humor, which undermines a reader's sense of superiority and unveils her or his tendency to reduce everything and everyone to objects of an ironic gaze. Octavio Paz, in *Los hijos del limo: Del romanticismo a la vanguardia,* describes this self-reflexive, humorous irony as "metairony," a suspended state beyond affirmation and negation when we look at ourselves looking. Metairony is the moment when "criticism becomes creation" and performs a "'renversement' of the modern era by means of its own weapons: criticism and irony" (Phillips, 112).[1] Paz's notion of "metairony" resonates with many French poststructuralist defenses of humor as a means of challenging logocentrism and its essentialist conception of language. Candace Lang, in *Irony/Humor: Critical Paradigms,* argues that while Anglo-American critics have tended to characterize irony as a means of conveying authorial intent, French poststructuralists such as Roland Barthes, Paul de Man, and Gilles Deleuze have focused more on the play of language that undermines "the dichotomies that ground the classical concept of irony" (61). Lang calls this latter type of irony "humor" because it is "the affirmation of a self constituted in and out of language" and "is not a choice of appearance *instead* of reality, signifier *instead* of signified" (60). Like Paz's metairony, Lang's notion of critical "humor" offers a self-reflexive alternative to irony's "dialecticization" (35). In other words, humor does not enforce a hierarchy of readership, nor does it risk reproducing the violence of the other.

Vega's stories and essays oscillate between irony and humor. Like Luis Rafael Sánchez, Vega does not relinquish her agency as an author with a serious political commitment to Puerto Rican national identity. However, her texts can also scrutinize the very textuality that constitutes her authorial persona. Her use of irony serves as a subversive critique of machismo, racism, and class conflict. She deploys irony's rhetoric of negation in order to affirm a Puerto Rican national identity that intersects with feminism, Afro-Caribbean culture, and class consciousness. Yet her ironies run the risk of reproducing the very discourses she sets out to demystify, putting oppressed subjects even further at the margins. In order to redress such dialecticized discourse, Vega takes her irony to another level toward metairony, or humor, which allows her texts to reflect on their own deployment of irony and to consider the repercussions of irony's superiority complex. Irony can enforce a "discourse of mastery" between the subject and the other (Lang, 56). On the other hand, when a subject uses irony to examine her or his subjectivity and looks on the self as if it were other, then that subject places irony at the service of humor and its ability to blur the lines between selfhood and otherness. Vega's texts perform a *jaibería* between irony and humor as a means of reclaiming authorial agency while exploring the play of language that constitutes the authorial persona.

Like so many other Puerto Rican writers, Vega's texts also perform a *jaibería* between the insular and the eccentric. Her feminist critique informs the interplay of these two tropes to show how women and women's writing have challenged the paternalist culture of enforced domesticity. Vega's eccentric texts often represent the figure of the female tourist, who travels independently to foreign countries and encounters her cultural, racial, and sexual others. These traveling women deploy what John Urry has called a "tourist gaze": an objectifying mode of perception that distances the subject from the foreign, exotic other. The tourist gaze easily intersects with the ironic eye, for both see the other as a surface and an object lacking any knowledge of itself. The tourist/ironist authorizes herself as the arbiter of meaning, reading in the other a ready-made script that strips it of its agency. To a certain degree, this combination of the tourist gaze and irony demystifies machismo, racism, and class hatred, but as it articulates a feminist discourse it can also propel the eccentric sensibility back toward an insular vision, isolating the female subject from alterity. It is then that humor intervenes with its blurring of selfhood and otherness. Some of Vega's stories negotiate this humor more successfully than others, yet in all cases her *jaibería* between irony and humor and between the insular and the eccentric challenges readers to reexamine the position from which they find the comic in others. Vega's humor turns the reader's ironic gaze back to its source, allowing for a self-examination of one's own superiority complex and quest for mastery.

Revenge of the Diaspora: "Pollito Chicken" and the Bilingual Nation

One of the oldest theories of laughter and the comic is the superiority theory, which operates on the premise that a subject perceives an object as comic because of some physical, mental, moral, or ethical shortcoming. In Plato's *Philebus*, Socrates argues that persons who are ignorant of themselves and powerless to defend themselves against attack are the prime targets of ridicule and laughter. He states: "For ignorance in the strong is hateful, because it is hurtful to everyone both in real life and on the stage, but powerless ignorance may be considered ridiculous, which it is" (qtd. in Morreall 1987, 12). According to Socrates, the pleasure a subject takes in laughing at a comic object is a mixture of malice and pain, because delighting in the misfortunes of one's enemies is malicious, but "malice is a pain of the soul" (13). Similarly, in the *Poetics*, Aristotle defines theatrical comedy as "an imitation of people worse than average" (V.i). In ancient Greek comedies the braggart, ignorant of himself or his station, played the role of the *alazon*, while the underdog, who saw through the *alazon*'s pretensions and unmasked them to the audience, played the role of the *eiron*. Like Socrates, who used his famous method of feigning ignorance in order to unravel his opponent's arguments, the *eiron* demonstrated his superiority over the *alazon* by having him unmask his own shortcomings and inferiority. The *eiron* would take the *alazon*'s logic to its absurd extreme, revealing its incongruity and thereby making it ridiculous.[2]

Another well-known superiority theory of laughter and the comic comes from Thomas Hobbes' *Leviathan*, in which the seventeenth-century philosopher argues that humans are in constant struggle with one another. One way a person demonstrates superiority over another is through laughter, which Hobbes defines as a "sudden glory" that the subject either causes through his or her own actions or apprehends in the rival. Hobbes characterizes those who take pleasure in others' misfortunes as those "who are forced to keep themselves in their own favor by observing the imperfections of other men." Therefore, "great minds" are not prone to laughter because they are self-aware and "compare themselves only with the most able," not with those they consider inferior to themselves (qtd. in Morreall 1987, 19). Laughter does not always convey malicious intent, yet Hobbes' superiority theory of laughter underscores the incongruity that subjects perceive between themselves and other members of their society. While incongruity is at the heart of all forms of the comic, the superiority theory helps to explain the negative affect that often suffuses laughter (Morreall 1987, 190–92). Such laughter or "sudden glory" is the pleasure that subjects take in perceiving or representing their rivals as smaller than what they imagine themselves to be.

Ana Lydia Vega's short story "Pollito Chicken" has often been interpreted as a malicious satire of Puerto Ricans who migrated to and make their homes in the United States. The story presents a caricature of these diasporic Puerto Ricans in Suzie Bermiúdez, a Puerto Rican who migrated to New York as a young girl and has since adopted an assimilationist attitude. The story ridicules Suzie's bilingual consciousness by reproducing an exaggerated form of Spanglish—the hybrid speech of many U.S. Latinos and Latinas who grew up code-switching between English and Spanish.[3] Vega depicts Suzie as a woman deluded by the American Dream, ignorant of the futility of erasing her Puerto Rican heritage and exchanging it for a false sense of "whiteness." Suzie shows her ignorance by returning to Puerto Rico as an adult and attempting to hide her Puerto Rican identity behind her economic independence, her impeccable English, and her dyed, straightened hair. Although she dreams of seducing a white man while on her vacation, Suzie winds up succumbing to the hypermasculinity of a black Puerto Rican bartender with a kinky afro. The story ends with this "mamitólogo" recounting to his friends how he brought Suzie back to her people by giving her the most liberating orgasm possible: "¡VIVA PUELTO RICO LIBREEEEEEEEEEEEEEEE!" (*Vírgenes* 79). When Suzie utters these words during her orgasm, the macho applies his superior lovemaking skills ostensibly to free her from her deluded assimilationism, reinscribing her into the fold of the national community. He serves as the *eiron* to Suzie's *alazon* and exposes the "true," Spanish-speaking Puerto Rican behind her mask of Anglo whiteness. The battle for national identity is played out on Suzie's body, with an Africanized Puerto Rican nationalism acting as the law of the phallus.

Several critics have disapproved of Vega's story, considering it a cheap shot at the communities of Puerto Ricans who reside in the United States and who are raised in a bilingual environment. Nicholasa Mohr, a New York Puerto Rican novelist and short-story writer, has harshly criticized this story for its portrayal of Spanglish, calling it "ludicrous and incorrect" (1987, 90). She refers to the story line as "stupid" and "like a cartoon" and, refusing even to name Vega, rebukes the writer for having "very little knowledge of who we are here" and for holding "quite a bit of disdain and contempt for our community" (90). Myrna García Calderón, in *Lecturas desde el fragmento: Escritura contemporánea e imaginario cultural en Puerto Rico,* also disparages this story as an example of a failed satire, for its personal attack against Suzie undermines the story's sociopolitical critique. For García Calderón, the text appears to blame Suzie for her doubly marginal status: not truly Puerto Rican nor Anglo-American (186). Both Mohr and García Calderón take exception to the way the story ridicules Suzie's bilingual, bicultural identity. From the point of view of a phallically and racially enforced monolingual nationalism, Suzie's hybridity is an obscene moral flaw, which can only be corrected through a sexual discipline meted out against her female body.

However, another way to read this story is through humor; that is, a reader can take Vega's use of irony to another level and see how it turns back on its textual source and its ideal audience. Diana Vélez, in *"Pollito Chicken*: Split Subjectivity, National Identity, and the Articulation of Female Sexuality in a Narrative by Ana Lydia Vega," provides an astute analysis of the different narrative levels encoded in Vega's story and how their interplay affects the reading of irony. Vélez points out that the story is told, not by Suzie, but by an extradiegetic narrator whose voice "is inflected with the emotional structure of the character" yet also regards that character with irony (70). Vélez writes that Suzie's voice is "always mediated, quoted as it were, by the narrator, although there are no syntactic markers to indicate this" (71). This ambiguity destabilizes the reading of irony, since not only does the narrator parody Suzie's bilingualism in its ridicule of assimilated Puerto Ricans, the narrator also uses the same language to satirize the island's own economic disparities, internal racism, and sexist culture of machismo. In this way the text employs the eccentric strategy of using an "outsider" to critique Puerto Rico's internal problems. This narrator speaks in a self-consciously heteroglossic voice when it addresses the readers: "Todo lo cual nos pone en el aprieto de contarles el surprise return de Suzie Bermiúdez a su native land" [All of which puts us in the tight spot of telling you [plural] about the surprise return of Suzie

Bermiúdez to her native land] (*Vírgenes* 75). This narrator speaks as the implied author, who distances herself from Suzie through irony, but the narrator also speaks in the plural to and for the insular Puerto Rican nation, the story's ideal audience.

For Diana Vélez this story is a "revenge narrative" that reflects back on Puerto Rican islanders and their desire for national cohesion (74). In this reading, the story's denouement becomes an obscene joke told in the male character's voice, and he gets to deliver the punch line at Suzie's expense. The obscene joke, or smut, told in the company of men, is a demonstration of male sexual aggression, as Freud explains in *Jokes and Their Relation to the Unconscious* (115–16): "Smut is thus originally directed towards women and may be equated with attempts at seduction. If a man in a company of men enjoys telling or listening to smut, the original situation, which owing to social inhibitions cannot be realized, is at the same time imagined. A person who laughs at smut that he hears is laughing as though he were the spectator of an act of sexual aggression." The bartender's punch line inscribes the complicitous reader into the text as a witness to Suzie's orgasmic moment, which is also the moment of her reintegration into the national, phallogocentric family. Unlike humor, the joke form separates the subjects of laughter from their comic object. This is the "tendentious joke" that Freud describes as either "a *hostile* joke (serving the purposes of aggressiveness, satire, or defence) or an *obscene* joke (serving the purpose of exposure)" (115). As a revenge narrative, this ironic undoing of Suzie's assimilationism reveals her "authentic" Puerto Rican self, declaring her spasmodic nationalism in the mother tongue. National cohesion is achieved by negating in Suzie that which made her other: her hybrid, bilingual identity.

However, by negating Suzie's bilingualism, the readers admit to their comprehension of it. Like ethnic jokes, this story projects onto the other that which the subject wishes to deny in her- or himself. Christie Davies, in *Ethnic Humor Around the World*, writes: "Ethnic jokes 'export' a particular unwanted trait to some other group and we laugh at their folly, perhaps glad or relieved that it is not our own" (7). Similarly, the Puerto Rican readers who take Suzie as an object of derision desire to negate in themselves the bilingualism that allows them to be in on the joke. Vélez writes that Suzie represents the return of the diaspora that has "put into question the much fought for cultural and national identity of that island colony" (75). Suzie's comeuppance at the end of the story reflects an islander's resentment toward the diasporic community, but Vélez argues that the nation, "like Suzie, like the reader, is a house divided against itself" (75). That division not only separates island and mainland Puerto Ricans but also fractures any notion of a cohesive, pure national identity.

The "revenge" in this narrative can also belong to the diasporic community, whose bilingualism and bicultural experience hold up a mirror to Puerto Rico's fragmented national identity. Vega's story opens itself up to such a reading through its use of irony, which risks destabilizing its own attempt to convey meaning. Dustin Griffin, in *Satire: A Critical Reintroduction*, argues that when some satirical texts use irony, they go beyond their moral imperatives when their aesthetic function takes over as the dominant source of comic pleasure. Sometimes "the satirist may simply be unable to resist a joke" (65). The use of irony—a rhetorical strategy that already operates through ambiguity—becomes unstable, and the reader cannot determine with certainty which of irony's levels of meaning coincides with the satirist's ethical stance. Griffin argues against Wayne Booth's *A Rhetoric of Irony* (1974), which contends that satiric irony is usually stable, in that the satirist directs readers toward a "true" meaning that must be recovered from a superficial, "false" statement. Griffin questions the stability of irony when the reliability of the narrator is in doubt, and he states that "when a satirist seems to speak to us through an assumed mask, it is difficult to apply any set rules like Booth's to determine when and to what extent the author 'agrees with' the apparent speaker" (66). Vega's text takes a risk using irony because its ambivalent narrator sometimes ridicules Suzie but sometimes sees Puerto Rico's problems through Suzie's tourist gaze. Despite its objectification of Suzie, the narrative voice turns out to be the agent of Suzie's revenge; that is, Suzie's voice—the voice of the other—speaks in the discourse of Puerto Rican nationalism as it reflects on itself.

Vega's story offers the possibility of a humorous laughter from two other perspectives: Puerto Rican islanders who see their own fragmented nationalism in Suzie, and diasporic readers who see in Suzie their own frustrated desire to return to the Puerto Rican national family. In other words, a humorous reading of this story sees an incongruity that has escaped the dialecticized order of meaning/language, signified/signifier. That incongruity is the inherent otherness of the self—the voice of the other that articulates itself in the subject's discourse. Candace Lang argues: "The assumption and affirmation of the discontinuity and inherent otherness of the self is humor; the denial of it, irony" (25). Readers who find Suzie laughable might harbor malice toward the diasporic community that this character represents, thus reading her ironically. Such readers assume they possess direct access to the meaning behind the narrator's ironic statements. They also assumes that Suzie is wholly other.

Humor, on the other hand, shows that Suzie always was part of the Puerto Rican national identity, and her linguistic and cultural bifurcation reflects the island's own internal, insular society. As Diana Vélez points out in her essay on "Pollito Chicken," the title of the story refers to a nursery rhyme that was popularized on the island—not the mainland—in an attempt to impose English on several generations of Puerto Rican children (69).[4] Vega herself recounts her own bilingual language experience in her essay "Pulseando con el difícil" [Wrestling with English]. As a student in Puerto Rico, she attended a Catholic school run by Irish American nuns, and her textbooks were imported from the United States. She was prohibited from speaking Spanish except in Spanish class, but at home her father made a point of speaking only in Spanish and forbade his children to call him "Papi," a term he considered an anglicism. Vega grew up with two languages, but they were far from equal in status. She writes:

> Little by little the view that English was the language of prestige, progress, and modernity began to consolidate itself. In English was all the technical, scientific, and literary vocabulary that we incorporated in order to discuss the most diverse aspects of knowledge. Spanish, with its delicate odor of antique furniture, was reduced to the domestic and intimate spheres. I remember when I arrived at the University of Puerto Rico, years later, I urgently had to rush to the dictionary in search of mathematical terms, names of historical figures, or exotic countries that I did not know how to say in Spanish. (*Esperando a Loló* 12)[5]

Vega's bilingual experience is the result of a privileged education, middle-class upbringing, and urban environment, while Vega's character Suzie encounters English as the child of the Puerto Rican diaspora—the successive waves of migration that displaced tens of thousands of working-class, disenfranchised families from Puerto Rico's interior to mainland U.S. cities. However, one can surmise from Vega's own example that a generation of Puerto Ricans raised and educated on the island were not exempt from the interference of English, which remains to this day the language of the United States's colonial presence on the island. The idea that a pure, unadulterated Spanish has been the exclusive language on the island is an inaccurate account of Puerto Rico's colonial history. Suzie's bilingualism is a reflection of the islanders' own struggles with language and national identity, and Puerto Rican readers arrive at this humorous doubling if they perform the metaironic—or humorous—reading that looks at the self looking.

Yet a diasporic reader, like Nicholasa Mohr, might take offense at the grotesque caricature of Suzie and the obscene joke made at this character's expense. The bilingual, bicultural Puerto Rican who grew up in the United States would feel the sting of an islander's ridicule, and Suzie is similar to the kind of assimilated character that often inspires fear and abjection in works by U.S. Puerto Rican writers and artists. Judith Ortiz Cofer offers a particularly striking example in her memoirs, *Silent Dancing: A Partial Remembrance of a Puerto Rican Childhood*. Narrating her childhood in Paterson, New Jersey, Ortiz Cofer remembers one of her grandmother's stories about a young aunt who disparages her Puerto Rican heritage and desires to pass as white. This aunt dates a married white man and is eventually forced to abort the unborn child that results from her adulterous affair. She is sent back to Puerto Rico as a disgrace, to "a place so far away from civilization that you have to ride a mule to reach it" (97). The grandmother mocks the assimilationist aunt, saying: "But believe me, the men in Puerto Rico know how to put a saddle on a woman like her. *La Gringa*, they call her. Ha, ha, ha. *La Gringa* is what she always wanted to be" (97). The author/narrator experiences the negative affect of that mockery, since she, too, is assimilated in ways the grandmother is not. The grandmother's mocking words, aimed at the aunt, serve as a warning to the young Ortiz Cofer—a lesson in what happens to young women who defy nationalism's phallogocentric order. The grandmother's laughter consumes the author/narrator: "The old woman's mouth becomes a cavernous black hole I fall into. And as I fall, I can feel the reverberations of her laughter. I hear the echoes of her last mocking words: *La Gringa!, La Gringa!*" (97). Much in the way that Vega's story ridicules Suzie and reinscribes her into the national family via her body, Ortiz Cofer feels herself being swallowed by her grandmother's laughter. In both cases the negative affect of laughter's superiority complex overwhelms the U.S Puerto Rican subject and silences her bilingual, bicultural identity. Her identity is marked as wholly other, and only through a refusal of that otherness can she be reincorporated into the national family, in which there is no room for hybridity or ambiguity.

However, humor can allow the diasporic subject to appropriate the mocking discourse of the other and overcome the pathos of the "Gringa"

stereotype. In the case of Vega's story, the ironic narrative can be reformulated through humor as a critique of monolingual nationalism, because the
story forces readers to examine the position from which they perceive
irony. Charles Baudelaire in "On the Essence of Laughter" underscores the
self-reflexive nature of certain kinds of laughter: "The man who trips
would be the last to laugh at his own fall, unless he happened to be a philosopher, one who had acquired by habit a power of rapid self-division and
thus of assisting as a disinterested spectator at the phenomena of his own
ego" (154). A diasporic reader who confronts the caricature of Suzie might
experience negative affect, as Nicholasa Mohr expresses in her condemnation of this character. In that case, the reader would not laugh at Vega's
representation of the disaporic community because that ridicule originates
from another community—the island—that is wholly other. Yet like the
island Puerto Rican reader who deploys a metaironic gaze and sees in Suzie
a reflection of fragmented selfhood, Suzie reflects back to a diasporic
reader the otherness that suffuses her or his own subjectivity. Looking and
laughing at their own fragmented selves, diasporic readers also look and
laugh at the incongruities that fracture the cohesion of monolingual nationalism. Ostensibly the victims of irony, diasporic readers can use humor
to destabilize the text and show that its object of ridicule—Suzie's bilingual struggle—is actually a shared experience between islanders and U.S.
Puerto Ricans. This metaironic—or humorous—gaze allows Suzie to become an object of laughter for the diasporic reader, and the negative affect
of ridicule is displaced and resituated as an affirmation of self, a "triumph
of narcissism."[6] Like the Baudelairean philosopher, the diasporic reader is a
"spectator at the phenomena of [her or] his own ego." By laughing at the
self, the reader who identifies with Suzie's bilingualism—but not her
assimilationism—overcomes the ridicule and refusal of a mocking, phallogocentric nationalism, while at the same time reinscribing the diaspora
into a bilingual national family.

Perhaps this is not the "ideal" reading that Vega intended when she
wrote "Pollito Chicken," but one of the risks of literary irony is that it
opens the text up to multiple ambiguities. The other risk is that irony functions by appealing to a particular interpretive community, and therefore is
inherently political.[7] Linda Hutcheon, in *Irony's Edge: The Theory and
Politics of Irony*, writes that "irony can be provocative when its politics are
conservative or authoritarian as easily as when its politics are oppositional
and subversive: it depends on who is using/attributing it and at whose
expense it is seen to be" (15). However, there is no "guarantee" that irony

will successfully reach its intended audience, or that it will be perceived and interpreted as intended. Hutcheon writes:

> Those whom you oppose might attribute no irony and simply take you at your word; or they might make irony happen and thus accuse you of being self-negating, if not self-contradicting. Those with whom you agree (and who know your position) might also attribute no irony and mistake you for advocating what you are in fact criticizing. They may simply see you as a hypocrite or as compromised by your complicity with a discourse and values they thought you opposed. They might also, of course, attribute irony and interpret it precisely as you intended it to be. (16)

As Hutcheon suggests, an ironic text risks misinterpretation when it speaks in the voice of that which it attempts to negate. And as Diana Vélez has shown in her analysis of "Pollito Chicken," the multivoiced narrative destabilizes a reader's attempt to attribute irony "precisely" to a univocal source. Therefore, the "true" meaning behind Vega's ironic representation of Suzie is just as slippery and fraught with contradiction as the "surface" text that engages the reader. This ambiguity allows Suzie to function as a comic object for readers with different, perhaps incompatible, investments in the question of Puerto Rican national identity. A character like Suzie can inspire malicious laughter from those who consider themselves superior, but she can also elicit the laughter of those Puerto Ricans who see in Suzie a reflection of themselves. This self-reflexive, humorous laughter emerges from either side of the eccentric Puerto Rican nation and articulates a political challenge to the oppressive discourses of conformity, homogeneity, and linguistic purity.

The Afro-Caribbean Slideshow: "Puerto Príncipe abajo"

Suzie is not the only character that Vega portrays as a Puerto Rican tourist, although Suzie is a tourist whose gaze does not possess the capacity for self-reflection. She remains unaware of herself throughout the story and thus fulfills the traditional role of the *alazon*. It is perhaps for this reason that this character does not readily appeal to a diasporic reader, who would find Suzie an unsympathetic figure. However, Suzie resembles another set of Puerto Rican characters that Vega portrays as tourists in her story "Puerto Príncipe abajo." Suzie's condescending attitude toward her homeland is very much like the dismissive attitude taken by a group of boorish middle-class tourists who travel from Puerto Rico to Haiti. These Puerto Rican tourists consider themselves economically, racially, and culturally superior to the Haitians they encounter while on vacation, but their superiority complex blinds them to their own colonial condition and Afro-Caribbean heritage. Vega employs a different narrative technique in her portrayal of these characters, for although they are unable to reflect on themselves, they are accompanied by another young Puerto Rican woman who is highly aware of her status as a tourist and how her tourist gaze frames her encounters with her Haitian others. In many ways this diegetic narrator takes the place of the extradiegetic narrator of "Pollito Chicken": it is her voice that tells the story and it is through her ironic perspective that the reader sees the other tourists as ridiculous. Yet unlike the narrator of "Pollito Chicken," the protagonist in "Puerto Príncipe abajo" also turns her ironic gaze on herself, seeing herself as other. Her self-reflexive narrative—told alternately in the first and second person—makes her a much more sympathetic character, for she overcomes the negative affect of her tourist gaze through humor.

In a discussion of literary representations of Puerto Rican tourists, it is important to recall Emilio S. Belaval's classic collection of short stories, *Cuentos para fomentar el turismo* [Stories to promote tourism]. When we compare the title of Belaval's collection to the stories contained within, we immediately perceive an intended irony. The stories depict the degradation and misery of the Puerto Rican *jíbaro*, a victim of the rapid industrial expansion on the island and ensuing loss of an agricultural way of life. The tragic scenes depicted in these stories are far from the picturesque images that promote tourism, yet the narrator imparts a compassionate tone for these victims of cruel, accidental ironies. Belaval's stories reflect an insular vision, for they imagine the *jíbaro* as the static object of a tourist's gaze. Vega's female characters, on the other hand, are the tourists who consume other cultures. They travel in order to escape their insular lives, their mind-numbing careers, or their suffocating relationships with men. In traditional Puerto Rican society, a woman risked either her reputation or herself if she left the house unescorted, let alone traveled to foreign countries without a male chaperone. The representation of tourism in Puerto Rican literature has gone from Belaval's island-bound *jíbaros* to Vega's globetrotting modern women. In Vega's fictions the female tourist becomes a symbol for the independence that Puerto Rican women have achieved through education and employment. Yet, as a tourist, a woman attains a privileged status in regard to the "natives" she encounters during her travels, and her sense of superiority can cloud her vision to her exploitation of others as well as the exploitation that is being enacted upon her.

A character who struggles with this superiority complex is the unnamed Puerto Rican schoolteacher in the short story "Puerto Príncipe abajo," which appeared in the collection Vega copublished with Carmen Lugo Filippi, *Vírgenes y mártires* (1981). The story's title refers to the Haitian capital, Port-au-Prince, which the protagonist visits on a package tour in the company of a less than congenial group of middle-class, middle-aged Puerto Ricans. The story is told as a series of ten slides—*diapositivas*—and in each narrative image Vega offers a derogatory comment made by someone from the tour group, followed by the ruminations of the main character. The diction that characterizes these voices serves to distance the protagonist from her compatriots, since the passages attributed to the schoolteacher mix Spanish, English, and French, while the statements made by her compatriots are caricatures of the popular Puerto Rican dialect. While the Puerto Ricans vocalize their criticisms of Haitians' blackness and poverty, the narrator/protagonist internally criticizes the narrow-mindedness of her travel companions. Her ironic perceptions allow her to distance herself from them, but her sense of superiority is deflated by a series of events that lead to an accidental irony, of which she is the unwitting victim.

She rationalizes her feelings of superiority over what she sees as the crass behavior of the other tourists: "Excuse me, but how can one not feel like a *vedette* [diva] in the middle of this delegation of urbanized matrons: profusion of Chanel No. 5 and mops of hair saturated with enough hairspray to withstand a hurricane" (92).[8] The narrator sees herself as having much more cultural cachet than her boorish compatriots. However, she is black, and her African heritage places her in a subordinate position to the other tourists, who see themselves as white, especially in comparison to the black Haitians. The protagonist knows that during the unavoidable small talk that she will have to endure with her déclassé companions, the subject of her ancestry is bound to come up: "Pick through my afro in search of the fatal ancestor. The status is at issue" (92).[9] Vega cleverly alludes to the question of Puerto Rico's political status by means of the English word "issue." One is reminded of the series of status plebiscites in which Puerto Ricans voted to decide their political future—a vote that was nonbinding because the fate of the island, as a U.S. commonwealth, ultimately rested with the government in Washington.[10] The protagonist transposes that debate onto her own status as a black Puerto Rican, implying that Puerto Rico's political status and the racial inequalities suffered by

Afro-Caribbeans derive from a shared history of colonialism. The protagonist's awareness of her racial identity distances her from the other tourists, who see the Haitians as black but themselves as white. The protagonist makes the connection between her national identity and race in a way that threatens the other tourists' sense of superiority, for Puerto Rico and Haiti share a history of colonialism, slavery, and U.S. intervention that these tourists would rather ignore.

The protagonist perceives her travel companions with a heavy dose of irony. While the tourists look on her with a mixture of pity and contempt, she uses her marginal status to gain a vantage point that the self-deluded tourists do not achieve. One of the narrative "slides" begins with a rude comment by one of the unenlightened Puerto Rican tourists: "Nena, ¿y tu marido te deja viajal sola?" [Honey, your husband lets you travel alone?] (92). The condescending remark—rendered in the characteristic Puerto Rican diction that alters terminal *r* to *l*—allows the other tourists to use marriage as a trump card to remind the protagonist of her socially inferior status. However, marriage does not necessarily protect a woman from being exploited; quite the contrary, the false security that marriage provides can blind a woman to the shallowness of her bourgeois mentality. The segment of the story that follows the rude comment details an encounter between the protagonist and a Dominican prostitute, Altagracia, who has just had sex with the husband of one of the other tourists. As Altagracia tells her story, the narrator/protagonist sees the seduction play out before her cinematically, imagining the clumsy, brutish treatment the Puerto Rican husband inflicts. At that point in Altagracia's story, the man's wife arrives and the narrator/protagonist, armed with the information of her husband's infidelity, describes the other tourist ironically, showing how the woman is contented but is in reality being deceived. She describes the woman as

> all expanse of fat rolls rearranged by the girdle, all fanfare of charm bracelets, showing off the five identical ashtrays for her five best friends that she got through her indefatigable haggling for five American cents. She complains about the sun, about the humidity, about Créole, about the noise, about the lemon vendors. And it's as if her eyes moisten with the air-conditioned memory of a day of shopping at Plaza Las Américas. (93)[11]

The last line in this passage offers a good example of the internalized verbal irony that the narrator deploys in order to ridicule her traveling companions. Rather than portray the wife as a sentimental woman given to nostalgic reminiscences of home, the narrator presents her as a shallow consumer whose level of emotional maturity does not supersede her consumerist self-indulgence. Clearly, the protagonist identifies more closely with the Dominican prostitute than with a fellow Puerto Rican from the same social class. She distances herself from the other tourist and depicts her as a caricature of the bourgeois matron, whose married status is compromised by her philandering husband. Ironically, the marriage that supposedly secures her social legitimacy is the main cause of her exploitation. Irony functions here as both a negation and an affirmation: it negates the unsympathetic tourist's superiority complex, but it affirms an egalitarian relationship between the marginal subjects of the Caribbean.[12]

The protagonist scorns the Puerto Rican tourist for her willful blindness to her husband's infidelity, while she tries to empathize with the sexual freedom of the prostitute. However, her alliances with oppressed others are compromised by her inability to see the world through their eyes. When she imagines Altagracia's sexual encounter with the Puerto Rican husband, the image she conjures borders on the pornographic, placing her in the position of an intrusive voyeur. The protagonist comes to recognize that despite her disassociation from the other tourists, she cannot shed her own privileged tourist status. Although the protagonist's ironic perspective distances her from the unsympathetic characters, it does not automatically bring her closer to the black Haitians. She attempts to see a more authentic Haiti than those around her, but the protagonist's gaze also deploys a frame of signification in which she constructs her Haitian others.

Vega's use of narrative "slides" highlights the visual aspect of tourism and the voyeuristic impulse to capture the cultural authenticity of the other. John Urry, in *The Tourist Gaze: Leisure and Travel in Contemporary Society*, argues that photography structures the relation between the tourist and the object of her gaze by appropriating the object being photographed. While photography seems to transcribe reality, it is an active signifying practice that constructs idealized images. According to Urry, the photographic image attempts to miniaturize the real, and the quest for the perfect image gives shape to travel, being the reason in and of itself for stopping at any particular site/sight. Yet a hermeneutic circle obtains when tourists seek to recreate the images that they have already consumed from travel brochures, posters, and the like (139–40). The tourist gaze, mediated through photography, brings the subject in proximity to the "foreign," yet it engages its objects only within predetermined frames of signification.

Any notion of authenticity emerges from the photographic encounter, which situates tourists in a position of superiority in relation to the objects of their gaze. Not only does the tourist gaze choose which objects to frame with a photographic lens—making some objects visible and others invisible—the tourist gaze confers cultural authenticity on the objects it captures on film.

In "Puerto Príncipe abajo" the narrator/protagonist employs the tourist gaze to construct her Haitian others, but she also visualizes herself within the photographic frame. Vega illustrates this effect in a scene in which the protagonist barters with a Haitian man for a souvenir photograph:

> "How much for the photo?"
> "Twenty, *madame*."
> "Dollars? You're crazy."
> "Ten goud', *dix*.
> "Too expensive. Better if I take your picture."
> And before you point your homicidal lens at him, he disappears at the speed of his injured pride. His T-shirt: a small white dot at the end of the alley. (93)[13]

The scene pits two Afro-Caribbean subjects in an antagonistic relationship, with the Puerto Rican woman taking the upper hand. Not only does she refuse to buy the tattered photograph from the Haitian man, she miniaturizes him with her own photographic lens, reducing him to a consumable object that nevertheless resists the appropriating power of her tourist gaze. The last sentence in this passage reproduces the visual image captured by the tourist as the man runs away, and its smallness and remoteness heighten the social chasm that separates the tourist from the "natives," even if they do share an Afro-Caribbean heritage. However, the narrator employs the second person to refer to herself in this narrative "slide," placing herself within the frame of her photographic lens and visualizing herself as an object of her own tourist gaze. The second-person perspective functions here as a form of self-reflexive humor, for the narrator/protagonist sees herself through the same ironic lens with which she has negated the superiority complex of her travel companions.

By alternating between the first and second person, the narrator/protagonist uses humor to blur the line between self and other more successfully than if she simply employed irony. Brian Richardson, in "The Poetics and Politics of Second-Person Narrative," argues that when a protagonist is also the narrator and the narratee—the person to whom the story is told—a "slippage" occurs in the traditional structure of storytelling (311). With such a second-person narrator, the identity of that "you" becomes unstable, since it can refer to the protagonist as well as to the reader. Richardson writes: "The 'you' . . . also threatens the ontological stability of the fictional world, insofar as it necessarily addresses the reader as well as the central character" (312). Furthermore, the second-person narrator can establish a "heightened sense of engagement between the reader and the protagonist," whether the reader resists identifying with the story's "you" or sympathizes more fully with that protagonist (319). Irene Kacandes, in *Talk Fiction: Literature and the Talk Explosion*, also argues that the second-person narrative, which she identifies as a form of apostrophe, is a much more "empty" sign than the "I" of the first person (153). Because of this "emptiness," anyone can readily become the "you" in the text and respond to this direct address (153).[14] In Vega's story the "you" refers to the protagonist, who in other narrative "slides" speaks as the first-person "I." Yet she adopts the second-person voice when she visualizes her own gaze—she "looks at herself looking." She resumes the first-person voice when she casts her ironic eye on the other tourists. This double-voiced narrative not only destabilizes the protagonist's subjectivity, it also draws its readers more closely into the encounter with otherness. It aims its destabilizing discourse at them and prompts their own self-scrutiny. From what position do the readers perceive irony? Do they visualize their own reading practices? By alternating between the first and second person, Vega's story forces readers to move beyond the dialecticized discourse of irony and toward the playful ambivalence of humor, where the subject "looks at her- or himself looking."

The second-person voice narrates the story whenever the protagonist attempts to foster an intimate connection with Haiti. In one of the narrative "slides," when all the other tourists have gone in search of staged voodoo rituals, the protagonist lingers in the Champs de Mars and contemplates the statues of Louverture, Dessalines, and Christophe—heroes of the Haitian Revolution. Although she wants to break the time barrier and return to witness history in the making, she realizes that her daydreams are just "Romanticismo intelectual de ligas menores" [minor-league intellectual romanticism] (95). She turns on herself the ironic lens with which she has dissected her fellow tourists and her romanticism backfires, portraying the landscape not as a grandiose witness to history but as a bored spectator of the reality indifferent to her presence: "Up the hill Pétionville yawns. The moon watches television impassively. And you no longer commune with Boukman and Mackandal in the Caiman Forest. The howls of the living curdle your blood in Port-au-Prince" (95).[15] The protagonist wants to draw closer to the Haitians, but by romanticizing their history she would only blind herself to the cultural, political, and economic differences that separate her social reality from theirs. Her romanticism also blinds her to the present-day conditions in Haiti, whose "howls of the living" give testament to a less than heroic scene. The protagonist can get in touch with her Afro-Caribbean heritage and identify with the Haitians on that level, but her tourist status reconfigures just what it means for her to be black, Caribbean, and a woman.

Rafael Falcón, in "Aleluya a la caribeñidad: Los cuentos negristas de Ana Lydia Vega," argues that, despite her tourist status, the protagonist in "Puerto Príncipe abajo" feels at home in Haiti and finds the common Caribbean bond that the other tourists reject (40). However, Falcón does not take into account the protagonist's use of the second person, which functions at a humorous level to estrange the character from herself. The protagonist/narrator sees the irony of the culturally inauthentic tourist traps, like the voodoo rituals performed for the benefit of foreigners. Yet she recognizes that her attempts to gaze into the culturally authentic Haiti are already framed by the desire to visualize otherness through an ironic lens. It is only through the self-reflexivity of humor that the protagonist can see the otherness that penetrates and fragments her subjectivity and that destabilizes the position from which she deploys both irony and her tourist gaze.

The protagonist in "Puerto Príncipe abajo" deploys irony to distance herself from those she perceives as crass, and she fixes this ironic gaze on herself in order to avoid imposing her subjectivity on the Haitians, yet she also becomes the felicitous victim of an accidental irony that allows her finally to let down her guard and remove her ironic lens. Just as she is about to return to Puerto Rico, the protagonist loses a button from her blouse and goes to the open-air market to buy a replacement. The vendor immediately spots her as a tourist and tries to charge her five dollars for the first button she sees. The woman refuses and walks away, but to her surprise the vendor's young daughter catches up with her and hands her the button free of charge. In the earlier bartering episode, when the protagonist refused to buy the tattered photograph and instead snapped a picture of the fleeing man, she objectified him and appropriated his image without consent. In this instance, the Haitian girl also runs off and disappears before the woman can give her any money, but this time the girl gives something freely rather than having something taken against her will. The protagonist realizes the accidental irony of these events, since she expected the button vendor to be as uncooperative as the man in her previous encounter. She says, "Then you are overcome by an idiotic euphoria. And you return to the hotel, relic in hand, denying yourself an autopsy. Completely puzzled by this encounter between islands" (98).[16] Once again, this narrative "slide" is recounted in the second person, and the humorous effect—the protagonist's "idiotic euphoria"—is derived from a double irony: the narrator/protagonist ironizes her ironic gaze. The reader perceives her as a victim of irony and, in turn, takes pleasure in seeing the tables turned on a character whose unforgiving skepticism has refused enjoyment throughout the story. However, this euphoria is short-lived for both the character and the reader. The schoolteacher leaves Haiti with an overwhelming sense of regret—not because she failed to understand Haiti better, but because she realizes that Haiti will always resist her best efforts to empathize with its history. As she looks down at the island from the airplane, she reflects: "Haiti is a slap in the face to your synthetic kindness. A country that does not forgive. Every act is guilty and the penalty is a luxury that is paid at tourist prices" (98).[17] Although the protagonist has had an epiphany of sorts, she acknowledges that Haiti will continue to appear before her through the distorting lenses of irony and the tourist gaze. Only when she is caught off guard by the guileless actions of others can she afford to resist the habits of dissecting the world around her through irony and imposing predetermined frames of signification on otherness.

The final irony of the story, though, is that the crass, unrepentant tourists now set their sights on Spain as their next port of call: "Dicen que Ejpaña ej preciosa . . ." [They say Spain is lovely . . .] (98). By giving these Puerto Ricans the last word in the story, Vega returns her protagonist to her former ironic self, and this last statement from her traveling companions needs no comment from her for the reader to perceive its irony. The bourgeois tourists detested Haiti because they saw in its poverty and degradation a reflection of themselves, but their sense of superiority allowed them to distance the Haitian reality from their own colonial condition. They desire to go to Spain, which is whiter and more economically developed, but where, most likely, they will be the "inferior" subjects from a former colony. Their use of Spanish will be the object of someone else's ridicule, and their racial difference will be more noticeable among Europeans. By ending the story in this way, Vega fuses the perspective of her protagonist with that of the reader, since both are complicitous in detecting the irony of the final line. Vega has provided the reader with an obsessively self-aware character who ultimately, through humor, overcomes irony's investment in negation and the obscurantism of the tourist gaze. This satirical portrayal of Puerto Rican tourists inscribes clear ethical lines between colonized subjects who are in touch with history and those who have been deluded by their bourgeois longings for economic privilege. The readers are always "in on the joke" as long as they identify with the protagonist. They can securely laugh at the portrayal of the other tourists because, unlike the protagonist, these characters do not undergo an awakening of consciousness—an anagnorisis—and, in fact, appear to pull the veil of self-delusion even more tightly over their eyes.

The ironic eye can allow the subject to unmask hypocrisy and disempower the superiority complex of an antagonistic other, but a second-level ironic perspective—as in metairony or humor—focuses the subject's gaze back on its own use of irony. This othering of the self blurs the lines between superiority and inferiority. Once again, Charles Baudelaire's "The Essence of Laughter" can shed light on how the irony in "Puerto Príncipe abajo" functions self-reflexively. Baudelaire identifies two forms of the comic: the significative and the absolute. The significative comic occurs between subjects, when one takes another as an inferior comic object. The absolute comic occurs when "laughter is still the expression of superiority—no longer now of man over man, but of man over nature" (157). In other words, the absolute comic is not so much an intersubjective discourse as it is the laughter of a subject at the otherness that permeates its own selfhood, "nature" understood here as the subject's own internalized alterity. Paul de Man, in "The Rhetoric of Temporality," interprets Baudelaire's notion of the absolute comic as a "dédoublement" of the subject, in which "the so-called superiority merely designates the *distance* constitutive of all acts of reflection. Superiority and inferiority then become merely spatial metaphors to indicate a discontinuity and a plurality of levels within a subject that comes to know itself by an increasing differentiation from what it is not" (213). Using Baudelaire's terminology, one can see that the narrator/protagonist in "Puerto Príncipe abajo" alternates between the significative and absolute forms of the comic. This textual *jaibería* uses irony satirically to unveil Puerto Ricans' blindness to their own colonial condition. Yet the *jaibería* also allows for a self-reflexive humor in which the subject's position as ironist comes under scrutiny as it reflects on the discontinuities and pluralities that constitute its knowledge of self. The narrator/protagonist refocuses her superiority complex through humor to visualize the fragmentation of her own subjectivity, even as she trains her unremitting ironic eye on the hypocrisy of her fellow Puerto Rican tourists.

Vega's "Puerto Príncipe abajo" demonstrates the possibilities of integrating irony and humor. The narrator/protagonist remains critical of others while aware of her own capacity for error and incongruity. Yet what happens when a text takes entire literary genres as its comic objects while reflecting on its own textuality? In "Pasión de historia," Vega expands the lateral movement between irony and humor in order to excoriate the culture of machismo and its violence against women, while at the same time estranging the text from itself in order to avoid reinscribing that violence. The story parodies the literary genres that have constrained women's writing and readership in Puerto Rico in order to "smuggle" both feminism and nationalism in as political subtexts. "Pasión de historia" forms part of a textual politics of opposition that engages oppression obliquely. It recognizes the risks it takes when it parodies the discourses of oppression, for its negation of those discourses often carries with it the oppressor's ideological baggage. Humor allows the text to undermine its own superiority complex while continuing to postulate a discursive agency for the marginal subject. Ultimately, "Pasión de historia" directs the ironic charge of its multiple parodies to debase machismo's violence and the violent storytelling that disciplines and punishes unruly women. Yet it also reflects on its own textuality and its citation of that violence as a means to forestall the "death of the [female] author" in Puerto Rican literature.

A True-Crime Gothic Fairy Tale: Parody, Violence, and Storytelling in "Pasión de historia"

Poststructuralism did not kill the author, but a few well-known French critics have enthusiastically postulated the author's death. When Roland Barthes declared "The Death of the Author" in 1968, he did not consider the author as a person, but as a subject position that imposed a "limit" on a text that would "close writing" (147). To do away with the author is to allow for "the birth of the reader" (147–48); that is, the devaluation and the negation of authorial presence in a text brings forth a reader liberated from the constraints of an "ultimate meaning" (147). Like Foucault, whose "author-function" clears the way for a new set of critical questions indifferent to the origins of discourse, Barthes with his notion of the "death of the author" posits a textuality in which meaning defies unicity and proliferates in fragmentation.[18] Jacques Derrida, in *Limited Inc.*, also de-authors the text, partly as a response to an essay by John Searle, but also partly as a larger theory that denies authorial intent as immanent and self-evident in a text.[19]

These theories of writing replace the author's authority with the reader's appropriation of a text, signaling an interpretive practice that denies limits to signification. In many ways, these theories of the death of the author offer a liberating critical practice by conferring interpretive authority on the reader. Yet the authorial subject that these theories imagine as "dead" is, or was, neither a marginal nor a subaltern subject; these theories imagine the author as an enforcer of phallogocentric law. For those "scriptors," as Barthes would call them, who take risks with their writing, who deliberately deploy the ambiguity, double meanings, and self-reflexivity of irony and humor as an oppositional discourse, it is in the text's incongruities and multiple meanings that the writing subject inscribes her- or himself as an authorial persona. For a Puerto Rican woman writer, an authorial persona can negotiate the ambiguities of irony and humor to give voice to an oppositional literary discourse, one that confronts the discourses of sanctioned violence against women. Perhaps the "Vega" that one finds in Vega's texts is as fictional as the "Borges" of "Borges y yo," yet it is that authorial persona, that textual Vega, who intervenes in literary discourse to unmask and negate the culture of machismo while it reaffirms a Puerto Rican national identity—which is not an easy negotiation, given that the discourse on Puerto Rican national identity often inflicts its own forms of violence against women, both literally and figuratively. In "Pasión de historia" the protagonist is a Puerto Rican woman writer who meets her literal death so that the text's authorial persona can be born along with the reader.

Vega has consistently asserted her feminist and nationalist politics as part of her authorial interventions in Puerto Rican literary discourse. In what can be considered her personal statement as a writer, her essay "De bípeda desplumada a Escritora Puertorriqueña (Con E y P machúsculas)," Vega exposes the frustrations Puerto Rican women writers encounter in a rigidly controlled national canon.[20] From the very title, we see Vega's characteristic use of parodic citation and wordplay, whose comic element is often difficult to translate from Spanish to English. "Bípeda desplumada" refers to Plato's famous classification of man as a featherless biped.[21] This first parodic citation already carries a feminist statement that appropriates a universal classification of "man" and resignifies it to refer to a singular woman: the Puerto Rican woman writer Ana Lydia Vega. Rendering "bípeda desplumada" as "featherless biped" does not fully capture Vega's play on the word *pluma,* which can refer to a feather or, either literally or figuratively, a writing pen. Vega combines the parodic citation with the pun to imply that universalist definitions leave her without a scriptive agency. She is a woman without a pen who must somehow become a Puerto Rican Woman Writer. Yet she is not just any writer; her authorial persona must be consecrated by the paternalist literary establishment, thus her wordplay "machúscula," which combines *mayúscula* (upper-case letter) with *macho,* implying that the official title "Escritora Puertor-riqueña" carries with it a phallogocentric privilege even though the words are gendered as feminine. In sum, Puerto Rican women writers must undergo a tortuous process of gender sublimation and adaptation in order to join the ranks of nationally recognized authors.

Vega describes the nearly impossible task that Puerto Rican women writers often face in negotiating their triple identities: as Puerto Ricans, as women, and as writers. Although each identity carries with it certain presuppositions, these designations are not independent of one another. As a Puerto Rican, a writer is obliged to tackle what Vega calls "las tres nobles metas" [the three noble goals] of Puerto Rican literature: "Save the Nation from the Clutches of Yankee Imperialism, Affirm the Culture, and Accelerate the Advent of the Socialist Revolution" (27).[22] In addition to these prerequisites, women who write in Puerto Rico are expected to express themselves as "women"; that is, they are compelled to stay at home and rummage through their grandmothers' dusty trunks for sentimental souvenirs—what Vega calls "reliquias falopianas" [fallopian relics] (27). This kind of writing elicits approving nods from the male-dominated literary critical establishment, which offers such pet phrases as "finísma sensibilidad" [refined sensibility] or "cordialidad de tono" [cordiality of tone] (27). On the other hand, feminist criticism deplores this kind of writing with the accusation that it reaffirms stereotypes of the traditional, submissive woman. However, if women writers take to the streets and address feminist issues, they are then labeled unfeminine—"de ésas que queman brasieres y se meriendan a los niños crudos" [one of those who burn their bras and snack on raw children] (27).

Even within the notion of what characterizes a "woman" in Puerto Rico there lie myriad contradictions. More generally, Vega notes that all writers in Puerto Rico—men and women—are faced with scant publishing possibilities, but those works by women that do get published are often of a less than challenging nature: "cuentos para niños, libros de cocina y poesía de poetisas" [children's stories, cookbooks, and ladies' poetry] (28). Because of this narrowly defined space to which women's writing has been relegated, imposed on the one side by the male literary establishment and on the other by orthodox feminist critics, Vega says that women writers in Puerto Rico become their own worst enemies and consequently silence themselves after just one attempt at producing serious literature. Vega employs multiple allusions, puns, and comic interjections to describe the difficult decisions with which women grapple should they choose writing as their profession: "Pero, suponiendo que, por un milagro tecnológico de gran envergadura, esta heroína anónima logre tener su muy Woolfiano cuarto propio—¡ay!—tendrá que hacerle frente a las Siete Pruebas Terribles de la Censura y su infame hijastra la Autocensura, quien es tan mala como su madre pero además tiene auto" [But, supposing that, by a technological miracle of grandiose proportions, this anonymous heroine should succeed in attaining a very Woolfian room of her own—oh!—she will have to stand up to the Seven Terrible Tests of Censorship and her infamous stepdaughter Self-Censorship, who is as evil as her mother but in addition comes equipped with a self-propelled coach] (26).

Vega's use of wordplay accomplishes several critiques simultaneously, some of which are clearly impossible to translate into English. She alludes to Virginia Woolf's *A Room of One's Own* by making the English author's name into an adjective, a technique she employs repeatedly in her fiction as a way to humorously compress intertextual references.[23] Vega achieves the comic from this compressed allusion as one would with a witty remark, characterized by "brevity, eloquence and surprise" (Michelson 2000, 4). Vega also parodies the language of the fairy tale, with its heroines, evil stepmothers and stepsisters, as well as "the Seven Terrible Tests." Finally, the wordplay with "Autocensura" and "auto" cannot be adequately rendered into English because "autocensorship" is not a commonly used English word. The double meaning of *auto*—self and automobile—implies that self-censorship is much more highly charged than institutional censorship alone because it swiftly moves in to prevent the writing subject from embarking on a literary project.

Vega's own literary practice has consistently employed parodies of the genres that are sanctioned as "women's writing," but in "Pasión de historia" Vega once again has the protagonist's tourist gaze intersect with a proliferation of other gazes, each of which is conditioned by the numerous parodies that the text performs. The main plot revolves around an erudite teacher/novelist, Carola Vidal, who travels from Puerto Rico to visit her troubled friend Vilma in the French Pyrenees. When Carola arrives in France, she soon becomes an unwilling witness to Vilma's marital woes, but Carola interprets Vilma's story of domestic abuse and impending divorce through the plot of a true-crime narrative that she has been writing, about "el caso Malén." Carola accepted Vilma's invitation partly to work on this story of a crime of passion, but also to escape her own menacing former lover who stalks her outside her apartment. As a writer with a highly ironic sensibility, Carola interprets the people, places, and events around her as caricatures found in true-crime and detective fiction, the Gothic romance, and fairy tales, among other literary and cinematic genres. Yet her first-person narrative is also laced with several metafictional elements: allusions to the notions of authorship, textuality, and reading communities that extend beyond the diegetic world of the story. As Carola's, Vilma's, and Malén's stories all intersect, the text builds up suspense, and the reader anticipates a scene of erotically charged violence against the female protagonist. However, the story both fulfills and frustrates the reader's expectations, and by using self-reflexive humor the text resignifies its tales of terror to function as a feminist and nationalist intervention in Puerto Rican literary discourse. Ultimately, Carola's real terror is that she will be unable to write not only Malén's story but her own as well, and the scene of horror presented to the reader is not Carola's death but the obliteration of her discursive agency as an author.

When the story begins, Carola expresses her relief at having received Vilma's invitation to France just in time, since she has recently broken up with her unfaithful boyfriend, Manuel. She feels justified in calling off the relationship when she finds out that, ironically, the other woman is none other than Manuel's estranged wife. Carola moves out on her own to a studio apartment in Río Piedras and begins to feel at ease, but her neighbor, Doña Finí, warns her that a suspicious character has been watching her window. The stalker turns out to be Manuel, but rather than confront him, Carola accepts the unexpected invitation to visit Vilma at her in-laws' country home in the Pyrenees. She packs her bags, taking along the initial pages of the true-crime novel she has begun writing.

"El caso Malén" was an actual crime that took place in Puerto Rico in the early 1980s. Although it caused a scandal at the time, in many ways it was unfortunately consistent with a violent pattern of machismo's domination over women. This so-called crime of passion involved a vengeful lover who stabbed his ex-girlfriend to death in a jealous rage. Salvador, the spurned macho, surprised Malén making love to his best friend. The friend escaped, but Salvador stabbed Malén repeatedly. In Vega's story, Carola imagines how Malén must have stumbled down the hallway of her condominium, knocking on the doors, but to no avail: "Tun, tun no hay nadie, le contesta la muerte" [Knock, knock, nobody home, answers Death] (11). As Carola writes about Malén, she recognizes that her work-in-progress does not radically depart from just "otra pedestre historia de pasión" [another pedestrian story of passion] (10). The story is typical of tabloid journalism with its "carácter particularmente sangriento y su moraleja reaccionaria para mujeres chochicalientes" [particularly bloody nature and its reactionary moral for women with overheated cunts] (9).

Yet Carola cannot help but be seduced by the tabloid stories and, in particular, by the newspaper photographs of the beautiful Malén and her equally handsome lover/assassin. Carola narrates: "That's how I started to weave together the story of Malén, the novel of Malén, because every day the loose, unstitched scenes became more tangled, something was always missing: the decisive seam, the thread that would make them signify" (11).[24] Such a statement implies that Carola will embark on her own mission of detection and bring the criminal to justice, but Salvador has already turned himself in to the police. There is no crime to solve, but Carola compares the process of writing her novel to sleuthing. She is so engrossed by her work-in-progress that she ignores "the sworn testimony of [her] neighbor, a housewife with sleuthing in her genes,"[25] who tries to warn Carola that a mysterious male figure has been stalking her apartment (11). On the one hand, Carola's interest in Malén emerges from a visual confrontation with an especially lurid photographic image, and she begins to visualize the bloody details for her fictional account, thus acting as a voyeur. On the other hand, she is an unwilling object of her ex-boyfriend's gaze. As she collects loose bits of information to develop her narrative, she plays voyeur with the image of Malén. Yet Manuel plays voyeur with her, and the parallelism entices the reader to imagine that Carola's metaphorical sleuthing will lead to a real detective story.

The reader, too, plays voyeur, as she or he "watches" Carola write her novel. Becky Boling, in "The Reproduction of Ideology in Ana Lydia Vega's 'Pasion de historia' and 'Caso Omiso,'" offers an analysis of how Carola's complicity with the murderer's gaze gradually transforms so that it passes "from the distanced narrative of the 'whodunit' Carola is writing, set off by quotation marks, to her personal narrative, as part of her own diary" (91). We see in the mirroring between Malén's story and Carola's

the first instance of narrative suspense: will Carola come to an untimely
end like the doomed heroine of her true-crime novel? In "Pasión de historia,"Carola's life becomes of interest to the reader just as Malén's story
grabbed Carola's attention "in flagrante" (10). Vega establishes this mirroring to do more than create suspense. The fiction within a fiction also
creates a *mise en abyme* effect, which in turn reveals "Pasión de historia"
to be more than a pedestrian story of passion; it is a metafictional text
that parodies true-crime and detective fiction, refunctioning these popular
genres through irony and humor.

Linda Hutcheon, in *Narcissistic Narratives: The Metafictional Paradox,*
argues that metafiction turns the responsibility for the creative process
onto the reader:

> Reading and writing belong to the processes of "life" as much as they
> do to those of "art." It is this realization that constitutes one side of
> the paradox of metafiction for the reader. On the one hand, he is
> forced to acknowledge the artifice, the "art," of what he is reading; on
> the other, explicit demands are made upon him, as a co-creator, for
> intellectual and affective responses comparable in scope and intensity
> to those of his life experience. In fact, these responses are shown to be
> *part of* his life experience. (5)

Like many other writers of the Latin American "new novel,"[26] Vega places
demands on her readers as coconspirators in the narrative process. The
metafictional element in "Pasión de historia" serves to blur the line between Carola as a narrator and as a narrative mask for Vega, the authorial persona who engages the reader through this text. The reader detects
this duality between the first-person narrator and the authorial persona
through metafictional statements that force the reader to confront her or
his own reading practice. For example, when Carola first arrives in France,
Vilma surprises her with an antique desk, restored especially for "Carola
Vidal, la escritora con E mayúscula" [Carola Vidal, the writer with a capital
W] (14). This metafictional statement is an autointertextual allusion to
Vega's earlier essay "De bípeda desplumada." It signals to the reader familiar with Vega's writing that Carola can be read as a narrative mask for the
author. The text compels the reader to read at various narrative levels, including the extradiegetic level in which irony is turned on itself to operate
as a humorous critique of authorship.

Another metafictional statement occurs when Vilma ironically refers to
Carola's aspirations to "empollar la Gran Novela Puertorriqueña" [hatch

the Great Puerto Rican Novel], even though Carola admits to herself that her true-crime novel is not exceptionally original (13). When Vilma shows Carola the refurbished desk, she jokes, "Si no pares algo aquí es porque eres machorra" [If you don't give birth to something here, it's because you're barren] (14). Vilma's sardonic comments regarding her friend's literary aspirations reproduce the nationalist ideology that constrains women writers. They also function as metafictional statements for the reader who recognizes Carola as Vega's narrative mask. In this way, "Pasión de historia" confronts the same debates Vega addressed in "De bípeda desplumada": What kinds of writing constitute "great" literature? Do women have access to those kinds of writing through popular genres? Are Puerto Rican women writers capable of producing great literature when their popular writing is presumably apolitical?

By casting Carola as a writer, Vega allows her parodies to intersect at various narrative levels; unlike a straight parody in which one text imitates another, "Pasión de historia" can perform several parodies simultaneously and have the reader continually question the ethics of their intersections. Margaret A. Rose, in *Parody: Ancient, Modern, and Post-Modern*, argues that as a species of the comic, parody shares with irony the ability to "confuse the normal process of communication by offering more than one message to be decoded by the reader and this duplication of messages can be used, in either case, to conceal the author's intended meaning from immediate interpretation" (87). In some cases, parody can double back on itself through the use of irony, resulting in a metafictional text that draws the reader's attention not only to the parody's mimetic refunctioning of another text or genre, but to the political implications of self-reflexive textuality. Rose writes: "While the ironist may also use parody to confuse a meaning, the parodist may use irony in the treatment of the parodied work and its messages in a variety of different ways—from, for example, the ironic use of the parodied text to conceal the parodist's identity or meaning to the use of irony in meta-linguistic or meta-fictional comments about the text and its place in the parodist's work" (87). In "Pasión de historia" the text uses irony to situate multiple parodies at a metafictional level, engaging the reader with a critique of the hackneyed forms of "women's writing" as well as with a humorous self-reflexivity that forces the reader to consider the position from which the text makes that critique: from the position of a "Puerto Rican woman writer." The intersection of parody, irony, and metafiction in this text allows the reader to perceive Carola's efforts as a writer—her struggle to make sense of "el caso

Malén"—as part of Vega's literary intervention in the discourse on Puerto Rican national identity, particularly the debates on who has access to literary discourse and how that access must be channeled within the confining parameters of the national canon.

As the reader follows Carola's adventures in France, she or he must read this character's own ironic gaze and deployment of parody at a humorous, metafictional level. When Carola arrives at Vilma's in-laws' rustic home in the French Pyrenees, the initial parody of the true-crime novel splinters into a series of other parodies. Vega layers the tropes of the Gothic romance genre in "Pasión de historia" as overt and covert references to reflect her metafictional concern with women's writing. The first reference to the Gothic occurs when Vilma confesses that she is having marital difficulties with her French husband, Paul, and that she suspects her mother-in-law of conspiring with her husband to torment her. Carola describes Vilma's story ironically as "tan conspiratoria, tan Daphne Du Maurier" [so conspiratorial, so Daphne du Maurier] (17). Carola also learns that Vilma is on the verge of having an affair with a married doctor who lives nearby. On several occasions Vilma alludes to a local woman, Maité, who has left her husband to run off with a mechanic, thus hinting to Carola that she is about to take the same action. As with du Maurier's Rebecca character (who has much in common with Bertha Rochester from Charlotte Brontë's *Jane Eyre*), Vilma's sexuality takes on a transgressive power that threatens to emasculate her husband. Later, when Paul's mother confronts Carola about Vilma's indiscreet flirtations with Doctor Rousseau, Carola refers to the sinister mother-in-law as "Mrs. Danvers," the notorious character from du Maurier's *Rebecca* (31). The story evokes this novel again after Vilma's attempts to seduce the doctor are thwarted by Paul and his family. Her adulterous plans foiled, Vilma pretends to take ill and locks herself in her room, like a "madwoman in the attic,"[27] while Carola becomes the center of attention for Paul and his parents: "They serve me, they indulge me, they spoil me. With my unflappable social docility, today I am the new daughter-in-law: the spare" (33).[28] Involuntarily, Carola is now Vilma's double—the childlike, naive second wife who, in *Rebecca* and *Jane Eyre*, struggles with the ghost of her knowledgeable, sexually voracious predecessor. And like her Gothic sisters, Vilma-the-first-wife still makes her presence known: "The rebel angel comes and goes in her room. We eat as if we couldn't hear the subtle protest of the floorboards" (33).[29]

The Gothic also intersects with Carola's tourist gaze, although the text presents this intersection as more covert references to the popular genre in general. Janice A. Radway, in *Reading the Romance: Women, Patriarchy and Popular Literature*, notes that the Gothic genre in its popular form offers middle-class women an escape from their daily routines and "creates a time or space within which a woman can be entirely on her own" (61). Joanna Russ, in "Somebody's Trying to Kill Me and I Think It's My Husband: The Modern Gothic," notes how the heroines of this popular genre invariably find themselves in exotic locations, and the novels' preoccupation with "food, clothes, interior décor, and middle-class hobbies" simultaneously avoids, glamorizes, and vindicates the work of a middle-class housewife (671–75). Vega parodies these elements of the Gothic romance in her story, and food plays a particularly important role in Vega's refunctioning of the Gothic. Carola describes the delicious French pastries and rich soups prepared for her much in the way a nonparodic Gothic heroine would. However, in a show of nationalist fervor, Vilma decides to countercommemorate July 25, the "infausta fecha" [infamous date] of the Puerto Rican "pseudoconstitución" [pseudoconstitution] and the "invasión yanqui" [Yankee invasion] (23). She usurps her mother-in-law's domain in the kitchen and prepares "arroz blanco medio amogollado y habichuelas Goya" [rather soggy white rice with Goya beans] (23). As she places the food on the table, she says to Carola in Spanish, "Esto les cae como bomba" [This will hit them like a bomb] (23). The two women begin to laugh uncontrollably until Paul finally intervenes in French with a curt "Ça suffit" [That's enough] (23). Although the staple food of Puerto Rican cuisine has its revolutionary moment at the French table, Paul the "Shadow-Male," as Joanna Russ would call him, quickly suppresses this Caribbean uprising. The scene acts as a covert metafictional device in that it forms part of Carola's story but also reinscribes the "Three Noble Goals" of Puerto Rican literature that Vega described in "De bípeda desplumada": "Save the Nation from the Clutches of Yankee Imperialism, Affirm the Culture, and Accelerate the Advent of the Socialist Revolution."

In addition to the Gothic romance, Vega also parodies the fairy-tale genre and its cautionary tales for women who defy male authority.[30] Carola makes frequent overt allusions to fairy tales, describing the abusive husband, Paul, as Bluebeard and his manipulative mother as the witch from Snow White (21). She also mockingly refers to Vilma as Sleeping Beauty (35). Her allusions to Charles Perrault's and the Brothers Grimm's fairy tales[31] serve to minimize the precarious situation in which she finds herself, a situation she shares with the murdered Malén and the abused Vilma. The disciplinary eye of their male companions has trapped these three women, and all three suffer the violent consequences of attempting to contest or break free from the authoritative power of the male gaze. The Bluebeard references remind the reader of the immurement, the interdictions against curiosity, and the bloody chamber full of dismembered former wives that waits for the woman who disobeys her husband's demands. Such tales that proscribe women from accessing secret knowledge hark back to the biblical Eve and the Greek myth of Pandora's box. In the Bluebeard tale, we see the sexual implications of that prohibited knowledge in the indelible stains of blood that incriminate the transgressive woman. She must protect herself from that sexual knowledge, not so much for her own sake, but as part of the proprietary bond that her husband holds over her. The assumption in these tales is that, once beyond the disciplinary purview of male authority, women inevitably disregard prohibitions and bring about their own downfall.

In "Pasión de historia," Malén, Carola, and Vilma all break a bond with their male masters, and these men in turn treat the women as property that cannot exist outside their control. As a writer with a highly developed sense of irony and a penchant for parody, Carola perceives in these male gazes the oppressiveness of the fairy-tale prohibitions against curious women, but the irony she uses to deflate the gravity of the real-life circumstances also gives her a sense of aloofness, as if the warnings against Bluebeard's revenge do not apply to her.[32] When Carola reads Vilma's domestic unrest as a parody of the fairy tale, she does so to diminish the anxiety it stirs up in her. Yet at the metafictional level, this parody goes one step further by drawing attention to the reader's hopes and expectations of a happy ending. Therefore, even though the reader encounters the parodic citation of fairy tales from Carola's ironic perspective, at the metafictional level the parodies also serve to reflect the limitations of "women's writing" as a fixed and stable category. As Vega argues in "De bípeda desplumada," the revisionist fairy tale appropriates the limited space in which women's writing has been confined. Vega inscribes such fairy-tale characters as Bluebeard into this story about sex and murder in order to demonstrate that much of the popular literature and cinema aimed at adults perpetuates the social norms that fairy tales instill in children. In this way Vega's authorial persona speaks through Carola's parodies to solicit a humorous reading: one that forces readers to reflect on their own reading practices.

Because the story presents Carola as an intelligent, ironic, and independent character, the reader identifies with her perspective and laughs along with her as she reduces everything and everyone around her to a collage of parodic references. Like us, Carola sees through the fairy-tale veneer of happy endings, and so we expect her to prevail. The reader assumes that such a witty, self-conscious character would not rely on these simplistic narratives as guides for her actions. Because she can see through them, as does the reader, she will escape Bluebeard's (Manuel's) clutches. Nor will she imagine herself as the damsel in distress who needs a man to save her. She contrasts herself with Vilma, who she believes has indeed projected herself into the plot of a fairy tale. For this reason she distrusts the veracity of Vilma's claims, calling her friend in one instance "Vilma Bovary"—that is, a woman whose appetite for fiction has clouded her perception of reality. The reader's disbelief in the fairy tale ironically casts Carola as the clever "third sister" who will outwit the sorcerer, save her sisters, and punish the villain. If the reader interprets Carola's irony and parody solely at the diegetic level, she or he risks reinforcing the textual patterns that have supposedly been negated.

This double bind becomes apparent as Carola reconstructs the scene of Malén's murder, for even though she intends to give Malén a voice, she inadvertently adopts Salvador's perspective, following his actions as he stalks Malén, breaks into her apartment, and stabs her to death: "Salvador pursues me. Once again I roam with him through the hallway of the ill-fated condominium. I see him stop in front of Malén's door. Loud music. The blind is broken, he forced it himself the day that Malén refused to open the door for him. The blind is broken and Felipe Rodríguez is singing inside a lament of offended machos" (25).[33]

Vega heightens the intensity of this passage by using the present tense, imbuing it with a much more visual immediacy. It also simulates Carola's writerly imagination at work, so that her narrative reconstruction takes on the visual qualities of an act of voyeurism. The gaze is still mediated by Salvador's presence, placing Carola in the position of a male-identified spectator. Carola becomes so engrossed by the scene of violence that she adopts the perspective of the male voyeur, whose gaze enforces his proprietary privilege over women. The reader must proceed warily if she or he is to avoid taking that position in turn, reading Carola's story as a male-identified voyeur who imposes disciplinary social and moral codes on the text.

Although Carola perceives the events around her unfolding as parodies of the true-crime novel, the Gothic romance, and the fairy tale, Vega's authorial persona intervenes to force the reader to read these parodies at a metafictional level. The culmination of all these parodies occurs when they converge in a scene of horror, one that imparts no vengeful or voyeuristic pleasures. Since her arrival at Paul's family home, Carola has noticed the proliferation of animal heads lining the walls. Paul is an avid hunter, and although he attempts to convince Carola of how hunting revives a man's primal instincts, she considers it "matar por matar" [killing for killing's sake] (26). Not satisfied with displaying his taxidermic trophies, Paul shows Carola a photo album in which he has collected the images of his victims, "antes, durante y después del estirón de pata" [before, during, and after they kicked the bucket] (34). The final page of the album paralyzes Carola, for in it she sees Vilma posing next to a dead antelope, bugging her eyes and sticking her tongue out as if she, too, were one of Paul's victims. The photographic image recalls the picture of Malén that has fascinated Carola, and it connotes the true-crime novel's obsession with verifiable pieces of evidence—in this case, the proof that betrays Paul's murderous instincts. As part of the parody of the Gothic romance, this scene represents the moment when the second wife confronts the image of the deceased first wife. As in the novels *Rebecca* and *Jane Eyre*, the confrontation causes Carola to suspect Paul of being capable of murder. Finally, the stuffed animals that hang from the walls recall the dismembered former wives from the Bluebeard fairy tale, with the photo album representing the "bloody chamber." By reading these parodies humorously—that is, at the metafictional level—the reader interprets their convergence over the female body as a textual violence, one that immobilizes the female body and presents it as an object of voyeuristic pleasure. Vega's authorial persona intervenes once again to forestall the reader from reenacting that violence and to resist the temptation to follow any voyeuristic impulses.

Extradiegetically, then, the reader confronts the incongruities between how Carola casts others and herself as characters in a story and how the text flouts the expectations that her parodic intertexts elicit. So although Carola deploys intertexts to read her surroundings as parodies, the reader reads those parodies at another level, what Gérard Genette in *Palimpsests* would call the "architextual" level, or reading through to the "generic quality" of a text (4–6). Read as intertexts, Carola's parodic reading plays out for the reader as part of the narrative process. Linda Hutcheon in *A Theory of Parody* argues, in response to Genette, that the reader's participation in this textual mirroring is crucial, since intertextuality is not entirely a matter of structure, but depends on reading and decoding (20–23). In that way, while Carola's parodies sustain an ironic perspective at the diegetic level, at the extradiegetic or "architextual" level the parodies function humorously to draw attention to the reader's engagement with the text. "Pasión de historia" asks its readers to identify with Carola's sense of irony at the level of diegetic parody, but also to deploy humor and interpret this character as an effect of textuality.

Humor, as Schopenhauer argues, "can be called the double counterpoint of irony," since it functions as a serious statement masked by a joke. Schopenhauer writes: "Irony begins with a serious air and ends with a smile; with humor, the order is reversed" (Morreall 1987, 62). In "Pasión de historia" the text oscillates between the two, sometimes using irony to undermine the seriousness of oppressive discourses, but at other times using humor to "smuggle" in a serious political statement. The text destabilizes readers' expectations through this textual *jaibería* so that they can participate in the negation of machismo, but also so that they can visualize the position from which they deploy an ironic gaze. The text constantly fulfills and frustrates the reader's normal reading habits. For example, after encountering the foreboding photographic image of Vilma, the reader expects any one of the parodied literary genres to take over and follow through with its inevitable denouement. Even Carola thinks she might have seen the last of Vilma. Yet her friend makes one more appearance just before Carola returns to Puerto Rico. Paul and his parents go to Mass, but Vilma and Carola skip out and take a last hiking excursion. They sing patriotic Puerto Rican songs, and Carola notices her friend has recuperated her strength, "con esa vitalidad inquebrantable que le sobra a mi gente, lactada en la desgracia" [with that unyielding vitality that overflows in my people, who have been nursed on misfortune] (36). Carola finally shows some solidarity with Vilma, and even proposes that Vilma return to Puerto Rico with her. "Eso viene," Vilma replies, that will come (36). At this point the reader foresees the happy ending that has been looming all along: Carola will save herself and her Puerto Rican sister, like the heroines of the popular genres she and the reader have thoroughly demythologized.

But like a good thriller, "Pasión de historia" has a twist at the end. There is no happy ending in the traditional sense. When Carola returns to Puerto Rico, she writes to Vilma, but her letters are returned, "DESTINAIRE INCONNU" [ADDRESSEE UNKNOWN] (38). Carola's heart tightens as she reads this ill omen. But her voice is then cut off, and her story ends where, according to Tzvetan Todorov in *The Poetics of Prose*, a classic whodunit begins: the crime has been committed, and now follows the story of the investigation (44). There is no investigation; all that follows is a short "Nota de la editora" [Editor's note], in which one Griselda Lugo Fuentes of

Ediciones Seremos informs the reader that Carola Vidal has been murdered, a victim of a sniper attack while celebrating New Year's Eve with
friends in her own apartment (38). The story has been published posthu-
mously as part of their series TEXTIMONIOS. The publisher's name,
Seremos, implies a statement of purpose: We Will Be. Carola's story will
stand as a testimony in this political imperative, but only through its circu-
lation as a text—a "textimonio." The text does what Carola found so difficult to do: bear witness and intervene in a cycle of violence against women.
Even if it remains on the level of provocation, Vega's text, in which the
reader engages Carola's story, offers a note of hope. Yet that optimism is
not necessarily part of Carola's story, which is tragic, to say the least. The
oppositional discourse that Vega's text "smuggles" into the story engages
the reader at the metafictional level, and it is the text's authorial persona
who asks readers to consider the ethical implications of their own reading
habits. The underlying ethos of "Pasión de historia" advocates solidarity
through textual practices, but the texts that comprise a testimonial exchange must not be consumed passively, and the reader should look to
texts for more than just an escape from mundane reality. The reader must
now assume the interpretive task that Carola originally set out for herself:
to stitch the bits and pieces of Malén's story together and make them signify. Carola's death as an author allows for the "birth" of the authorial
persona and the reader.[34]

Within the world of the story—that is, at the diegetic level of the text—
Carola deflates the seriousness of reality by constructing it as a parody of
previously consumed texts, thereby marking her parodies with the negating power of irony. She imposes this ironic reading on all that she perceives and experiences, often with a dismissive gesture. But when her life
begins to mirror the sordid details of the true-crime novel she is writing,
her sophisticated powers of deflection are not enough to save her from
sharing the fate of her novel's victim. Despite Carola's acuity and her ability to reduce everything and everyone around her to caricatures, her self-
awareness as a writer makes it difficult for her to take anything seriously,
even when her own person is in real, physical danger. In the end, she suf-
fers along with Malén and Vilma the vengeful punishment for contesting
the authority of a male's objectifying gaze, yet the text's metafictional
statements modify the story's final irony. Vega's text "reads" itself
through metafiction and exposes women's overdependence on hackneyed
popular literary genres, especially as a quick fix for the construction of an
identity. "Pasión de historia" not only condemns the real, physical violence

perpetrated against women, it also decries the narratives that reaffirm a violent, paternalistic order.

In *Narrative Irony in the Contemporary Spanish-American Novel*, Jonathan Tittler writes: "Spanish-American history does not become ironic until it is perceived as such by a subject who also views himself in terms of incongruity and contradiction" (192–93). We can apply this statement to the way Vega depicts her female tourists. In the case of "Pollito Chicken," Suzie is the victim of the reader's ironic gaze and the object of Puerto Rican nationalism's laughter, although if the Puerto Rican reader looks closely, she might see some of herself in that monstrous *pollito-chicken* hybrid. In "Puerto Príncipe abajo," although the Puerto Rican protagonist is more aware of history than her compatriots, she quickly recognizes that the air of superiority she experiences with them is not at all appropriate to her encounters with Haitians. Finally, "Pasión de historia" serves as an allegory of Puerto Rico's colonial condition. Like the women in Vega's text, Puerto Rico's autonomy rests in the hands of "benevolent masters,"[35] and any show of resistance is met with immediate reprisal. The irony for middle-class Puerto Rican women who have benefited from colonialism's economic legacy is that their increased independence, social mobility, and sexual freedom have not liberated them from a paternalistic order; rather, the limits to their freedoms have served to delineate even more clearly the oppressive nature of their historical reality. We see that Vega's title "Pasión de historia" refers both to the *historias de pasión* [tales of passion] parodied in the text and to the passion for Puerto Rico's history that has always informed Vega's literary practice (Galván 1993, 139). Vega inscribes this passion through humor, which takes the irony in the text to another level, so that the reader—unlike Carola—does not dismiss the historical realities represented in these fictions, no matter how ironic they might be. Vega's *jaibería* between irony and humor allows her as a Puerto Rican woman writer to demystify the discourses of social inequity and gender oppression, while keeping an eye on the role her authorial persona plays in the Puerto Rican literary canon.

Pedro Pietri's Absurd Scenes of Writing

Pero yo no entiendo a la gente que no se ríe. Deben tenel argo en el arma.
Argo que loh pone fúnebreh como difuntoh.

René Marqués, *La carreta*

Cruelty, injustice, and death are no laughing matters, particularly when one cannot grasp the meaning of the pain and affliction they cause. Yet a poet will often incite laughter with his words when the antagonism of the world resists understanding, when the only way to confront absurdity is to speak the dissonant language of the absurd. Pedro Pietri, the Puerto Rican poet, playwright, and short story writer from New York, consistently invoked this cruel laughter in his literary confrontations with the harsh realities of the Puerto Rican diaspora. The language of the absurd does not incite mirthful laughter. With its jarring surrealism that defies logic and reason, its expletive-laced protests that shout out in rage, and its abject images that speak from a hallucinogenic haze, Pietri's absurd humor summons the laughter that lies closer to madness than to gaiety. Yet Pietri, like many other Puerto Rican writers, has imagined a paradise beyond the dehumanizing experience of the diaspora. His early work, particularly his well-known poem "Puerto Rican Obituary," speaks the language of the absurd satirically to overcome absurdity and imagine a Puerto Rican utopia. However, when the written text becomes its own absurd reality, Pietri engages the language of the absurd as a self-reflexive humor. His later texts deconstruct the utopian space, revealing it to reside within textuality. His absurd humor is just as jarring, angry, and abject in these later works, but in a self-reflexive twist it targets the very texts that articulate its cruel laughter. Pietri's later poetic, theatrical, and narrative texts act eccentrically to imagine not a Puerto Rican utopia, but an absurd scene of writing that lies at the heart of the diasporic identity.

Pietri's eccentric texts deviate from the Puerto Rican literary tradition in which geographic determinism situates cultural authenticity on the island. The passage in René Marqués's *La carreta* that contains the epigraph to this chapter not only valorizes agrarian traditions over modernity and migration, it also shows laughter and gaiety as the exclusive provinces of those island-bound traditions. Don Chago—the *jíbaro* character who speaks the quoted words—represents the traditional agrarian values that his (illegitimate) grandson, Luis, is so eager to abandon in his quest to assimilate into the modern world. Luis is the overly solemn youth whom Don Chago describes as one of those who are like the dead—"como difuntoh" (17). Eventually Luis's obsession with urban life and modernization brings about his real death, yet his tragic end holds forth a utopian promise of return to the Puerto Rican homeland for his surviving family. By juxtaposing the jovial and old-fashioned Don Chago with the serious and modern Luis, Marqués invokes a trope in the literature of the Puerto Rican diaspora in which life-affirming laughter is associated with the island, while a deathlike solemnity accompanies those migrants unfortunate (or foolish) enough to abandon their traditional rural lifestyle. Yet the generation of Puerto Rican writers raised in New York, often known as Nuyoricans, has reinterpreted this geographic determinism in a variety of ways. For example, Tato Laviera's poetry collection *La Carreta Made a U-Turn* stands out as one of the most direct resignifications of Marqués's seminal play and the tropes of the telluric utopia. For Laviera, Nuyoricans have taken the helm of their own cultural production, and their hybrid language and cultural identity have redirected poetic discourse to celebrate rather than lament that hybridity.[1]

Pedro Pietri's writings also contest the notion that the diaspora can only be represented with solemnity, and his texts have used parody, caricature, and satire to condemn the degrading conditions that have afflicted Puerto Ricans in New York. As social protest, Pietri's satiric texts attempt to expel the colonialist and assimilationist discourses from the Puerto Rican communal psyche. A satiric text such as "Puerto Rican Obituary" also functions as a social corrective by imagining a utopian space that will offer the Puerto Rican community a safe haven from enslaving ideologies. Yet the absurd humor of his later writings serves to "other" the literary text to itself. This self-reflexivity results in a much less representational form of literary discourse, so that the poem, play, or fiction resists marking a clear line between the interior and exterior of its textual boundaries. Rather than project a utopian space for Puerto Ricans that transcends textuality, Pietri's absurd humor stages a scene of writing that allows for a literary negotiation between textual presence and disembodied performance, as well as between selfhood and otherness. The literary articulations of an absurd "nowhere" act as antidotes to the telluric discourse of Puerto Rican national identity, which associates an insular cultural autochthony with oral traditions, embodied performance, and literary realism. A self-othering absurd humor might appear to be a literature of solipsistic non-sense, yet it holds an important key to Puerto Rican identity, both on the island and on the mainland. Pietri's eccentric texts demonstrate that within every Puerto Rican self resides a strange yet familiar Puerto Rican other—a disturbing and distorting mirror image that speaks through si-lence, performs through absence, and writes through erasure.

This chapter will examine Pietri's use of the absurd in the expression of satire and humor. In Pietri's poetry, absurd satire serves to denounce social injustice and cultural alienation, while absurd humor scrutinizes the role played by writing in the construction of an oppositional discourse. Some of Pietri's theatrical texts also function satirically to expose the absurdity of Puerto Rican disenfranchisement, but others function humorously to question the political limits of performance. Finally, Pietri's short story "Lost in the Museum of Natural History" displays both satirical and hu-morous uses of the absurd, but its ending favors a humorous self-reflexiv-ity that blurs the line between the subject who writes and the object of his writing. The eccentric sensibility that all these texts articulate in their use of the absurd detaches Puerto Rican identity from its traditions of geo-graphic determinism. The "empty space" left behind redirects Pietri's liter-ary discourse toward an open-ended negotiation of subjectivity and other-ness, of interiority and exteriority, and of sense and nonsense.

Declarations of Discontent: Pedro Pietri and Nuyorican Poetry

In the fall of 1969 in the New York area called the Barrio, a militant group of Puerto Rican activists, the Young Lords, forcibly occupied the First Spanish Methodist Church on 111th Street (Morales 1998, 213). The Young Lords had already established themselves as a radical organization dedicated to bettering the living conditions of the disenfranchised Puerto Rican community in New York. In one demonstration, they gathered the piles of garbage that the sanitation department refused to collect and burned them in the streets so that the city would finally clean up the neighborhoods it routinely deprived of its most basic services (Guzmán 1998, 155). During the church takeover of 1969, much of the Puerto Rican community aided the Young Lords in their standoff against the police, and even matronly women helped to smuggle out the protesters' weapons in an effort to avoid an escalation in violence (158).

Another participant in this political action was Pedro Pietri, who read to the crowd his now famous poem "Puerto Rican Obituary" (Matilla Rivas 1992, xiii). The Young Lords' actions exemplified the political rage and discontent that many Puerto Ricans in New York felt during the late sixties and early seventies, and Pietri captured eloquently in free verse not only the anger of his community but also the hope for rebirth and renewal that has characterized the experience of Puerto Rican migration. Pietri's reading of this poem during the 1969 church takeover demonstrates the importance of an oral tradition in diasporic literature. The oral tradition represents a culturally legitimate form of expression, as Miguel Algarín writes in his introduction to *Nuyorican Poetry: An Anthology of Puerto Rican Words and Feelings*: "We have to admit that speech comes first" (19). Pietri did not abandon his commitment to oral, live performance, as his many subsequent theatrical productions and poetry readings testify, yet his later poems, particularly those in *Traffic Violations*, reveal a change in attitude toward the primacy of the oral over the written. As he reoriented his poetic interventions from the oral to the written, Pietri's use of comic forms also moved from the satirical function of a social corrective to the humorous function of a self-reflexive critique.

In "Puerto Rican Obituary," orality is a direct emanation from the poet and his community, while writing represents the repressive grammar of the state. The oral is the presence of a communal identity in language, while the written is the absence of a Puerto Rican voice. "Puerto Rican Obituary" characterizes writing as a discursive medium imposed on the Puerto Rican community from the outside as part of the ideologies of capitalist exploitation. Again, this reflects Algarín's assertion that if the "rules" that govern authentic Nuyorican expression "do not legitimately arise from the street people, the rules and regulations will come from outside already existing grammatical patterns that are not new but old systems of rules imposed on new patterns of speech" (19). Pietri's use of comic forms and the absurd in "Puerto Rican Obituary" functions satirically to situate that exploitative grammar on the outside of authentic Puerto Rican discourse.

The social corrective offered in Pietri's "Puerto Rican Obituary" is similar to the dramatic plot of Marqués's *La carreta* in that both works imagine a utopian space for the Puerto Ricans of the diaspora once they reclaim their Hispanic heritage. However, Marqués's play promises its characters rebirth and renewal on the condition that these uprooted migrants traverse the geographic breach between the United States and Puerto Rico. In Pietri's "Puerto Rican Obituary," a number of poetic characters die and are reborn in a utopian space, but the poem places that rejuvenating homeland in the realm of the imagination rather than in the fixed geography of the island. Pietri has reworked Puerto Rican literary traditions to confront the feelings of loss and displacement—*el abandono*—that characterize the diasporic experience. Efraín Barradas, in "'De lejos en sueños verla . . .': Visión mítica de Puerto Rico en la poesía neorrican," compares the ways Puerto Rican poets in the United States, like Pietri, Miguel Algarín, Sandra María Esteves, Tato Laviera, Víctor Hernández Cruz, and Miguel Piñero, have represented the Puerto Rican homeland in terms strikingly similar to those of canonical island poets. The title of Barradas's essay refers to a poem by José Gautier Benítez, a romantic poet par excellence from the nineteenth century who imagined Puerto Rico from afar: "y para saber quererla / es necesario dejarla" [and to know how to love her / it is necessary to leave her] (quoted in Barradas 1998, 74). For many Nuyorican poets, whose memories of the island (if they have any at all) are of a distant childhood, their rejection of Anglo-American culture impels them to yearn for the island as lovingly as did Gautier Benítez. Barradas writes that the Puerto Rican poet in the United States, by yearning from afar for the island where he wishes to find his origins, joins in that literary tradition that arises at the very beginnings of Puerto Rican literature. However, the reencounter with those origins can be traumatic, and the emigré usually meets with rejection by Puerto Ricans from the island who consider the Nuyorican to be North American. As a result, Barradas argues, the Nuyorican poet transforms the old myth of Puerto Rico as the lost Eden and converts it into an internal utopia (74).[2] Among the Nuyorican poems that Barradas analyzes as examples of this tropic shift, he cites Pietri's "Puerto Rican Obituary" because it constructs just such an "internal utopia" in order to combat the difficulties and problems that the Puerto Rican subject faces while living in the antagonistic world of New York (73).

Pietri's poem decries the cultural death that that world has inflicted on the diasporic community. The poem employs its first comic form in the title as it parodies the obituary that announces the deaths of Juan, Miguel, Milagros, Olga, and Manuel, poetic characters who represent the Puerto Rican Everyman and Everywoman. These poetic characters resemble very closely the "docile" Puerto Ricans Marqués described in his essay "*El puertorriqueño dócil*," for they labor without complaint or resistance until the day they die. And like Luis from Marqués's *La carreta*, Pietri's poetic characters succumb to the workings of the capitalist machine that eventually grinds them down. The poem conveys the mundane, mechanized lives that these characters lead with a staccato rhythm of "They worked / They worked / They worked / and they died." Their deaths are the uneventful and inevitable consequence of their dehumanized existences, yet the poem suggests that these deaths are symbolic, for they "All died yesterday today / and will die again tomorrow." These "deaths" are a daily occurrence because the characters live as if they were already dead. As the obituary narrates a life gone by, its writing inscribes the subject with absence. The written obituary marks that absence from the outside and collaborates with other written texts that impose a dehumanizing grammar on the Puerto Rican community.

The poem performs that textuality in English, which places it outside and anterior to the authentic, Spanish speech of the utopian promise it makes at the end. Miguel Algarín describes a similar linguistic split in the consciousness of the Nuyorican, particularly one who must function as a laborer in an English-speaking society: "The factory laborer reads instructions in English but feels in Spanish" (18). Pietri's poem also ascribes English to an exterior, written discourse, while Spanish belongs to the authentic "latino" soul that the English text erases. In another stanza we find a similar condemnation of writing in English:

They saw their names listed
in the telephone directory of destruction
They were train [*sic*] to turn
the other cheek by newspapers
that misspelled mispronounced their names
and celebrated when death came
and stole their final laundry ticket. (5–6)

This series of absurd images, in which ostensibly banal objects from everyday life take on ominous, destructive qualities, conveys a satirical condemnation of the hostile environment in which Puerto Ricans in New York are forced to live. The "telephone directory of destruction" functions from the exterior and places Puerto Ricans in a written order not of their making. The "newspapers" represent another antagonistic institution that utilizes writing to erase the Hispanic traditions that are part of Puerto Rican identity. The "laundry ticket" is yet another form of false identification, a written text whose meaning circulates independently of the Puerto Ricans who tentatively possess it. Using satire as a social corrective, the poem calls on Puerto Ricans to resist the enslavement of the English text that writes them into absence: "If only they / had used the white supremacy bibles / for toilet paper purpose" (10). Finally, in the utopian hereafter—"where you do not need a dictionary / to communicate with your people"—a spoken language brings the "they" into the immediate presence of "you." The oral discourse that reconstitutes the Puerto Ricans' "latino souls" expels the written discourses of exploitation from the internal utopia, yet a closer look at the poem reveals that the utopia is always already scripted, and that the oral performance emerges from the space of writing.

The poem has little use for the dictionary, since it is a written text that fixes meaning and establishes lexical standards. The poem implies that authentic Puerto Rican speech exceeds the limits of a standard lexicon. The dictionary's written text would interfere with the open and direct communication that this poem situates in its internal utopia. An oral tradition, then, acts as an oppositional discourse for Puerto Ricans who reject assimilation into U.S. mainstream culture. They refuse the written text that would mediate the erasure of their cultural heritage. By saying that Puerto Ricans, once reborn, will "not need a dictionary" to communicate with one another, the poem reinforces the notion that a standard lexicon is a foreign, written imposition on the authentic, oral discourse that communicates the spirit of the people—something Algarín suggests when he describes Nuyorican speech as "the way people talk in the raw before the spirit is molded into 'standards'" (16). "Puerto Rican Obituary" associates writing with death, absence, and obscurity while associating speech with life, presence, and transparency. So even though the poem performs the finite, written text of the obituary in English, that very text announces (in diacriticless Nuyorican) the infinite, spoken exchange of Spanish: "Aqui Se Habla Espanol all the time."

Paradoxically, the written English text becomes the precondition for the rebirth of the oral Spanish discourse. The poem cannot describe the utopian promise without recourse to an interplay between English and Spanish, between writing and speech. The final lines of the poem perform bilingually to reveal the utopian "Aqui" to reside within writing: "Aqui Que Pasa Power is what's happening / Aqui to be called negrito / means to be called LOVE" (11). Román de la Campa, in "En la utopia redentora del lenguaje: Pedro Pietri y Miguel Algarín," argues that the poem's bilingual ending speaks the language of migratory groups like Puerto Ricans, for whom cultural and linguistic assimilation become improbable, if not impossible, given their marginal economic and racial status. For de la Campa, the Spanish of that "Que Pasa" is important not for its linguistic purity nor as a symbol of an intact Hispanism that does not exist even in the migrants' countries of origin; that Spanish does, however, act as a hybrid culture of resistance, as a utopian space between languages (56).[3] Yet in its performance of that hybrid linguistic utopia, the poem takes on the role of a dictionary—that written arbiter of language—that it had already relegated to the exterior of direct speech and salutation. "To be called" implies the utopian subject receives its name—"negrito"—from a communal voice that calls out through the voice of the poet. "Negrito" is a term used affectionately among Puerto Ricans and, as it is used in this poem, functions as a communal name reclaimed from the racially pejorative "Negro" of English. Rubén Ríos Avila, in "El arte de dar lengua en Puerto Rico," argues a similar point: "When Pedro Pietri, in his now classic 'Puerto Rican Obituary,' ends with 'Aqui negrito means to be called LOVE,' that 'aquí' establishes another space for Puerto Rican literature. That 'aquí' expands affective space to make room for a complete world of the Puerto Rican experience that has been denied poetic dignity" (334).[4] Yet that reconstituting voice calls out from the poem's bilingual dictionary; thus the utopian "Aqui" is declared and situated within the space of writing.

These observations owe much to Jacques Derrida's reading of Rousseau in *Of Grammatology*. Derrida performs a deconstructive reading of the tradition in Western philosophy and linguistics that separates speech from writing. His readings of Rousseau and Saussure in *Of Grammatology* examine why and how philosophers and linguists characterize the voice as closer to the mind, while writing arrives from the exterior as a technique or artifice, and is therefore a less reliable form of representation than the voice. In this tradition, sound is opposed to the grapheme, or written sign, but this opposition generates a series of other oppositions, including presence versus absence, interior versus exterior, nature versus culture, pure versus corrupt, life versus death. Derrida points out that although this tradition, or logocentrism, privileges the spoken word over the written, it cannot describe speech without recourse to the terms associated with writing. In his analysis of Rousseau's *Essay on the Origin of Language*, Derrida argues: "There is therefore a good and a bad writing: the good and natural is the divine inscription in the heart and soul; the perverse and artful is technique, exiled in the exteriority of the body" (17). In his analysis of Saussurian linguistics, Derrida discusses in more detail the categories of outside and inside as they relate to writing and speech: "But has it ever been doubted that writing was the clothing of speech? For Saussure it is even a garment of perversion and debauchery, a dress of corruption and disguise, a festival mask that must be exorcised, that is to say warded off, by the good word: 'Writing veils the appearance of language; it is not a guise for language but a disguise'" (35). In Pietri's "Puerto Rican Obituary," writing is also exterior to the "latino soul," for it is associated with the English, institutional discourses that are imposed on Puerto Ricans and alienate them from their truer selves, which are articulated within their community by a Spanish voice.

Yet, as Derrida argues, the "outside bears with the inside a relationship that is, as usual, anything but simple exteriority. The meaning of the outside was always present within the inside, imprisoned outside the outside, and vice versa" (35). In Pietri's poem, that exterior writing—the dictionary—that interferes with Puerto Rican discourse is constituted by the voice that speaks as an act of translation: "Que Pasa" is "what's happening"; "negrito" means "LOVE." Therefore, the English writing that was relegated to the exterior of the Puerto Rican utopia resides in the Spanish voice that interpellates from within English. The plenitude of that spoken language is already split as it represents itself as a form of writing. This is similar to what Derrida finds in the texts by Rousseau and Saussure:

> Representation mingles with what it represents, to the point where one speaks as one writes, one thinks as if the represented were nothing more than the shadow or reflection of the representer. A dangerous promiscuity and a nefarious complicity between the reflection and the reflected which lets itself be seduced narcissistically. In this play of representation, the point of origin becomes ungraspable. There are things like reflecting pools, and images, and infinite reference from one to the other, but no longer a source, a spring. There is no longer a simple origin. For what is reflected is split *in itself* and not only as an addition to itself of its image. (36)

So although Pietri's poem has ripped the Puerto Rican utopia from its geographic determinism and situated it in language, the oral performance of that language is no more a pure origin than the deathly written text it opposes to itself. The "homeland" to which Puerto Ricans return after their "obituary" resides in the poem as a written text. Its presence is constituted by the absence associated with writing, by that play of representation that substitutes one word for another, one language for another. At the heart of that unified community lies the difference that enables one subject to call out to another in language. Thus writing performs the voice, just as English frames and defines the Spanish of the affective communal bond.

A dual pedagogical intent emerges from the poem's satire: demystify the ideological paradigms that enslave the Puerto Rican community in the United States and reveal the possibility of a communal reunification that lies outside the discourses of "false consciousness." Throughout the poem, Pietri ridicules and caricatures the oppressive forces that have brought about the cultural death of the Puerto Rican laborer. William Rosa, in "La vision humorística del espacio en la poesía de Pedro Pietri," writes that Pietri uses ironic humor as an effective way to call attention to the limits that obstruct Puerto Rican progress in New York, but that Pietri is also guided by a positive force that seeks to generate alternatives for change (108). Yet this pedagogical intent constructs a utopian discourse that places the poet and his community outside the deathly reach of writing, since this ostensibly codified form of language serves to erase the community's living name. As we have seen, though, the poem resorts to a metaphor of writing in order to pronounce that name.

With his later work, as Pietri moved away from the pedagogical intent that constructed a utopian space, he also incorporated self-reflexive humor in his poetry. His use of the absurd continued to target the harsh realities of life in the city, but it also placed writing in the foreground as the means with which to articulate a demystifying critique. Arnaldo Cruz-Malavé argues a similar point in "Teaching Puerto Rican Authors: Identity and Modernization in Nuyorican Texts":

> Although there is an elimination of the utopic element in Pietri's later works, there is no disappearance of the other pole that constitutes the 1960s dialectic that we have been discussing: the pole of demythification. If anything, there is an increased emphasis on exposing "false consciousness," "false illusions," or the "colonized" mentality. But the critique of ideology is not from without, as in Pietri's previous work, but from within. (49)

I would like to take Cruz-Malavé's argument further and analyze how the poems in Pietri's second volume, *Traffic Violations*, are eccentric texts that use humor to construct Puerto Rican identity from both within and without. That is, these poems challenge the reader to discover the space in identity in which otherness resides. This rupture creates an empty space rather than a utopia, yet that emptiness allows for a continually renewable source for poetic discourse. With *Traffic Violations*, Pietri (con)fuses the categories of outside and inside, and he inscribes his poetic texts as the written traces of a discourse that has no point of origin. In other words, the poem enacts its own erasure so that presence and absence occupy the same textual space. These poems underscore the otherness that permeates identity by means of an absurdist, self-reflexive humor. Because humorous discourse others itself and incites pleasure by undermining its own authority, we can see how Pietri's later poems deconstruct the oral, embodied utopia of "Puerto Rican Obituary" and replace it with a written, disembodied nothingness. This eccentric deviation produces poetic texts that disappear at their own inscription, staging an absurd scene of writing in which the self appears as the graphic traces of the other. Humor, with its blurring of the line between self and other, also functions in tandem with the absurd to destabilize exteriority and interiority, the "here" and the "there," as well as the said and the unsaid.

The "absurd" in literature can refer to a comic manipulation of language that disrupts logic and the separation of sense from nonsense. In *Jokes and Their Relation to the Unconscious*, Freud argues that absurdity produces a pleasurable release from the "compulsion of logic and reality" (154). Freud calls the absurd a type of "faulty reasoning," which creates a comic effect in jokes by appearing incongruously as sense in nonsense (69). Similarly, J. A. Cuddon notes in his dictionary of literary terms that nonsense in verse can evoke mirth in order "to dispel fear and apprehension, to evade and combat the question: To what end?" (428). Martin Esslin, in *The Theater of the Absurd*, concurs with Freud and further contends that verbal nonsense is more than just playfulness in literature: "In trying to burst the bounds of logic and language, it batters at the enclosing walls of the human condition itself" (341). Yet the absurd has also come to be associated with a type of existentialist philosophy, in particular the twentieth-century notion of "the meaninglessness of life" that one finds in Albert Camus' *The Myth of Sisyphus*. Camus writes that the absurd is a sensibility, a way of perceiving the world. A man perceives the absurd when his everyday routine becomes mechanical and loses its meaning, when he realizes that he "belongs to time" and is struck by his own mortality, when the objective world becomes "dense" and negates his existence, when human actions become a "meaningless pantomime," and when man sees himself as a stranger (12–15). The purpose of Camus' enumeration of these kinds of absurdities is to ponder whether life is worth living, given that it is meaningless. Camus argues that he cannot know meaning beyond his own condition: "This heart within me I can feel, and I judge that it exists. This world I can touch, and I likewise judge that it exists. There ends all my knowledge, and the rest is construction" (19). Camus advises man to live in the absurd, which offers neither hope nor despair, yet does provide him with the liberty to live in the present and thus avoid renunciation or suicide.[5]

Gilles Deleuze, in *The Logic of Sense*, makes a clear distinction between verbal nonsense and the philosophy of the absurd. Deleuze argues that "for the philosophy of the absurd, nonsense is what is opposed to sense in a simple relation with it, so that the absurd is always defined by a deficiency of sense and a lack . . ." (71). With verbal nonsense—the kind Deleuze finds in Lewis Carroll's *Alice in Wonderland*, for example—the absurd "is always too much sense: an excess produced and over-produced by nonsense as a lack of itself" (77). For Deleuze, nonsense "has no sense" and is therefore "opposed to the absence of sense" (77). In other words, both sense and nonsense are effects of language and its structure. A "lack" of sense implies that an immanent meaning lies behind language, so that nonsense would constitute a "lack" of that meaning. Deleuze points out that the absurd and its deployment of nonsense capitalizes on the structural interplay of sense—that is, it "is always too much sense." Therefore, the philosophy of the absurd, as articulated by Camus, construes nonsense as meaninglessness when, to the contrary, nonsense is a radical displacement of the categories of presence and absence that stabilize meaning within the logic of sense. Understood this way, Camus' philosophy of the absurd functions as a satirical critique of life's incongruities, while Deleuze's structural notion of the absurd operates as a humorous irresolution of incongruity.

Pedro Pietri's texts oscillate between these two notions of the absurd. On the one hand, as in "Puerto Rican Obituary," Puerto Ricans mourn their cultural "deaths," and their existence in a hostile world is meaningless. It is only through a reappropriation of language that Puerto Ricans can restore sense to their lives and give a voice to their community. On the other hand, many of the poems in *Traffic Violations* displace the utopian desire for an identity that emerges from immanent sense. In "7th Untitled Poem," one in a series of thirteen "untitled" poems, the title immediately destabilizes the line between presence and absence, sense and nonsense. The title declares itself as an "untitle," which is not the same as saying that the poem has no title. The poem simultaneously articulates and disarticulates its title in the same utterance. The poem that follows continues this absurd deployment of nonsense that traverses the line between affirmation and negation:

I am not here now
I am sure I am not here
Nor have I been here before
Or after I have not been here

I recognize the furniture
And the dust on the floor
And the fingerprints on the ceiling
(somebody tried to escape)

The legs of the chair are weaker
Than they were the last time
I remember not being in this place

The window curtains have fallen
The walls need a new paint job
There is garbage all over the floor
Inside this room I am not in now

Electricity has been cut-off
So has the gas and running water
If you try running out of here
You will end up right back inside

The same thing will happen
Should you jump out the window

Don't ask me why or how come?
I am not here to answer you
I am always somewhere else—always
Insisting I am somewhere else

Should I see a half filled glass
Suspended in midair I will lie
About not being in here and
Make myself comfortable.
    (*Traffic Violations* 51–52)

On the one hand, the poetic voice makes this uninviting room visible and establishes a sense of familiarity with it while, on the other hand, the voice repeatedly denies its presence in that room. Normally one would say, "I am not there," designating one's absence from a place that is the opposite of "here," the space from which the voice speaks. Yet this poem (con)fuses the "here" and the "there," and the poetic voice speaks simultaneously from both spaces. Not only do these stanzas paint a verbal picture of a squalid, prisonlike room, the line "(somebody tried to escape)" visually inscribes an enclosure around absence with the use of parentheses. The "somebody" who left the traces of his escape attempt can be read as the poetic "I" who speaks eccentrically from both inside and outside the room. When the poetic voice declares he is not "here," then the "there" from which he speaks collapses into the "here." In this way we can read the room as an allegorical representation of the poem's textuality, and its words are like "the fingerprints on the ceiling" that mark a desperate struggle for freedom from that textual space. Once the poetic voice writes the poem, it no longer occupies that space. This becomes clear when the poetic "I" displaces this struggle for freedom onto a second person by saying:

> If you try running out of here
> You will end up right back inside
>
> The same thing will happen
> Should you jump out the window.

The poem destabilizes subjectivity in its eccentric slippage from first to third to second persons, yet all three have tried or continue to try to find an aperture through which they can escape the dirty room (the poem) where they are trapped.

Why do these imprisoned subjects attempt to escape the very textuality that engages them in poetic discourse? Is not poetry a means of constructing a discursive community? It is at this point that the poetic voice bluntly states, "Don't ask me why or how come?" The poetic voice engages the reader with an aggressive posture of nonresponse, yet the question mark at the end of this line punctuates both the reader's question and the poetic voice's refusal to answer. The question mark erases the origins of these articulations through its grammatical ambiguity. In this way Pietri's poem performs the absurdist irresolution of contradictory statements. Unlike irony, which presents a false statement whose true meaning must be decoded from its opposite, the absurd allows contradictory statements to collapse into each other without any reversal of meaning. Sense is conflated with nonsense. The poetic voice can be in the room while always insisting he is somewhere else. Although this voice speaks from several subject positions, any one of those subjectivities can negate the voices of its other "selves." Furthermore, if we refer back to the title of this "untitled" poem, we see that it names by unnaming, thus articulating a humorous aesthetic of incongruity. The poetic voice forces his interlocutor to suspend any demands for rational discourse as he imprisons the "you" in the very room from which the "I" is presumably absent. If the "you" refers to the reader of this absurd poem, he or she inhabits the space that the poetic "I" has already abandoned. Therefore, no one can answer the reader's questions of "why or how come" because the poem erases its discursive origins and leaves only the textual traces—"the fingerprints on the ceiling"—that mark an ongoing struggle against an unnamed enclosure. In the essay "Freud and the Scene of Writing" in *Writing and Difference*, Jacques Derrida argues: "Traces thus produce the space of their inscription only by acceding to the period of their erasure. From the beginning, in the 'present' of their first impression, they are constituted by the double force of repetition and erasure, legibility and illegibility" (226). In Pietri's poem the tension between inscription and erasure performs an absurd scene of writing, in which the writing and reading subjects occupy the same textual space even though neither one of them is fully present in that space. Like the poetic voice, the reader occupies the scene of writing through absence.

Although the poem's images create a space of uneasy isolation and describe the desperate, futile struggle to escape those confines, the last stanza introduces a surreal image that contradicts the unease and desperation of the previous verses:

Should I see a half filled glass
Suspended in midair I will lie
About not being in here and
Make myself comfortable.

The surreal image of "a half filled glass / Suspended in midair" once again suspends any attempt to understand this poem rationally. Is this glass part of the allegorical structure that equates the poem's textual space with the prisonlike room? Does it have its own symbolic significance outside that allegorical construct? Its very ambiguity allows the poetic voice to deny his previous declarations of absence so that he can reoccupy the room and make himself "comfortable." The comfort that the poetic voice takes in his dissembling discourse reveals the poem's humor, because what was up to this point an uneasy prison of ambiguity becomes a source of pleasure. This poem plays a trick on the reader, trapping him or her in a hermeneutic circle that resists logical explanations. Once the reader—along with the "I" who stands as his or her poetic other—"sees" but does not understand the poem's absurdity, then the "you" will also enjoy the pleasurable nonsense of the absurd. Although the poem lays a trap for the reader, its textual space is a relief from the dictates of reason and sense. It opens a door to nothing, which alleviates the discomfort of occupying the stifling space of the here and now. These textual displacements are but a few of the many "traffic violations" committed by Pietri's poetry.

Yet what is most conspicuously absent in this poem is any mention of Puerto Rican or Nuyorican identity, a consistently present theme in everything from Pietri's "Puerto Rican Obituary" to his later plays and one published short story, "Lost in the Museum of Natural History." The structural absurdity of Pietri's texts adds a new dimension to an understanding of Nuyorican language, since the humorous destabilization of self and other that appears in a poem like "7th Untitled Poem" does not inscribe the clear delineations between interiority and exteriority that marked the identity politics of "Puerto Rican Obituary." Efraín Barradas, in *Partes de un todo: Ensayos y notas sobre literatura puertorriqueña en los Estados Unidos*, argues that the irrational experiences depicted in Pietri's "surrealist" poems confirm the equality of all the inhabitants who live in the absurd and grotesque world of New York City (145).[6] Barradas finds that the poems in *Traffic Violations* develop the absurdist tendency even further. He writes: "The poet is no longer the bard of the obituary of exploited Boricuas [Puerto Ricans], but rather the being who destroys the established intellectual order, who goes against social flow, who violates that predetermined route" (135–36).[7] As Pietri's texts become more structurally absurd, they initiate a self-reflexive, humorous critique that explores the creative possibilities of sense in nonsense, and of nonsense in sense. By erasing the borders between "here" and "there," Pietri redirects the literature of the Puerto Rican diaspora toward a pleasurable openness. This new cultural horizon becomes visible from the discursive apertures created by his eccentric texts, which at one and the same time enclose the reader in an endless play of language, yet free the reader from the imperatives of making sense. Without "sense," the nationalist discourse that situates Puerto Rican identity exclusively on the island destabilizes, so that one enclosure in the construction of identity always leads to another discursive opening and another negotiated textual performance.

Pietri's "7th Untitled Poem" critiques the notion of an immanent identity in a scene of writing where the absurd irresolution of contradictory statements, surreal images, allegory, ambiguous grammar, and the disruption of sense all contribute to the humorous pleasure of othering the self. Yet Pietri was a polygraph in the sense that he was a writer of many or various works, so the analysis of one poem does not by any means fully explore the complexity of Pietri's poetry, theater, and narrative. Pietri uses humor in conjunction with an eccentric sensibility to destabilize Puerto Rican identity from its geographic determinism. Pietri's polygraphic writing extends to creating hybrid texts, in which poetic orality reveals its scriptural economy, performance fuses with textuality, and narrative collapses the border between fiction and reality. Pietri participates in and deviates from Nuyorican poetry's aesthetic concerns and political engagements. Pietri's works participate as foundational texts in the articulation of a diasporic identity, yet their eccentric sensibility also critiques the very notion of cultural foundations, dislodging Nuyorican identity from its rootedness in geographic determinism. His various poetic practices reflect a shift from an island-oriented construction of identity to a more culturally open-ended negotiation of selfhood and otherness. One also finds this shift in Pietri's plays, in which the absurdist performance of empty space culminates in theatrical texts that (con)found the possibility of performance. Here Pietri likewise uses humor as a disruption of logic and sense, which serves to blur the lines between presence and absence, performance and text. Finally, Pietri's short story "Lost in the Museum of Natural History" incorporates absurd humor and textual hybridity in a narrative that deconstructs the author as a self-determining authority, thus exposing identity as a negotiated—and often subverted—text.

Performing Absence and Absent Performances: Pietri's Absurd Theater

Like many other Latino theatrical and performance enterprises, early Nuyorican theater and performance engaged its audience as a political discourse. Alberto Sandoval-Sánchez, in *José, Can You See? Latinos On and Off Broadway*, writes that Latino theater has often been marginalized from mainstream venues: "Being primarily a community-based form of theater with a pedagogical agenda, it has been produced mainly for the Latino community and has been limited to venues that foment 'Hispanic' cultural affirmation, ethnic pride, Spanish language and/or bilingualism, and identity politics" (118).[8] As a political tool, Nuyorican theater took live performances to the people, as in the case of the Puerto Rican Traveling

Theater, whose mission was to provide politically engaged entertainment to those who could not afford the high ticket prices for Broadway or even off-Broadway productions (106). Such efforts have opened up multiple spaces in which Latinos and Latinas can perform their identities and see their hybrid cultures and languages come to life on the stage. Pedro Pietri participated in this politically engaged form of theater from the 1960s on, yet he also deconstructed the very notion of theatrical space by taking the separation between performance and text to its absurd extremes. Some of his plays perforate the theatrical stage with a performance of absence, while others stage absence through performative writing. In both cases, these plays use self-reflexive humor to blur the line between performance and text and to inscribe otherness in the discourses on identity. Pietri's absurd theater remains a political intervention that continues to address the affective fallout of *el abandono* even as it reflects on its own performance space and its spatialization of language.

When Anne Ubersfeld writes in *Reading Theater*, "Stage space exists, period!" (114), she reminds the reader that theater is more than just a text; it is a performance within space and time, in which light, sound, movement, and depth play as active a role as the dialogue between characters. For Ubersfeld, theater functions as a negotiation between text and performance, in which text consists of dialogue and *didascalia* (stage directions) while performance "is made up of a set of verbal and non-verbal signs" (8–14). The theatrical text can be further divided into the author's manuscript (T) and the staging or mise-en-scène (T'), and it is the gaps in T (what the author leaves out) that the director and actors fill in with T'. This negotiated text leads to but is not equivalent to performance, which must take into account the audience's ability to understand the play's deployment of a "multitude of codes" (14). Ubersfeld argues that theater obeys the laws of communication, but that the spectator's role should not be as a passive receptor of the theatrical message, for

> it is the spectators, much more than the director, who create the spectacle: they must reconstruct the totality of the performance, along both the vertical axis and the horizontal axis. Spectators are obliged not only to follow a story, a fabula (horizontal axis), but also to constantly reconstruct the total figure of all the signs engaged concurrently in the performance. They are at one and the same time required to engage themselves in the spectacle (identification) and to back off from it (distancing). (23)

Theater that attempts to reproduce reality through transparent mimesis misconstrues the role of the spectator, for one of the goals of theatrical communication is to induce "the spectator to possible action" (24). Theater must engage the spectator with texts and performances that draw attention to their own devices, thus communicating with the audience as coagents in the production of meaning.

In order for theater to accomplish this unmasking of itself as theater, the audience must read both text and performance space as negativities: "The essential characteristic of theatrical communication is that the receiver considers the message to be unreal, or more precisely, untrue" (24). In this self-aware theater, the language of the text and the verbal/nonverbal signs of the performance are "marked with a minus sign" (24). The risk of relying on transparent representation is that the spectator "contemplates without taking action, is implicated but not involved" (26). Even street theater, which often seeks to represent dramatically real events that have just occurred previously in that same location, figuratively drags along the footlights of the proscenium stage, so that "yesterday's arrest or strike becomes unreal" and the poor and oppressed of "kitchen-sink drama" are exoticized (27). Ubersfeld argues that realism "cannot be created through textual and stage phenomena" and insists that a spectator becomes an active participant in theater when "a divorce is effected between language and the limiting forces of reality" (27). Both text and performance emerge from the absences that permeate their discursiveness and materiality; in other words, the theatrical text and performance space exist because of what they are not. Pedro Pietri, with his use of the absurd, engaged the spectator and reader of his plays with a radical devaluation of language and a deconstruction of performance space. Yet it is through humor that Pietri blurs the line between theater and reality, so that the spectators perceive not only the textual and performance devices of theater but also the theatricality of their own daily existence.

As in his poetry, Pietri uses absurd humor to politicize the negative spaces in theater. In his stage play *The Livingroom*, Pietri adapts the late-twentieth-century tradition of the Theater of the Absurd, in particular Samuel Beckett's *Waiting for Godot*, in a farcical representation of a Puerto Rican family and their absent son, Vitico. Vitico has lived for the past year inside a tent in the family's living room, having vowed not to come out until he has repaired the record player. The text provides this information in the opening stage directions, yet at the beginning of the performance the spectator would only notice the incongruous tent in the living room and an empty record player stand with a record rack alongside it. It is through the ensuing dialogue among the other characters—Manolo, the father; Adela, the mother; Violeta, the sister; Chencho and Chencha, the compadres; Tremenda, the neighbor; and Dr. Rod/Dr. Rodríguez, the psychiatrist/chauffeur—that the spectator learns why the tent is in the middle of the room. The only indications that Vitico is actually inside the tent are his hands. The spectator sees his hand place an "escupidera" [chamber pot] full of "piss and mojones" [turds] outside the tent (75), and the spectator hears Vitico applaud Tremenda's loud, operatic singing (85). At one point Vitico places a letter outside the tent, telling his parents he is "having a nice time at camp" (93). Only when the characters normalize the tent, commenting on how good it looks in the living room, does Vitico finally emerge with the functioning record player. Vitico's self-imposed exile in the tent ends with an upsurge of music, and his appearance unites the family and neighbors in a festive *guachafita*. Yet his presence could only be realized with a precondition of absence and alienation from the family, and the celebratory sense of community that the play invokes is a result of the characters' normalization of incongruity.

Before Vitico does finally emerge at the end of the play, the characters argue incessantly over whether to have him committed to a mental institution. As the stage directions tell the reader, this is "a play about the world's oldest pastime—mental illness" (63). As the action unfolds, the reader and spectator come to realize that the other characters are no saner than Vitico. In the following exchange, Violeta and Manolo contradict one another as they try to persuade Adela to have Vitico committed:

ADELA: (Angry) Vitico will come out . . . (Calmed) when the record player plays again.

VIOLETA: Adela, you do not believe that any more than we believe it! (Pause) Even your best friend, Tremenda, who is completely spaced out, agrees that Vitico should be institutionalized.

ADELA: Tremenda's madness is premeditated, I've caught her reading books many times.

MANOLO: There is nothing wrong with increasing your intelligence.

ADELA: If you were born intelligent, learning will only make you ignorant. (70)

Reason begets madness in this exchange, and Adela's absurd arguments imply that Tremenda is ignorant because she reads, yet she betrays her feigned insanity through reading, which makes her intelligent. According to Adela's twisted logic, madness becomes a relative behavior rather than a certifiable condition, which supports her claim "THERE IS NOTHING WRONG WITH VITICO!" (72). This sense in nonsense performs the "radical devaluation of language" that Martin Esslin, in *The Theatre of the Absurd*, marks as one of the defining characteristics of this particular theatrical genre (26). The play not only inscribes absence in the performance space (the tent), it also performs absence in its text by detaching language from any notion of immanent meaning. Through absurd humor, both text and performance show the empty spaces that underlie their own structures.

Yet Pietri's use of absurd humor also functions as a politically engaged discourse on Nuyorican language and its power to disrupt linguistic purity. One of the play's most absurd characters, Dr. Rod, is the psychiatrist the family has secretly consulted without Adela's permission. Dr. Rod speaks a ludicrous version of Spanglish with a comical gringo accent:

DOCTOR ROD: . . . Moo show goose toe amigos, como everybody has been? . . .

TREMENDA: I see he speaks English fluently.

Even though all the other characters speak English, Dr. Rod insists on addressing everyone in this murderous corruption of Spanish (native Spanish speakers would say *habla matao*). Tremenda's ironic retort reveals the condescending posture that Dr. Rod takes with the Puerto Rican family. He tries to address the Puerto Ricans in what he thinks is their language, but his linguistic performance only further establishes the cultural and economic divides that separate him from the working-class characters. Eventually the family and friends conspire against Dr. Rod and force him to speak correct English in a moment of rage. Dr. Rod leaves but later returns as Tremenda's chauffeur, Dr. Rodríguez, who speaks perfect English. Alfredo Matilla Rivas, in "Algunos aspectos del teatro de Pedro Pietri," argues that Dr. Rod/Dr. Rodríguez is the truly grotesque figure of the play. His name in English, a shortened version of the Spanish surname with phallic implications, reinforces the ridicule aimed not only at North American figures of institutional authority but also at the Anglophile façade of the assimilated Puerto Rican (94). Pietri has inverted the usual way in which Puerto Ricans subvert condescending, monolingual Anglos. Rather than have his characters speak Spanish to confuse their adversary, Pietri allows them to undermine Dr. Rod's authority with English—the language that supposedly belongs to the oppressor. When this character lapses into his own language, he loses his power over the truly bilingual Puerto Ricans. When he reappears as Dr. Rodríguez, he takes the subordinate position of a chauffeur, but he also integrates himself into the Puerto Rican community by speaking clearly in English, not Spanish. Matilla Rivas writes: "the caricature once again inverts itself, now that it transports us, like the revolving door, from one closed boundary to another, completing the spin that allows us to perceive the disfiguration of the Puerto Rican in his own collectivity" (94).[9] In other words, the absurd Dr. Rod/Dr. Rodríguez blurs the line between text and performance because his stage presence becomes an effect of language, and his language performs within theatrical space as a political intervention in the discourse on Puerto Rican identity.

The performance of absence allows the characters in *The Livingroom* to found a sense of community in nonsense—that is, in the incongruities of absurd humor. As a rewriting of *el abandono*, Pietri's play also shows that the diasporic identity of Puerto Ricans living in the United States finds its most powerful articulation in the performance of absence. Vitico's obsession with the record player invokes René Marqués's character Luis from *La carreta*, who so blindly fetishized "la maquinah" that his obsession led to his death.[10] Pietri rewrites that tragedy as a comic reaffirmation of Puerto Ricans' ability to inhabit incongruity and overcome the social and material forces that conspire against them. It is only when the family normalizes the incongruity of Vitico's (present) absence on the stage that Vitico finally emerges from the tent, victorious in his struggle to fix the record player. That machine becomes not the engine of Puerto Ricans' destruction but the tool with which they articulate their culture and sense of community. Unlike the tragic characters in *La carreta*, the absurd characters in *The Livingroom* have appropriated the language and the technology associated with their oppressors and applied the *arte de bregar*; that is, they make do with the incongruity of their (absent) presence in the United States in order to set up a "living room" in the larger body politic.

Pietri also uses the performance of absence in his plays to address the issue of cultural assimilation. Like the poetic characters in "Puerto Rican Obituary," the characters in *The Masses Are Asses* dream of inhabiting a "Puerto Ricanless scene."[11] The protagonists, a nameless Lady and Gentleman, live in a tenement bathroom-turned-apartment, yet pretend to be dining in a fancy Parisian restaurant. Pietri's construction of theatrical space affects not only the way the characters move, gesture, and interact with the objects on stage; his complex, metatheatrical denial of the reality of stage space devalues the language the characters speak. While the Gentleman emphatically declares, "This is Paris not Paramus!" (3), the stage directions equivocate as to which is the real space, indicating that "this empty apartment or fancy restaurant" contains a table and chairs, drinking glasses, menus, and other restaurant paraphernalia, as well as a toilet with overhead tank, a roll of toilet paper on the floor, and a bathtub on the far left (1). While having bathroom fixtures in a restaurant seems improbable, there is, for many poor New Yorkers who live in small apartments with exposed plumbing, an element of realism to this absurd juxtaposition. Yet the inclusion of the toilet bowl and tank as visible stage objects transforms what might have been a typical "kitchen-sink drama" into scatological metatheater, conspicuously exposing the way theatrical staging constructs space as an illusion.

When the spectator of Pietri's play perceives the intentional unreality of the bathroom/restaurant space created on the stage, and sees the absurd actions of the well-dressed Lady and Gentleman as they rise out of the bathtub, cross the stage to sit at the table, and begin to toast one another with glass after glass of champagne, the spectator also confronts how language has been divorced from reality when the characters exchange absurd dialogue such as: "You look astonishing. . . . You look astonishingshinger. . . . You look flabbergasting everlasting. . . . You look everlastinger flabbergastinger" (5–8). Even in the Spanish translation the language is purposely stilted, and Alfredo Matilla Rivas does an excellent job of rendering these nonsensical exchanges as: "Te ves insuperable. . . . Te ves insuperabilísimo. . . . Te ves despampanantemente eternamente. . . . Te ves eternamentísimamente despampanantísimamente" (103–6). Pietri's characters exchange these increasingly absurd superlatives because they suffer from their own form of spatial denial, and their absurd language overcompensates for the fact that they are not in a Parisian restaurant but in a fetid bathroom.

The Gentleman is the more emphatic of the two, often forcing the Lady to readopt her role when she lapses into reality. He forbids her to flush the excrement-filled toilet, answer the telephone, or open the door, since any of these actions would betray their presence in the apartment. After all, they had told all their neighbors that they have gone to Paris and must maintain this pretence at all costs. As the characters continue to get more inebriated, they decide to "pretend" to act and talk like the "poor people" by exaggeratedly cat walking across the stage and using outdated slang such as "groovy" and "far out" (21–27). The Gentleman tries to reprise their upper-class comportment, but the Lady is unable to shake her ghetto persona. The action soon devolves into a struggle between the abusive Gentleman and his victim, the Lady, whom he prevents from escaping not only the apartment but also the imaginary Parisian restaurant his assimilationist dreams have constructed.

Efraín Barradas, in the essay "Pedro Pietri o lo 'surdo' del absurdo" in *Partes de un todo*, discusses how the possibility of an impending reality that waits outside the apartment door distinguishes *The Masses Are Asses* from other plays in the tradition of the Theater of the Absurd. He describes the spaces separated by the apartment door as two complementary planes that portend the possibility of abandoning the absurd, of its ceasing to be in the play itself. This implies that the absurd in this play is an essentially social and psychological phenomenon, not metaphysical (153). However, Barradas also notes that, despite all the activity and noises that signal the outside world offstage—gunshots, loud knocking at the door, even an over-heard rape scene—the play never resolves the issue of whether that off-stage plane is any more real than the absurd space onstage. The voices the Lady and Gentleman hear offstage are their own (that is, recordings of their own voices), implying that one reality is just as absurd as the other. Barradas writes: "The Lady and the Gentleman, especially the latter, who is more quixotic, retreat from the world and create their own because ours is grotesque and absurd. But the one the Gentleman creates is neither a uto-pia nor an ivory tower but a world that reflects class struggle. The world of the imaginary Parisian restaurant is the world created by a proletarian who wants to be bourgeois and who makes fun of his own class" (155).[12] Once again, Pietri's play uses absurd humor to blur the lines between text and performance as a political intervention in the discourse on Puerto Rican identity. As the dialogue performs an absurd devaluation of lan-guage, it opens a space in the text in which meaning empties out and sense and nonsense collide. Yet the performance space in which that absurd lan-guage is deployed also alternates between affirming and denying itself, revealing a slippage from the stage's unreality to the real world. If, as Ubersfeld argues, the mise-en-scène emerges from the theatrical text's gaps, then the text also emerges from the empty space between the stage and the street as it engages its audience. That is, the separation between

what lies inside and outside the space of performance is the gap that the
theatrical text fills in and simultaneously erases.

Pietri takes the separation between text and performance to its absurd
extreme, not only with plays that perform absence, but with plays in which
absence is the only means of performing. Plays like *Illusions of a Revolving Door* and *A Play for the Page and Not the Stage* fly in the face of the
twentieth-century theater of the avant-garde that revolted against the primacy of the text. For example, one of the most radical innovations of
Antonin Artaud's Theater of Cruelty was the spatialization of language,
which placed much more emphasis on mise-en-scène and cast speech as
just another physical object (Gaensbauer 1991, 18). In *Theater and Its
Double*, Artaud writes that "instead of harking back to texts regarded as
sacred and definitive, we must first break theatre's subjugation to the text
and rediscover the idea of a kind of unique language somewhere in between gesture and thought" (68). Artaud advocates a theatrical language
that would create "temptations" or "vacuums" around metaphysical ideas.
The theatrical stage should not be the space in which speech becomes the
primary means of communication. Artaud suggests that language must be
subsumed by the performance, which will estrange the theatrical message
and thus empty out the spectator's preconceived ideas. In *Writing and Difference* Jacques Derrida states that in Artaud's Theater of Cruelty "speech
and *its* writing will be erased on the stage of cruelty only in the extent to
which they were allegedly *dictation*: at once citations or recitations and
orders" (239).[13] The theatrical text will take a secondary role in the Theater
of Cruelty, and the performance space will be the primary means of establishing communication with the spectator.

Yet what about a text that writes performatively and takes the page as
its performance space, presenting the reader/spectator with a theater constructed entirely as a text? In Pietri's *Illusions of a Revolving Door*, the
text is its own performance and the theatrical message inscribes the
reader/spectator in the text as an absence. Although the play takes the
form of a theatrical text, it defies theatrical convention and even avant-
garde antitextuality by offering almost no opportunity for an embodied
performance. The *didascalia* indicate from the outset that this is a "No Act
Play," implying not only that there are no acts in it but that neither is there
any acting to be generated from it. The stage directions are as absurd as the
nondialogue that follows, and these vague bits of text offer very little with
which to imagine how to construct a theatrical space:

Characters: 13 speakers reading simultaneously 13 different speeches into 13 microphones. The speeches are excerpts from the wisdom and philosophy of famous men and women. (35)

The reader cannot trust the sincerity of these stage directions, since the text that follows completely erases the "speakers" and does not bother to provide the thirteen speeches they presumably read. What the reader does encounter is a list, "500 Things The Audience Can Do During This No Act Play," which includes:

1. You can leave before it starts
2. You can leave before it finishes

. . .

28. You can denounce the reality of the theater

. . .

88. You can goose the person in front of you

. . .

500. You can forget about doing any of these 500 things. (35–47)

Following these "Clues for Doing Something," the text moves on to a long "Intermission" comprised solely of repetitive phrases such as "HOW ABSENT IS ABSENT / HOW CONTENTED IS CONTENTED / HOW INCREDIBLE IS INCREDIBLE" (50). These phrases are made further ambiguous in that they can be read as either questions or exclamatory statements. It is as if these phrases celebrate their own incongruity. Finally, the play ostensibly resumes with another list, three hundred "Clues for Doing Nothing," such as "Look at the typewriter / Look at the endless blank page" (55). The text performs a scene of writing, but it is a writing that does not commence and remains an "endless blank page." One could imagine a production of this play in which the director follows the stage directions, hires thirteen speakers who recite their speeches simultaneously, and gives each audience member Pietri's "clues" for doing something or nothing. Would that constitute a performance, or would it subvert performance altogether by forcing all the participants to engage with a text rather than with the theatrical space? Such a staging would be even more cruel than Artaud's Theater of Cruelty, since the language of the thirteen speeches would become as solid as objects in their incoherence and impenetrability, and the text would force the audience to take action, even if that action took the form of a refusal or an absence. Finally, the text erases itself, thus performing an antitextuality within its own textual space.

With this play, Pietri places the focus on what the audience may or may not do during the performance. If the spectator leaves before the performance starts, his absence is still part of the theatrical message that the play communicates. Even the "Intermission," which normally offers the audience a brief return to the real world outside the space of performance, is in this play a moment constituted wholly within the theatrical text. There is neither an inside nor an outside for the spectator/reader who engages this play, and any attempts to negate it or even ignore it only serve to reinitiate the textual performance. Pietri takes the separation between text and performance to its absurd extreme, so that the play becomes a "revolving door" that leads to presence and absence simultaneously. This textual theater confounds the Theater of Cruelty's antitextuality, yet its absurdity in many ways accomplishes one of Artaud's main propositions: that theater incorporate the anarchic qualities of humor so that "HUMOUR as DE-STRUCTION can serve to reconcile laughter with our reasoning habits" (69). Pietri's humor functions to blur the lines between presence and absence, text and performance, theater and reality. It is anarchic in that it undermines the spectator's expectations of how theatrical space can manifest itself. But unlike Artaud's notion of humor in the Theater of Cruelty, which destroys logic from outside the text, Pietri's absurd humor is self-reflexive, so its critique reveals its own textual devices from within textuality. In Pietri's play, humor is also a deconstruction of the binary categories that place the spectator in opposition to the performance. The play's "revolving door" will always resituate the spectator within the performance space, even when he or she tries to leave.

Pietri also takes Artaud's notion of a spatialized language to an absurd extreme in *A Play for the Page and Not the Stage*. The text appears as a barely legible collage of handwritten monologue and *didascalia*, and the scenes are presented as triangular, rectangular, and rhomboidal fragments that lie adjacent to one another and flow in vertical and horizontal directions (211–14). The action revolves around a single character who, with agonizing difficulty, decides whether or not to open an envelope while he struggles to get out of bed and leave his apartment for work. The play also describes the character's breakup with his girlfriend in a very matter-of-fact way. It approaches the philosophy of the absurd in that it makes the mundane tragic and the tragic mundane. Yet it is closer to the Theater of Cruelty with its spatialization of language, for even though the stage is constructed entirely out of text, the play performed on that textual stage turns language into gesture and movement. The play also functions anarchically against notions of time and logic, since the text's multiple fragments do not follow any coherent, chronological order. They can be read forward and back and side to side, changing the script with every reading/performance. Pietri's title suggests that this is a play in which the page is the stage. It is both text and performance, in which the only embodied performer is the reader who must direct the action while watching the spectacle.

Anne Ubersfeld describes a similar form of theatrical communication as a "sign reversal," in which certain uses of language and performance objects "designate theatre as theatre" (28). Its effect is to make the spectator aware of theatricality. Ubersfeld writes that "the mechanism of this sign reversal is very complex. In large measure it is a function of the fact that the actors on the stage are at the same time spectators, spectators who observe what is happening in the space where theatricalization is taking place and send back to the audience, after its inversion, the message they receive" (28). While what Ubersfeld describes is a form of ironized performance, in which the actors conspire with the spectator to see through the false world of the theater to a message underneath, what Pietri does in *A Play for the Page and Not the Stage* is cast the reader in the triple roles of director, actor, and spectator. Like the letter waiting to be opened, this textual theater does not deliver its message but puts it in recirculation. It is a virtual performance that not only spatializes language but also textualizes the performance space. Like *Illusions of a Revolving Door*, this play could be produced and performed, but Alfredo Matilla Rivas (1989, 93) warns that "the so-called 'metatext' of a stage director could hinder Pietri's theoretical proposition, which here intends a writing independent (if it were possible) from 'interference,' or historicist alteration of the mise-en-scène."[14] Pietri's absurd scenes of writing allow performance to emerge whenever and wherever a reader engages with the text, so an enterprise that would mount a production of this play might disempower the reader/spectator.

However, Pietri's play does not foreclose the possibility of theatrical, embodied performance. While closer in appearance to concrete poetry than to a traditional dramatic script, the text nonetheless crosses these different genres so that each one emerges in the other. Derrida performs a similar type of textual cross-pollination and spatialization of language in *Glas*, which situates readings of Hegel and Jean Genet in two opposing columns on each page, sometimes embedding notes and asides in the columns, and incorporating different typefaces throughout. On the very first page, Derrida offers what could be the only "stage direction" that guides the reading: "Two unequal columns, they say distyle [*disent-ils*], each of which—envelop(e)(s) or sheath(es), incalculably reverses, turns inside out, replaces, remarks, overlaps [*recoupe*] the other" (1). While Derrida has often been criticized for his inaccessible style, *Glas* takes the notion of nonlinear writing to its extreme, spatializing language so that the text can never be read the same way twice. Jay David Bolter, in *Writing Space: Computers, Hypertext, and the Remediation of Print*, argues that *Glas* is a precursor to the kind of hypertext that challenges traditional reading patterns. Bolter writes: "In the printed *Glas* the network of relationships that normally remain hidden beneath the page has emerged and overwhelmed the orderly presentation we expect in a printed book" (110). Like Pietri's play for the page, Derrida's studies of Hegel and Genet perform a scene of writing in which meaning is detached from the tyranny of logic.[15] In the case of Pietri's text, the scene of writing also offers the possibility of embodied performance, with the various fragments of text acting as a form of "blocking." The play becomes a hyperperformance that resists static interpretation and destabilizes the border between theater and the "real time" world. Once again, this deconstruction of binary oppositions operates within the realm of absurd humor, which straddles incongruities without resolving them and opens up the gaps in language where sense and nonsense collide.

Both *Illusions of a Revolving Door* and *A Play for the Page and Not the Stage* are example of writing that performs. Della Pollock, in "Performing Writing," argues that performative writing, like the kind found in the texts of many poststructuralist critics, is not necessarily an exercise in obscurity; it is "writing as *doing*" rather than "writing as meaning" (75). Pollock writes that

> writing becomes meaningful in the material, dis/continuous act of writing. Effacing itself twice over—once as meaning and reference, twice as deferral and erasure—writing becomes itself, becomes its own means and ends, recovering itself the force of action. After-texts, after turning itself inside out, writing turns again only to discover the pleasure and power of turning, of making not sense or meaning per se but making *writing* perform. (75)

Performative writing takes on the difficult task of analyzing itself within the limits of its own medium. Like humor, in which a subject others him-

or herself in the realm of play, Pollock argues that "a performative perspective tends to favor the generative and ludic capacities of language and language encounters—the interplay of reader and writer in the joint production of meaning" (80). Likewise, the absurd humor in Pietri's plays breaks with the notion of writing as meaning and offers instead a Nuyorican version of *el arte de bregar*: writing as making and making do. His plays perform writing and his writing performs, and the self-reflexivity of his texts functions ludically to engage the reader/spectator in the production of meaning. Pietri's theatrical texts inscribe and erase themselves, and his theatrical performances simultaneously represent presence and absence in the same space. This eccentric sensibility detaches Puerto Rican identity not only from its geographic determinism but from the dictates of reason and logic altogether. Nevertheless, Pietri does not negate the Puerto Rican experience; his eccentric texts allow for a renegotiation between writer and reader that casts identity not in meaning but in performance and play. Pietri takes his absurd humor even further in his short story "Lost in the Museum of Natural History," which not only blurs the lines between sense and nonsense but also collapses textuality in on itself so that the reader can no longer discern the border between fiction and reality.

The Black Hole of Humor in "Lost in the Museum of Natural History"

Jorge Luis Borges's story "Las ruinas circulares" (The circular ruins) articulates allegorically the literary trope of the creator who not only confronts and is confronted by his own creation but faces the reality of his own createdness; that is, he realizes that he, too, is someone else's creation. Borges's story is very similar to Miguel de Unamuno's novel *Niebla* (Mist) and Luigi Pirandello's play *Six Characters in Search of an Author*. All three of these literary works blur the line between reality and dream, they stage the confrontation between the creator/author and the figments of his imagination, and they cast the author/creator as a being whose existence is only a dream, fiction, or drama. For example, in *Niebla* the protagonist, Augusto, has an interview with his author, Unamuno, who reveals to his character the unfortunate truth of his fictional existence. Yet Augusto turns the tables on his author and asks, "May it not be, my dear Don Miguel . . . , that it is you and not I who are the fictitious entity, the one that does not really exist, who is neither living nor dead? May it not be that you are nothing more than a pretext for bringing my history into the world?" (Fite 295).[16] Unamuno's novel brings into question the notion of a literary work's origins, casting doubt on the author as a self-determining subject. Pirandello's *Six Characters in Search of an Author* poses a similar question, which undermines the univocity of a coherent, stable subject. One of the characters in search of an author, the Father, says to the theatrical director:

> And therein lies the drama, sir, as far as I'm concerned: in my awareness that each of us thinks of himself as *one* but that, well, it's not true, each of us is many, oh so many, sir, according to the possibilities of being that are in us. We are one thing for this person, another for that! Already *two* utterly different things! And with it all, the illusion of being always one thing for all men, and always this one thing in every single action. It's not true! Not true! (84)

There are philosophical, psychological, and metaphysical ways to interpret the ludic and oneiric elements in these various works, but perhaps what makes them so compelling is that these are texts that reflect on their own textuality.[17] Whether in the form of a fantastic allegory ("The Circular Ruins"), a philosophical dialogue (*Niebla*), or comic metatheater (*Six Characters in Search of an Author*), the text that reflects on its own textuality and that questions the univocity of the authorial subject performs what Jacques Derrida calls a "scene of writing." For Derrida (1978), the writing subject is never whole or univocal: "We must be several in order to write and even to 'perceive'" (226). Derrida contests the notion that writing functions according to a linear, communicative model in which the sender transmits his or her perceptions via the text to the receiver. Writing is more like a stage (*scène* in French) on which multiple levels, or strata, of perception and articulation converge. According to his view, it is of little use for the "sociology of literature" to search for "the first reader: i.e., the first author of a work" (227). Because writing is the stage on which a multitude of voices converge, Derrida argues, "The *sociality* of writing as *drama* requires an entirely different discipline" (227).

Pedro Pietri's short story "Lost in the Museum of Natural History" performs an absurd scene of writing that combines textual circularity with black humor. Like the texts by Borges, Unamuno, and Pirandello, Pietri's story reflects on the paradox of the writer who is both agent and object of his writing. The story depicts the absurd, often violent and cruel events that occur at the beach when a "record-breaking crowd from all corners of the metropolitan disaster areas where it stays very cold all year around came out on this extremely hot Saturday to socialize with the sun, whose fever was incredible" (1).[18] In many ways, Pietri returns to the satirical representation of the Puerto Rican experience in the city that he addressed in "Puerto Rican Obituary," offering a harsh portrayal of the economic and cultural disenfranchisement that Puerto Ricans suffer in even the simplest social relations and most mundane activities. The main characters in the story are a little lost girl, who walks on the beach wearing a white communion dress, and the girl's abusive mother, who beats the girl and tries to get rid of her. The struggle between these two characters intersects with the comings and goings of an absurd cast of misfits and degenerates, but the character who has the most impact on the story is the writer, a man dressed in black who appears at the diegetic and extradiegetic levels of the narrative and writes the characters and himself into existence. Efraín Barradas, in the essay "Pedro Pietri, narrador" in *Partes de un todo*, argues that in this story, as in Unamuno's novel and Pirandello's play, the characters eventually rebel and confront their creator, but unlike in these earlier texts, in Pietri's story the narrator is irremediably trapped in the very chaos he narrates, which makes the title of the story ambiguous as to who exactly is "lost" in the narrative (147). In an ironic denouement reminiscent of Borges's "The Circular Ruins," Pietri's story ends with the little girl dreaming of her creator but also confronting him and, in the end, negating him. With this absurd scene of writing, Pietri undermines the notion that a politically engaged Nuyorican writer presents the reader with a transparent message or an accurate depiction of the Puerto Rican experience in New York. Textual circularity and black humor combine in this story as part of a literary negotiation in which the writer and reader are absurd fictions of one another's imaginations.

One of the ways in which Pietri blurs the line between fiction and reality in his story is through black humor, which focuses on the most painful, tragic events of everyday life and portrays them comically. André Breton, in his preface to *Anthology of Black Humor*, describes this particular variant as "the mortal enemy of sentimentality" (xix). While many critics have used the term "black humor" to identify trends in North American literature of the 1960s,[19] Patrick O'Neill in *The Comedy of Entropy: Humour, Narrative, Reading* offers a more comprehensive definition. Black humor, unlike sympathetic humor or derisive humor, is not self-congratulatory or self-reassuring; black humor "is the humour of uncertainty, lost norms, lost confidence, the humour of disorientation, the comedy of entropy" (50). In Pietri's story, black humor serves to depict "the endless miserable living conditions" of the "poor people and poorer people" (1). Many of the scenes involve grotesque representations of violence, gluttony, drunkenness, and lechery, yet these disturbing images are devoid not only of sentimentality but of any narrative "realism." Using the poetics of sense in nonsense, Pietri makes the mundane seem tragic and the tragic seem mundane, all of which lends a surreal quality to the scenes of abjection and degradation:

> Old teenagers and young senior citizens were having a nice time. Everywhere you looked, everybody was busy eating and talking about what they were going to eat next. People ate on the boardwalk, in the sand, asleep and awake, taking a sun tan; they ate swimming above and under water; they ate regardless of what recreational activities they indulged in. (2)

Pietri defamiliarizes common words and phrases by juxtaposing them with their opposites: "Old teenagers and young senior citizens." It is as if no one at this beach is who he or she is supposed to be, and this ambiguity and disorientation contributes to the story's black humor. Through repetition, Pietri also takes a mundane activity—eating at the beach—and represents it as a grotesque absurdity. The constant eating continues in the most incongruous places until it becomes an inescapable obsession. The beachgoers indulge themselves in order to stave off returning "to the vicinity where destruction is inevitable"—that is, the "miserable living conditions" of their poverty (1). What Pietri depicts in this story is far from epic or melodramatic; it is the banal, disaffected reality of the marginal classes. Yet through absurd poetics this mundane reality takes on the dark, sinister shade of black humor.

The darkest and most sinister figure in the story, though, is the writer, who sits "alone on the seat of a table with an opened beach umbrella on top, writing down notes for future references and eating an imaginary heroe [sic] sandwich" (2). The writer drinks from a pint of Puerto Rican rum as he observes the beachgoers and writes about their actions. When some of these characters rebel against their author, however, he omits or erases them from the story. He is a shadow figure, and when the little lost girl approaches the table at which he supposedly writes about her, "she sees nobody there, and walks onto the boardwalk, desperate for help" (2). Like the other characters in the story, the writer refuses to intercede and help the little girl find her mother. When the girl and mother reunite, the mother begins to beat the child mercilessly. The writer states:

The little girl begs me to stop being so negative with my imagination and write about the bright side of life. I pay her no attention because I am totally broke. This story has to be written regardless of whose feelings get hurt. This is the way I make my living. If I am unreliable to my fantasies the rent will not get paid. (6)

In this instance, Pietri represents the world of the imagination and fantasy as the most mundane reality. His writing is simply a means of paying the rent, and although he is the godlike author of this text who controls the fates of his characters, he is as poor and disaffected as they are. As in *The Masses Are Asses*, this story (con)fuses the plane of reality and the plane of fantasy so that the reader can no longer discern a clear boundary between the interior and the exterior of the text. The narrator/writer crosses several narrative levels as well, performing metalepses from the extradiegetic to the diegetic level and back again. He also performs analepses (flashbacks) and prolepses (flash-forwards) throughout the story, especially when he repeatedly writes that he is taking "notes for future reference."[20] Finally, the narrative voice switches between the third, first, and second persons, heightening the sense of disorientation by inscribing the reader into the story with the use of "you" when the narrator refers to himself. Barradas (1998) argues that, ultimately, the person who is "lost" in the story is the narrator/writer, but if the narrator gets lost, then the characters and the reader must be lost with him (148).[21] In this way Pietri's story becomes a black hole of humor, depicting comically the mundane tragedies of everyday life while pulling the reader into an inescapable textual circularity.

As Barradas suggests, the narrator/writer of this story is as lost in his fantasy world as his characters and the reader, but in a Borgesian twist the writer realizes that he is also a figment of someone else's imagination. The writer narrates how the little girl dies from the beating her mother has given her, but because she is bored in heaven, she begs the writer "through mental telepathy to bring her back to life, so that she can grow up to become a good sinner and go straight to Hell the next time she gets lost at the beach" (8). The writer decides to make the change while riding home on the subway, fixing the story so that the little girl appears in a hospital intensive care unit. She recovers with the help of a leather-clad motorcycle gang and returns home to her mother, who turns out to be her grandmother. Her real mother comes home from the movies and asks the grandmother how the day went. As this conversation takes place, the writer re-fers back to himself as he redacts the text: "The train stops at the station where I'm supposed to get off. I purposely miss my stop to finish this story" (10). The story completely transgresses the diegetic and extra-diegetic levels with this metalepsis, since the writer becomes a part of the story he supposedly concocts in his imagination. The different narrative levels collapse into one another when the little girl wakes up screaming and says, "I had a dream that a man dressed in black was writing a strange story about me" (10). Finally the little girl crosses over from her side of the story and confronts the writer on the train:

> When the train stops again I have all intentions of getting off, but when I try to move nothing happens, my body is motionless, I am unable to move. The little girl I am writing about enters the train to distribute gypsy business cards. When she comes to where I am hope-lessly seated she hands me one of the cards she is distributing, and quickly draws her hand back when I reach out for it, and proceeds to the next passenger coming home from the beach. (10)

Paradoxically, the writer is immobilized within his own text—a moving train that crosses the border between fantasy and reality. Yet with this ending, Pietri destabilizes the positions of the writer, the narrator, the char-acters, and the reader. The little girl becomes the figure in which all of these narrative positions converge, and her final negation of her own creator acts as a form of empowerment for the reader, who even more than the writer can choose to inscribe or erase any part of this story. However, that refusal is already part of the text, so even the reader becomes "lost" in the transi-tory space between fact and fiction.

This scene of writing fractures the false univocity of realism and per-forms subjectivity on the negotiated stage of the text. The "message" of this story is infinitely deferred as the little girl moves from one passenger to the next, refusing to release her "gypsy business cards." Pietri's absurd humor resonates with Derrida's philosophy of writing in *Writing and Dif-ference*: "we are written only as we write, by the agency within us which always already keeps watch over perception, be it internal or external. The 'subject' of writing does not exist if we mean by that some sovereign soli-tude of the author. The subject of writing is a *system* of relation between strata" (226–27). The writer in Pietri's story is written as he writes, just as the dreamer in Borges's "The Circular Ruins" is the dream of someone else. However, Pietri, like Canales and Sánchez and Vega, uses the self-reflexivity of humor in his eccentric text to empower writing as an intervention in the discourse on identity. Although both writer and reader may get "lost" in the infinite play of textuality, humor allows them to perceive incongruity as a source of pleasure, even if the most radical incongruity is their own Puerto Rican identity. Humor acts as the triumph of narcissism for the writing subject, and the eccentric text functions as a destabilized scene of writing, so that the text creates an "empty space" in which the writer and the reader constantly negotiate meaning. Humor and the eccentric text join forces in Puerto Rican literature, founding an identity in incongruity and finding empowerment in movement, thus performing *el arte de bregar* in tandem with *jaibería* on the space of the page as well as on the stage of the Puerto Rican nation.

Afterword

The Ends of Humor

Puerto Rican humor draws from many literary and cultural traditions, from Spanish satire to Afro-Caribbean *guachafita*, from *jíbaro* folklore to modernist and postmodernist language games. Yet perhaps in every Puerto Rican humorist one can find the traces of the quintessential *jaiba*, Juan Bobo. A *jaiba* in Puerto Rico is a clever fool, a picaresque good-for-nothing whose foolishness invariably trips him up, but whose cleverness sometimes allows him to triumph over his adversaries.[1] In many stories Juan Bobo takes people's advice and precautions too literally, resulting in a comedy of errors, but sometimes leading to violence and death. He causes all sorts of calamities for his mother, who will often beat him for his mistakes and misdeeds. In one story he thinks the family pig wants to go to Mass, so he dresses it in his mother's finest clothes. He also mistakes the soft spot on his baby brother's head for a boil and sticks a pin into the infant's cranium, killing him but thinking he has just put the child to sleep. In other stories he gets the better of haughty politicians, tricking one candidate for governor to parade through the town with a turd on his head. Some writers have tried to clean up Juan Bobo and make him more suitable to a nationalist valorization of Puerto Rican culture or to U.S. multicultural discourses of racial hybridity, but Juan Bobo is not a politically correct figure, and in Rosario Ferré's *Los cuentos de Juan Bobo* (1981) the character appears in all his foolishness, gluttony, and cruelty.[2] His naïveté is sometimes tragic but sometimes strategic, disarming his foes with their own sense of superiority. His boorishness during solemn occasions shows his ineptitude, but it can also unmask the arbitrariness of social customs. Juan Bobo is both trickster and fool, and when we Puerto Ricans find humor in his foibles, in many ways we laugh at that rebellious child that resides in our own subjectivity. Freud suggests in "Humour" that when one adopts a humorous attitude toward oneself to ward off suffering, one "is treating [oneself] like a child and is at the same time playing the part of the superior adult in relation to this child" (114). For a Puerto Rican humorist, that child is like Juan Bobo, whose indomitable naïveté often needs to be corrected, but whose playful rebelliousness can be a source of pleasure and freedom from social constraints.

Still, laughter and humor remain elusive terms to define, and when reviewing the broad range of theories that I have incorporated into my analysis of Puerto Rican literature, the incongruities quickly emerge. Laughter can be cruel and corrective (Plato, Aristotle, Hobbes, Bergson), but it can also be a soothing balm or a release (Freud, Pío Baroja, Portilla). Humor can be sympathetic (Freud) but can also be the "triumph of narcissism" (Freud again). As a species of the comic, humor functions within the realm of play (Eastman, Huizinga), yet it can mask a serious statement behind its comic façade (Schopenhauer). Finally, humor can be a form of destruction that tears down the codified structures in society and art (Artaud), but it can also be a form of philosophical self-reflection and critique of the subject's own authority (Baudelaire). The Puerto Rican texts I have discussed in the previous chapters display one or several of these humorous qualities, but the common thread that ties all of these literary interventions together is their ability to find the incongruities not only in national identity but in their own textuality as well. It is from this unstable, fragmented, and self-reflexive position that these eccentric texts resituate the discourse on Puerto Rican national identity. The eccentric text breaks the bounds of the insular vision, not as a means to "universalize" Puerto Rican culture and literature, but to take pleasure in the diverse, often incongruous Puerto Rican voices that speak from multiple points of origin.

Notes

Introduction

1. See also Antonio S. Pedreira's account in *El periodismo en Puerto Rico*, 50–51.

2. The Generación del Treinta (Generation of the Thirties) is considered one of the most influential generations of writers in Puerto Rican literary history. Along with Pedreira, writers such as Tomás Blanco, Enrique Laguerre, Emilio S. Belaval, Juan Antonio Corretjer, Salvador Tió, Manuel Méndez Ballester (and many others) helped to canonize the insular vision (*insularismo*) and Hispanicism as the authentic national identity, particularly in the idealized figure of the *jíbaro*. Palés Matos, while writing contemporaneously, is the exception in that his best-known poetry recognized Puerto Rico's Afro-Caribbean culture as central to national identity. See Josefina Rivera de Alvarez's *Literatura puertorriqueña*, 320–480, and Lillian Guerra's *Popular Expression and National Identity*, 45–66.

3. Ríos Avila's description of *Tuntún de pasa y grifería* favors the Bakhtinian notion of the carnivalesque as a comic spirit of upheaval, communal participation, and the material bodily lower stratum. See Bakhtin, *Rabelais and His World*, 11–12.

4. These ideas resonate with Nietzsche's notion that a constant tension between Apollonian and Dionysiac forces lies behind all artistic creation. See *The Birth of Tragedy*, particularly the passage that describes the Prometheus myth: "We may express the Janus face, at once Dionysiac and Apollonian, of the Aeschylean Prometheus in the following formula: 'Whatever exists is both just and unjust, and equally justified in both terms.' What a world!" (65).

5. Alejandro Tapia y Rivera (1826–1882), considered the father of Puerto Rican letters, set a unique precedent in his 1882 novel *Póstumo envirginiado: Historia de un hombre que se coló en el cuerpo de una mujer* [*Posthumous becomes Virginia: Story of a man who sneaked into the body of a woman*]. This satirical novel is the sequel to Tapia y Rivera's *Póstumo el transmigrado* (1872), which tells the tale of a headstrong young Spaniard, recently deceased, whose spirit transmigrates into the body of his rival so that he can keep tabs on his former girlfriend. In the second part, Póstumo decides to transmigrate once again, but this time into the body of a beau-

tiful Sevillian girl he sees at random on the street. A comedy of errors ensues as Virginia (a.k.a. Póstumo *envirginiado*) attracts the attentions of both men and women.

6. See also Juan Manuel García Passalacqua's essay "The Puerto Ricans: Migrants or Commuters?" which argues: "If there is one quality that characterizes us as a people, it is our imperative to commute, our transient nature" (103).

7. Several anthologies and annotated bibliographies have presented a broad scope of humor theory. See Morreall, *The Philosophy of Laughter and Humor*; Goldstein and McGhee, *The Psychology of Humor*; and Roeckelein, *The Psychology of Humor*.

8. Robert L. Latta, in *The Basic Humor Process*, argues against the premise that amusing incongruity initiates the humor process—from cognition to the experience of pleasure and, finally, to laughter. Instead Latta turns the focus of his theory, which he calls Theory L, toward the states of "unrelaxation" and relaxation that allow the humor process to take place. For Latta, incongruity is only one among many "stimulus events" that can trigger the cognitive shift from "unrelaxation" (expectation) to relaxation (35–44). Latta's argument differs from the Incongruity Theory advanced by philosophy mainly in shifting attention away from the humor stimulus to the perception and reaction to that stimulus. By doing so, Theory L does not adequately address the issues of language and signification. Therefore, the Incongruity Theory provides the critical means for analyzing the shifts not only between cognitive states but between different realms of signification and how a comic object undergoes a displacement in meaning.

9. "En un país húmedo y frío, donde han de producirse fácilmente el artritismo y la dispepsia, ha de haber malhumoristas, y los ha de haber donde las bruscas oscilaciones de temperatura y de presión traen de continuo al corazón en jaque."

10. "El humor cancela el patetismo, que es una actitud de desesperación ante la acción. El patetismo lleva implícita la afirmación: 'no hay nada que hacer'; quiere consagrar, como insuperable, un estado del mundo. El humor destruye esta consagración y devuelve su carácter transitorio a la situación que el patetismo quería hacer definitiva."

11. "El humor es una actitud de estilo estoico que muestra el hecho de que la interioridad del hombre, su subjetividad pura, nunca puede ser alcanzada o cancelada por la situación, por adversa que ésta pueda ser; muestra que el hombre nunca puede ser agotado por su circunstancia."

12. Juan Gelpí in *Literatura y paternalismo en Puerto Rico* writes: "Del paternalismo habría que destacar ante todo una 'topografía' particular que lo caracteriza: el hecho de que supone una relación jerárquica entre sujetos, uno de los cuales se constituye en 'superior' al relegar al otro o a los otros a la categoría de 'subordinados'" (2).

13. "La estrategia del *bregar* consiste en poner en relación lo que hasta ese momento parecía distante o antagónico. Es una posición desde la cual se actúa para dirimir sin violencia los conflictos muy polarizados. En ese sentido, connota abrirse espacio en una cartografía incierta y hacerle frente a las decisiones con una visión de

lo posible y deseable. Implica también—es crucial—el conocimiento y la aceptación de los límites. . . . Es el arte de lo no trágico, sin la fatalidad ni la blandura del ¡Ay bendito!" (*Note*: In Puerto Rico, *¡Ay bendito!* is an exclamation of resignation, as if there were no solution to a difficult situation.)

Chapter 1. The Self-Mocking Satirist: Nemesio Canales and the Politics of Humor

1. The critic who has compiled the largest and most diverse collection of Canales's texts is Servando Montaña Peláez, whose edition of the *Antología de Nemesio Canales* was republished in 2000 (its first appearance was in 1974). Montaña Peláez has also written two critical studies on Canales, in addition to editing the first volume of the complete works, *Obras completas, Meditaciones Acres* (1992). To date, this is the only volume published. Interestingly, Montaña Peláez indicates the disappearance of a critical apparatus—introductions, notes—that interpreted, situated, and added a personal tone to this edition ("aparato crítico—introducciones, notas—que interpretaba, situaba y daba tono personal a esta edición"). Nevertheless, the volume includes an anatomy ("anatomía") of the contents, an analysis of the editorial process, and a biography/chronology ("biocronografía") of Canales's life and times (15–105).

2. "Nemesio R. Canales fue un ingenio malogrado. Su personalidad hubiera destellado en cualquier campo de nuestra literatura. Su fina observación, su talento claro y su facilidad expresional son factores claramente distintivos de la obra literaria suya que conocemos. Pero pretendió en toda su vida cultivar el humorismo filosófico que, si bien granjeó aplausos y popularidad en su época, lo coloca en posición desventajosa frente a los demás literatos de nuestra patria."

3. ". . . ha de poseer suma perspicacia y penetración para ver en su verdadera luz las cosas y los hombres que lo rodean. . . . es forzoso, además, que las circunstancias personales lo hayan colocado constantemente en una posición aislada e independiente, porque de otra suerte, y desde el momento que se interesa más en unas cosas que en otras, difícilmente podrá ser observador discreto y juez imparcial de todas ellas."

4. "En la política y en la vida se irritaba . . . contra los que achacan sus desgracias a su mala estrella y pregonaba que cada uno se forja el destino que quiere. . . . Y sabiéndolo, no supo o no quiso someter la circunstancia a sus intereses. En lo más íntimo era quizá débil, demasiado idealista para ello, desgarrado entre su racionalismo certero y su temperamento romántico. Larra es el caso del hombre inteligente, bien dotado, al que de alguna manera por oscuras razones le falla la voluntad."

5. "Yo no sabía que era cosa tan difícil encontrar un nombre pero, desde que me he visto pasando las de Caín para buscarle un epígrafe a mi gusto a esta sección del periódico que se me ha encomendado, estoy hasta por perdonarle a mi padre el feísimo delito que cometió conmigo llamándome «Nemesio»."

6. Canales also used many pseudonyms throughout his journalistic career, but he did not develop a lasting literary persona in that manner as José Mercado did with

"Momo," Leopoldo Alas with "Clarín," and Larra with "Fígaro." See *Obras completas*, 49–69.

7. "Amigo mío, comprendo la inmensidad de la carga de su aburrimiento, y me asocio a su pena, pero no veo más remedio para usted que el suicidio. Si no tiene usted valor para emanciparse del yugo de su respetabilidad dando, a la vista de todo el mundo, unos cuantos saltos y volteretas para curarse esa terrible anquilosis espiritual que padece, comprenderá usted que le hago un bien recomendándole el veneno o la horca."

8. "No sentimos el humor, y hasta debemos decir, sinceramente que nos molesta, que nos inquieta, que tememos, sólo con verlo pasar a nuestro lado, que manche o disminuya nuestra propia seriedad, de la que estamos enamorados y que ponemos gran celo en vigilar, porque nos parece que perder algo de ella, es como perder algo de nuestro honor. Y muchas veces, en efecto, cuando queremos afirmar que alguien ha perdido su decencia, decimos que ha perdido su seriedad."

9. Larra takes up the issue of honor in "El duelo," in which he condemns the practice of dueling as a way for a man to reclaim his slighted honor. He traces the code of honor back to the Middle Ages when, if a person of inferior rank showed disrespect to a superior, the lower ranked would be dishonored. However, in his "enlightened" day Larra sees that

> Ahora es enteramente al revés. Si una persona baja o mal intencionada le falta a usted, usted es el infamado. ¿Le dan a usted un bofetón? Todo el mundo le desprecia a usted, no al que le dio. ¿Le roban a usted? Usted robado queda pobre, y por consiguiente deshonrado. El que le robó, que quedó rico, es un hombre de honor. Va en el coche de usted y es un hombre decente, un caballero. Usted se quedó a pie, es usted gente ordinaria, canalla. ¡Milagros todos de la ilustración! (356)

> [Now it is entirely reversed. If a low or ill-intentioned person disrespects you, you are the discredited one. Someone punches you? Everyone despises you and not the one who hit you. Someone robs you? You have been robbed and are now poor, and therefore dishonored. The one who robbed you, who is now rich, is a man of honor. He rides in your coach and is a decent man, a gentleman. You are now left on foot, you are a common person, riffraff. All miracles of the Enlightenment!]

Larra scorns the kind of abusive behavior that confers honor upon a dishonest man, as well as the public ridicule to which the victim of this abuse is inevitably subjected. The code of honor isolates neighbors from one another and perpetuates a society in which one's reputation depends not on one's laudable qualities but on how well one can abuse others and escape public censure. He describes in all seriousness the sad state of affairs that the code of honor has wrought in Spanish society, but the tagline—"¡Milagros todos de la ilustración!"—functions as two types of irony. The first and most obvious irony is verbal, for Larra means the opposite of what he says: the injustices caused by the code of honor are not miracles but common occurrences.

The second irony is situational, a paradox in which the expected outcome of a series of events is not fulfilled, but rather its opposite takes place. The Enlightenment was supposed to bring about liberty, equality, and fraternity, but the code of honor has made the Spanish less enlightened than their medieval forefathers.

10. I have used the "Biocronografía" that appears in Servando Montaña Peláez's edition of the *Obras completas* for these dates, but a typographical error reads "1886" for 1896 in reference to Canales's departure for Spain (84).

11. "Yo estaba en San Juan, yo estaba entre ellos mis simpáticos y patrióticos compañeros graduados y asociados; y oyéndoles se me caía la baba de gusto—el gusto de ver el pleito de la patria puesto al fin en manos competentes, en manos de abogado—, y de la baba pasé al palmoteo y al hurra, y tiré siete veces el sombrero, y todo trémulo me disponía ya, convencido y conmovido, a caer en brazos de la Portorrican. . . ."

12. For an extended discussion of the linguistic properties of humor, see Nash, *The Language of Humour*, 125–72.

13. "Y lo peor es que este pueblo tiene en la masa de la sangre la afición a la guasa, y que, cualquier día, siguiendo el ejemplo pernicioso del Heraldo, se le va a ocurrir a cualquiera, a un limpiabotas, pongo por caso, gritarnos con sorna y hasta con betún, alguna pesadez por el estilo de la que sigue:

—Mire usté, mister: ¿De cuándo acá pa defendel un idear político se necesita er grado americano?"

14. ". . . no es un secreto para nadie aquí—como en todas partes—[que] no son nuestros conciudadanos los que nombran a uno, sino *uno el que hace que le nombren los conciudadanos.*"

15. "Todo derecho, sea cualquiera su índole o naturaleza, concedido por las leyes en vigor en Puerto Rico a los ciudadanos varones y mayores de edad, se entenderá concedido también a las mujeres, y regulado en su ejercicio y aplicación en la misma forma y condiciones que si se tratara de hombres."

16. Josefina Rivera de Alvarez (1955) notes that de Diego won fame for his "vehemente oratoria castelarina, retórica y erudita, llena de imágenes esplendorosas, de descripciones cautivadoras y de efectos teatrales que arrancaban delirantes ovaciones a las electrizadas muchedumbres que lo escuchaban" [vehement oratory in the style of (Emilio) Castelar, rhetorical and erudite, full of resplendent images, captivating descriptions, and theatrical effects that drew delirious ovations from the electrified crowds that listened to him] (61–62).

17. ". . . Deje el autor de este Proyecto a la mujer el pleno y dulce imperio que la Naturaleza le ha formado y Dios le ha concedido; no la despoje de su corona, de su trono y de su cetro en el hogar; no la saque del amor y la calma de la familia al odio y a las pasiones de las luchas viriles, no la saque de la serenidad beatífica del hogar al estrépito a veces infernal de las contrariedades políticas . . .

". . . ¡Mujer! ¡Santa mujer puertorriqueña! Tú no tienes el derecho de votar, como los hombres, pero tienes el derecho de hacer votar a los hombres por la fuerza irresistible de tu debilidad, de tu belleza y de tu amor: de tu sagrado vientre nacerán las futuras generaciones, y en tu santo regazo aprenderán a amar la patria y a luchar y quizás a morir por el triunfo de sus ideales!"

18. "Señor Muñoz Rivera: este pequeño hombre de cara gorda, irregular y aburrida, nacido en Jayuya, a quien usted sin duda recuerda y admira en silencio por su pasada campaña en pro de la mujer puertorriqueña, le sale al paso a usted en este luminoso día de hoy para gritarle su entusiástica adhesión y sincera admiración por sus hermosos propósitos en beneficio de la noble causa de la noble mujer puertorriqueña (cuyos menudos y graciosos pies, bien lavaditos, no me cansaría nunca de besar)."

19. Note the different spellings, "Cuasimodo" in Spanish and "Quasimodo" in French and English.

20. "Mi sino cruel me condenó a ser feo, y he sido feo hasta más no poder, pero tenía en la sangre una gotita de la sangre gloriosa del glorioso antepasado, y he seguido sus pasos, los pasos resonantes, los pasos épicos del inmenso don Juan, persiguiendo en cada boca de mujer una nueva emoción y en cada nueva emoción un fugaz vislumbre del divino misterio inefable de la vida."

21. ". . . no hay más remedio para este infeliz pecador que sentirse romántico esta noche hasta la mismísima médula."

22. "Yo quisiera exprimir, en el vaso
    Tosco de mi rima, zumos de locura,
    Que quemasen tu carne de raso
    Con el fuego impuro que a mí me tortura.

    Cortante, mi frase, como un puñal sea
    Que de tus pudores los velos desgarre . . .
    Que mi estrofa arda con furor de tea
    Evocando raptos de insano aquelarre."

23. After receiving severe criticism for this poem, Canales published a response to the general condemnation four days after the appearance of "En tu oído." See the essay "La moral de una poesía" in *Antología*, 80–83.

24. "¿Cómo se explica la apatía mortal que os mantiene tranquilas, impávidas, calladas como estatuas entre el fragor grandioso de la magna refriega que tienen empeñada las mujeres de ahora para rescatar su alma y asegurar el porvenir?"

25. "—No siga usted, por Dios, no siga usted. Todo se lo he tolerado en el terreno de la discusión, pero esto último es demasiado ya y no se lo tolero. Hacer dimanar la poesía de la mujer, la belleza física y moral de la mujer, . . . confesarse todavía abogado de la embustera y envilecedora tradición romántica que hace de la mujer un juguete, un instrumento para el recreo del hombre . . . ¡Oh! no le tolero a usted ni una palabra más. Farsante o ciego, no tengo nada que esperar de usted. Déjeme usted pasar, que el tiempo vuela y la tarea es urgente y hay en mi sangre llamaradas de impaciencia, de coraje y de fe."

26. According to Gerald Prince's *A Dictionary of Narratology*, "diegesis" refers to "The (fictional) world in which situations and events narrated occur (in French

diégèse)" (20). "Extradiegetic," then, means "External to (not part of) any DIEGESIS (*diégèse)"* (29). See also Gérard Genette's *Narrative Discourse: An Essay in Method*.

27. "Y volé más que corrí a la otra acera, donde ya podrán ustedes figurarse la algazara latina que armaríamos con nuestros saludos y preguntas y repuestas."

28. See *Memoirs of Bernardo Vega: A Contribution to the Puerto Rican Community in New York*, in which Vega recounts the early efforts of Latin Americans from many different nations to establish social, cultural, and political communities in New York.

29. Canales does not specify precisely the decade in which the story is set, but he mentions a profusion of Ford automobiles and the popular dance the foxtrot, which suggest that the story takes place during the Roaring Twenties. Interestingly, although the characters consume much alcohol during their festivities, there is no mention of Prohibition or the speakeasy, which suggests that Canales's depiction of New York nightlife reflects his own experiences in the United States from 1899 to 1902, well before Prohibition. One must also remember that Canales wrote the story while in Argentina, which suffered no such restrictions on drinking.

30. "¡Oh, árbol, cuán inefable compañía la tuya! ¡Cuán sosegadamente te vas transfigurando en el silencio, hasta parecer que tienes alma y que la brindas."

31. In 1891 George Schum published an English translation of Tolstoy's play.

32. "Ven, Raquel . . . Así, juntitas. Ahora . . . haga usted, caballero, el favor de besarnos con un solo beso."

33. "Pero . . . ¡cómo! ¿no entiendes? . . . ¿Y tú, Raquel, me crees irónica también?"

34. "¡Lucy, mi Lucy; ahora te admiro más que nunca!"

35. See Gustavo Pérez Firmat's essay "The Spirit of the Letter" on the importance of writing in Zorrilla's *Don Juan Tenorio*. He argues that Don Juan's letter to Inés sets the action of the play in motion, and that it is "a treacherous gift that circulates from hand to hand disseminating its poison. It is also an instrument of usurpation, a gift that possesses the receiver rather than being possessed by her" (5).

36. ". . . mientras don Quijote, repito, imaginaba el amor en lugar de sentirlo, y se valía de él como un juguete o embeleco para imitar con mil fingidos ayes, suspiros, letanías y aleluyas de enamorado platónico las congojas amorosas de los caballeros andantes, don Juan seguía paladeando, en vivas y desbordantes ánforas de amor, mieles exquisitas, sin apagar jamás la sed inmensa de su alma de brasa."

37. "Encastillado en la brutalidad ancestral que hace del amor una inmolación— bárbara si es sincera e hipócrita si es falsa—de un espíritu a otro, no vi de pronto que era mi vanidad la que se sublevaba ciega ante la sola idea de que mi Lucy no se mostraba, como todas, celosa y furibundamente avara de la propiedad exclusiva de mi corazón."

38. This was the question Antonio Pedreira posed to readers in 1929 in the journal *Indice*. Mercedez López Baralt, in her introduction to Pedreira's *Insularismo*, writes that most of the reponses to that question were negative, and even though Pedreira argued that there did indeed exist a Puerto Rican "soul," his characteriza-

tion of it was pessimistic (12–13). See also Juan Flores's analysis of *Insularismo* in *Divided Borders*, 13–57.

39. "Yo pido de rodillas a éste mi querido y cicatero país (el más cicatero de la tierra), que medite bien sobre lo que he hecho y sobre lo que puede esperar que yo haga todavía como artista y pensador, y si es que tiene idea de que mañana me ha de prodigar adjetivos y ha de glorificar mi pluma, que no cometa ¡que no cometa, Dios santo y bendito, la estúpida crueldad de sentarse a esperar tranquilamente a que yo reviente de fatiga o de miseria, para salir después babeándose de ternura ante mi cadáver y llamándose mi admirador y mi amigo!"

40. "El humorista indica con su actitud el hecho de que no podemos cancelar nuestra responsabilidad, es decir, nuestra libertad, simplemente porque la vida sea dura; señala que el hombre está avocado, siempre en franquía, para tareas que son una exigencia inaplazable, aunque la vida sea 'un mar de dificultades.'"

Chapter 2. Humor and *Jaibería* in the Novels of Luis Rafael Sánchez

1. "Las carcajadas amenazan desnivelar la presión que sirve a la guagua aérea" (*La guagua aérea* 12).

2. Vázquez Arce argues that a sociolect differs from the more general category of an ideolect in that it expresses the elements of a dialect that are determined by social class, which includes such factors as (national) origin, education, profession, economic status, race, or religion (23n).

3. See Joseph Chadwick's "'Repito para consumo de los radioyentes': Repetition and Fetishism in *La guaracha del Macho Camacho*," as well as Arnaldo Cruz-Malavé's "Repetition and the Language of the Mass Media in Luis Rafael Sánchez's *La guaracha del Macho Camacho*."

4. Aparicio draws her definition of metaphoric isotopes from Laurent Jenny's essay "La strategie de la forme," which states that the intertexts "servent à éclairer le sens d'un passage, à l'enrichir d'un jeu de souvenirs associatifs, à indiquer par la voix d'un autre une direction de lecture" (quoted in "Entre la guaracha y el bolero," 76).

5. "La guaracha abre el cuerpo, autoriza el desplazamiento, muestra en diligentes remeneos las partes más deseables, los tramos a humedecer. Los estrechos a despulpar. El bolero cierra el cuerpo, prohíbe el desplazamiento, reduce la rotación a la tentativa de una muerte vivificante."

6. Sánchez's comparison between the guaracha and the bolero also resonate with Mikhail Bakhtin's notion of the centripetal and centrifugal forces in language. In *The Dialogic Imagination* Bakhtin writes: "Every concrete utterance of a speaking subject serves as a point where centrifugal as well as centripetal forces are brought to bear. The processes of centralization and decentralization, of unification and disunification, intersect in the utterance" (272).

7. Sánchez takes these lines from "La cogida y la muerte," a section of *Llanto por Ignacio Sánchez Mejías*, Federico García Lorca's lament over the death of a bullfighter. The poem describes the tragic event as time standing still; as the poem re-

counts the actions that lead to the bullfighter's death in the ring, each action is coupled with "a las cinco de la tarde," which heightens the sense of a collective presence that witnesses the tragedy.

8. By stopping the narrative clock in this way, Sánchez also alludes to Francisco de Quevedo's *La hora de todos y la fortuna con seso*, in which Fortune, forced by an angry contingent of Roman deities, turns the world upside down precisely at four o'clock in the afternoon. What follows in Quevedo's text is a satirical catalogue of individual scenes in which the unjust are punished and each sinner meets his or her due.

9. Luce López Baralt, in *"La guaracha del Macho Camacho,* saga nacional de la «guachafita» puertorriqueña," argues that La Madre and Doña Chon become the novel's tropical version of Don Quijote and Sancho Panza. La Madre's obsessive compulsion to dance, enjoy life, and avoid taking anything seriously acts as a defense against the harsh reality and emptiness of her life. Her flight into fantasy is very much like Don Quijote's, but rather than escape through literature, La Madre gives herself up to the sexual fantasy world represented by Macho Camacho's guaracha. Doña Chon, as Sancho Panza, often attempts to bring La Madre back to reality, as López Baralt suggests: "Doña Chon pugna por volver a la realidad a La Madre, afianzada en su voluntariosa defensa contra la vida. Hay un caso en el que el diálogo resulta inesperadamente cervantino: Doña Chon emerge como sensato «Sancho» frente al ambiguo personaje de La Madre, complejo Quijote de los trópicos cuya fuerza vital parecería radicar justamente en su fuga hacia la imaginación" (115). Although López Baralt finds this reference to Cervantes unexpected, Sánchez has consistently engaged this and other Spanish writers of the Golden Age in his text.

10. "Luis Rafael Sánchez parece burlarse de algo indudablemente serio: su propio quehacer literario."

11. "Si se vuelven ahora, recatadas la vuelta y la mirada, la verán esperar sentada, una calma o la sombra de una calma atravesándola. . . . La verán esperar sentada en un sofá: los brazos abiertos . . ." (*La guaracha* 13).

12. In the French, Italian, and Portuguese, translators have focused on the literal meaning of the English title: *L'Importance d'être constant; L'Importanza d'essere serii;* and *Quanto importa ser leal.* In the German translation, *Ernst sein!*, not only does the pun take, it even surpasses the English original since there is no difference in spelling between "Ernst" as a proper name and "ernst" as a translation of "earnest."

13. See the Spanish translation by Risieri Frondizi.

14. "Después, solo y desconfiado, perfeccionándome la neurosis de la insatisfacción, entrevisté los fantasmas de mi libre hechura, forjé cartas con lejanas remitencias, mentí copias textuales de conversaciones apócrifas para que me nutrieran de especulación. Después concerté diálogos de una afectación verosímil y falsifiqué los dejes de la América amarga, la América descalza, la América en español que idolatra el personaje en que culmina su persona."

15. Diana Vélez analyzes this issue of the double-voiced text in "Bakhtin and

Puerto Rican Narrative: Heteroglossia in Luis Rafael Sánchez's *La importancia de llamarse Daniel Santos*": "This text of Sánchez's, then, rightly occupies a boundary, but it does so firmly within the genre of which it is a part, the novel. For what else does this text do but precisely what Bakhtin defined as novel, i.e., to 'artistically organize the diversity of social speech types and a diversity of individual voice'" (139).

16. As Sánchez notes in *Daniel Santos* (5), he takes this phrase from the composer Pedro Flores. The "palomas del milagro" refer to artistic inspiration.

17. "Mas, yo los invento a todos. Como un dios que, en páginas amarillas y rayadas, partea sus humanidades. Yo corrijo su predicación—dios que, con lápiz de carbón número dos, niega la visa a una coma, un vocablo inoperante, la preposición que agobia. Yo escucho sus talantes confianzudos—dios que lee, en voz alta, el escarceo de sus existencias y las doblega. Yo usufructo la tartamudez y la ríada de palabras que crecen a la mención solitaria de su nombre—dios que oprime la tecla de impresión si la escritura en la pantalla de la Silver Reed japonesa le parece eficaz, merecedora de mostrarse, suscitadora de placer. Lector, ¡oiga estos fantasmas explayarse!"

18. For concise definitions of these narratological terms, refer to Gerald Prince's *A Dictionary of Narratology*. For a more sustained discussion, see Gérard Genette's *Narrative Discourse: An Essay in Method* (227–52).

19. According to González Echevarría in *La ruta de Severo Sarduy* (39, 155), Sarduy's association with the French Tel Quel group of critics did not sit well with other Cuban and Latin American writers of the Left, who considered the author's disruptive, gender-bending fiction anathema to the anti-Eurocentric paradigms outlined by such institutions as the Unión de Escritores y Artistas de Cuba and Casa de las Américas.

The neobaroque, as Sarduy defines it in his 1974 essay *Barroco*, dethrones the harmonious order of the Golden Age baroque; structurally, it reflects disharmony, the breaking away from homogeneity and from the absolute Logos. The neobaroque's destabilizing effects are a reflection of a desire that cannot reach its object. He writes: "Al contrario, el barroco actual, el neobarroco, refleja estructuralmente la inarmonía, la ruptura de la homogeneidad, del logos en tanto que absoluto, la carencia que constituye nuestro fundamento epistémico. Neobarroco del desequilibrio, reflejo estructural de un deseo que no puede alcanzar su objeto, deseo para el cual el logos no ha organizado más que una pantalla que esconde carencia" (103). Sarduy's own literary practice, in novels such as *De donde son los cantantes* (1967) and *Cobra* (1972), reflects his ideas on the neobaroque, employing a fragmented narrative, repetition of passages, and doubling of characters. See also Adriana Méndez-Rodenas's *Severo Sarduy: El neobarroco y la transgresión* and Irlemar Chiampi's *Barroco y modernidad*.

20. This insult is translated by Edward Baker in *Caliban and Other Essays*, 36, as "the neo-Barthean flutterings," which neither accurately attributes "neobarthesiano" to the work of Roland Barthes, nor adequately translates the homophobic

connotations of "mariposa." See also Ricardo Ortiz "Revolution's Other Histories" (38–39).

21. The interview, originally published in the Mexican newspaper *La Jornada* on 21 January 1990, forms part of the collection *La guagua aérea* (89–93). The original Spanish reads:

> Mi tesis sobre lo soez, elaborada a partir de mi procedencia y experiencias de adolescente, no es fácil reducir porque está llena de implicaciones sociales y artísticas. No obstante, te podría adelantar, que siempre he tenido lo soez como una provocación, que creo que lo soez halla su dináminca expresiva en un medio social determinado y en una circunstancia histórica particular. De Valle Inclán a Edward Albee, de *La lozana andaluza* a las novelas de Henry Miller, lo soez literario ha querido operar como demolición moral. Esa teoría me permite hacer un viaje hacia mi origen, mi país y mi clase.

For other critical evaluations of Sánchez's *poética de lo soez*, see Carmen Vázquez Arce's *Por la vereda tropical* (156–57), and Myrna García Calderón's *Lecturas desde el fragmento* (202–4).

22. "Si termino de leer esta noche el Foucault que me ocupa, mañana me celebro en La Taza de Oro con un plato de gandinga."

23. Foucault takes his notion of the narrative "second self" from Wayne C. Booth's *The Rhetoric of Fiction* (67–77).

24. Similarly, Doris Sommer, in *Proceed With Caution, When Engaged by Minority Writing in the Americas*, argues that for subjects writing from/in the margins, a viable textual strategy is to alternate between universalist and particularist modes of discourse. She designates the "rhetoric of particularism" as a literary political engagement that simultaneously embraces the reader and sets up blockades against the reader's mastery. She writes: "To the extent that particularist writing is provocative, it is calculated to produce the desire that will then be frustrated" (15).

25. Castillo asks the question rhetorically, speaking in the first-person voice of the lover: "¿cómo hacer para matar al otro en mí, al otro que fue mi vida, que sigue siendo mi vida, sin matar al mismo tiempo lo que de más vivo en mí sobrevive?"

26. See also Iris Zavala's "De héroes y heroínas en lo imaginario social: El discurso amoroso del bolero" and Juan Gelpí's "El bolero: Poesía popular urbana."

27. In *Listening to Salsa*, Aparicio discusses the many well-known female *boleristas* and how their lyrics differ from the male bolero. In particular, she argues that boleros expressing a feminine point of view emphasize mobility and a desire for freedom after the end of a relationship (130–32).

28. María Vaquero has shown how *La guaracha*'s narrative technique simulates the performance characteristics of theater; she calls this technique "teatro novelado" (quoted in Vázquez Arce, *Por la vereda tropical*, 53). Sánchez reproduces this technique in *Daniel Santos*, while also offering its inverse—a *novela teatralizada*—in his play *Quíntuples*.

29. It is interesting to note that *Daniel Santos* was published in 1988, two years before the appearance of Judith Butler's influential *Gender Trouble* in 1990.

30. "Uno permanece en la piedra solitaria, inmovilizado, amparado en la ficción académica de la distancia crítica."

31. Laura Mulvey, in "Visual Pleasure and Narrative Cinema," discusses this narrative technique in classic Hollywood films, particularly the way a performing showgirl functions as an erotic object for the diegetic spectator (the male audience in the film) and the extradiegetic viewer (the male-identified audience in the theater) (19). Mulvey argues that this technique allows the two gazes to combine "without breaking narrative verisimilitude" (19). While Mulvey clarifies that these analyses are particular to cinema, her arguments shed light on how Sánchez incorporates the cinematic discourse into his literary text.

32. John Perivolaris, in *Puerto Rican Cultural Identity and the Work of Luis Rafael Sánchez*, makes a similar argument, particularly against the negative feminist reaction to *Daniel Santos*. He writes: ". . . opposed to masculine-gendered self-control the bolero's emotional exorbitance perhaps allows possibilities for women and homosexuals to recognize themselves in a space that ostensibly excludes their interests. Possessed by their pleasure in the music and singing, any listener may possess the bolero, so that each member of the audience, male or female, heterosexual or homosexual, rich or poor becomes their own authority in the realm of the senses" (132).

Chapter 3. Ana Lydia Vega's Tourist Gaze and the Eye of Irony

1. In the original, Paz describes "metaironía" as the moment when "la crítica se vuelve creación" and as a "renversement de la modernidad con sus propias armas: la crítica y la ironía" (156).

2. See J. A. Cuddon's *A Dictionary of Literary Terms* (21, 335–36) and Norman Knox's *The Word* Irony *and Its Context, 1500–1755* (38–42).

3. See Guadalupe Valdés's "Code-Switching as a Deliberate Verbal Strategy" and Ana Celia Zentella's "Returned Migration, Language, and Identity: Puerto Rican Bilinguals in Dos Worlds/Two Mundos."

4. The process of Americanization began in the public school system in Puerto Rico as early as 1900. See Aida Negrón de Montilla's *La americanización de Puerto Rico y el sistema de instrucción pública, 1900–1930.*

5. "Poco a poco se iba consolidando la visión del inglés como lengua de prestigio, progreso y modernidad. En inglés era todo el vocabulario técnico, científico y literario que incorporábamos para abordar los más diversos aspectos del conocimiento. El español, con su olorcito a mueble antiguo, quedaba reducido a las esferas de lo doméstico y lo íntimo. Recuerdo que cuando llegué a la Universidad de Puerto Rico, años más tarde, tenía que precipitarme urgentemente sobre el diccionario en busca de términos matemáticos, nombres de personajes históricos o de países exóticos que no sabía decir en español."

6. The assimilated Latino has been made the object of humor by many performers, including John Leguizamo, Luis Valdez and Teatro Campesino, and Culture

Clash. This kind of self-mocking humor has become a pervasive strategy among racial and ethnic minorities in the United States who confront the stereotypes that are normally used against them by other communities. Lois Leveen, in "Only When I Laugh: Textual Dynamics of Ethnic Humor," shows how Puerto Rican comedian Joey Vega mocks the very jokes that are used to denigrate Puerto Ricans. She writes: "Through the joke act, the joke teller acknowledges such jokes openly. By mocking jokes that are derogatory to Puerto Ricans, Vega, as the joke teller, undermines the stereotyping power of such jokes. For Vega, the opportunity to acknowledge and ridicule the stereotype outweighs the potential risk of confirming the stereotype" (36).

7. See Stanley Fish's *Is There a Text in This Class? The Authority of Interpretive Communities*.

8. "Perdón: pero cómo no sentirse vedette en medio de esta delegación de matronas urbanizadas: profusión de Chanel cinco y greñas saturadas de laca a prueba de huracán."

9. "Espulgar mi afro en busca del antepasado fatal. El status está en issue."

10. The story was written in 1978, and Puerto Rico has had three plebiscite votes: in 1967, in 1993, and in 1998. This most recent vote was also the occasion of the Ferré-Vega controversy, in which Rosario Ferré refashioned herself politically and wrote an op-ed piece for the *New York Times* (19 March 1998) in which she advocated statehood. Vega wrote a stinging rebuttal, denouncing Ferré's article as a sad apology for assimilation.

11. ". . . toda despliegue de chichos desplazados por la faja, toda fanfarria de pulseras de charms, mostrando los cinco ceniceros idénticos para sus cinco mejores amigas que su infatigable regateo le consiguió en cinco centavos americanos. Se queja del sol, de la humedad, del créole, del ruido, de los limoneros. Y como que se le humedecen los ojos ante el recuerdo acondicionado de un día de compras en Plaza Las Américas."

12. In "Fenomenología del relajo" Portilla writes: "La ironía se muestra así, por una parte, como algo demoledor. Es una negacíon. Pero, por otra parte, es una afirmación constructiva" (68).

13. This dialogue demonstrates the linguistic acrobatics that occur as different Caribbean subjects try to engage one another. English seems to be the lingua franca for the characters, but the Haitian man uses the French "Madame" and "dix," while the tourist barters in her native Spanish. The original text reads:

> —¿En cuánto me das la foto?
> —Twenty, Madame.
> —¿Dólares? You crazy.
> —Ten goud', dix.
> —Muy caro. Mejor te retrato yo.
> Y antes de que le apuntes con tu lente homicida, desaparece a velocidad
> de orgullo herido. Su camiseta: un puntito blanco al final del callejón.

The trilingual conversation hardly promotes understanding: the man is not asking twenty dollars, then ten, but "Ten goud'"—ten gourdes in Haitian currency, or two dollars.

14. See also Monika Fludernik's "Introduction: Second-Person Narrative and Related Issues" as well as Rita Gnutzmann's "La novela hispanoamericana en segunda persona."

15. "Allá arriba bosteza Pétionville. La luna mira televisión impasible. Y tú ya no comulgas con Boukman y Mackandal en el Bosque Caimán. Los aullidos de los vivos te coagulan la sangre en Puerto Príncipe."

The *houngans* (voodoo priests) Mackandal and Boukman led Haitian slave revolts in 1759 and 1791 respectively.

16. "Entonces te agarra una idiota euforia. Y vuelves al hotel, reliquia en mano, negándote a la autopsia. Toda rompecabezas de islas encontradas."

17. "Haití es una bofetada a tu bondad sintética. Un país que no perdona. Todo acto es culpable y la pena un lujo que se paga a precios de turista."

18. For a thorough comparison of Barthes' "The Death of the Author" and Foucault's "What Is an Author" see Peter Lamarque's "The Death of the Author: An Analytical Autopsy." Lamarque argues that, while both Barthes and Foucault offer innovative arguments for decentralizing textual meaning, their valorization of text over meaning, where the text is "an explosion of unconstrained meaning, without origin and without purpose, is a theoretician's fiction" (330). For Lamarque, writing is a speech act always performed in a purposive way.

19. Reed Way Dasenbrock, in "Taking It Personally: Reading Derrida's Responses," provides a detailed account of "l'affaire Derrida," a series of critical exchanges in which the French philosopher denied authorial intention in his readings of others' texts, but then later vigorously asserted his own rights as an author when his texts were scrutinized by other critics. Dasenbrock offers a measured evaluation of the problem of authorial intent in Derrida's early and later texts: "Writing inevitably involves a loss of authorial control, a symbolic death of the author. But the actions of the older Derrida remind us that being an author means to fight against that loss of control, to fight to stay alive. A theory of writing that brackets the intentional states of the author—leaving aside the intentions, hopes, desires, fears, and anxieties of meaning—leads to an extraordinarily impoverished because depersonalized view of the scene of writing" (276).

20. This essay originally appeared in 1985 in the Mexican journal *Fem* and was rewritten and published in the collection *Esperando a Loló*. I refer to the original version since some key passages were omitted in the later edition.

21. The classification appears in one of the Socratic dialogues in Plato's *Statesman* (15); it is also the basis of the anecdote in which the cynic Diogenes appears before a public forum with a plucked chicken saying, "Here is Plato's man!" See Benito Jerónimo Feijóo's *Teatro crítico universal* (179).

22. "Salvar la Patria de las Garras del Imperialismo Yanqui, Afirmar la Cultura y Acelerar el Advenimiento de la Revolución Socialista."

23. For a discussion of compression and allusion in humorous discourse, see

Nash, *The Language of Humour*, 13–25, 74–102. Freud calls this technique "condensation"; see *Jokes*, 45–50.

24. "Así empecé a tejer el cuento de Malén, la novela de Malén, porque cada día se iba enredando más la madeja de escenas sueltas, deshilachadas, donde siempre faltaba algo: la costura decisiva, el hilo que las pusiera a significar."

25. ". . . las declaraciones juradas de mi vecina, ama de casa con genes detectivescos. . . ."

26. See Raymond Williams's *The Postmodern Novel in Latin America: Politics, Culture, and the Crisis of Truth.*

27. See Sandra M. Gilbert and Susan Gubar's *The Madwoman in the Attic: The Woman Writer and the Nineteenth-Century Literary Imagination.*

28. "Me sirven, me añoñan, me malcrían. Con mi docilidad social a prueba de todo, hoy soy la nueva nuera: la repuesta."

29. "El ángel rebelde viene y va en su cuarto. Comemos como si no escucháramos la protesta sutil de la madera."

30. Bruno Bettelheim, in *The Uses of Enchantment*, encourages using fairy tales as a means of instilling moral and social codes, arguing that "the more deeply unhappy and despairing we are, the more we need to be able to engage in optimistic fantasies. . . . while the fantasy is *unreal,* the good feelings it gives us about ourselves and our future *are real,* and these good feelings are what we need to sustain us" (126). Ruth B. Bottigheimer, in *Grimms' Bad Girls and Bold Boys: The Moral and Social Vision of the Tales,* counters that Bettelheim tends to ignore how the "Christian values" expressed by many of the Grimms' tales "often occur, paradoxically, in connection with brutality, threat, and extortion" (144).

31. Although the Grimm brothers included a version of the Bluebeard tale in some of their collections, "La Barbe bleu" is attributed to Charles Perrault in his *Histoires ou contes du temps passé.* See Jack Zipes's translation of *The Complete Fairy Tales of the Brothers Grimm;* also see Sharon Rose Wilson's *Margaret Atwood's Fairy-Tale Sexual Politics,* 258.

32. The misogynist nature of the Bluebeard figure makes him an ideal target for feminist parody. The Canadian author Margaret Atwood, for example, has reformulated this fable in her short story "Bluebeard's Egg" and, to some extent, in her earlier novel *The Edible Woman.* See also Zipes, *Don't Bet on the Prince: Contemporary Feminist Fairy Tales in North America,* and Niebylski, *Humoring Resistance: Laughter and the Excessive Female Body in Latin American Women's Fiction.*

33. "Salvador me persigue. Vuelvo a rondar con él por el pasillo del condomino maldito. Lo veo pararse frente a la puerta de Malén. Música dura. La persiana está rota: él mismo la forzó el día que Malén no quiso abrirle. La persiana está rota y Felipe Rodríguez canta adentro un lamento de machos ofendidos."

34. Nancy K. Miller, in "Changing the Subject: Authorship, Writing, and the Reader," argues against Barthes' notion of the "death of the author," which strips women and writers from the margins of authorial agency. She writes (104): "The removal of the Author has not so much made room for a revision of the concept of

authorship as it has, through a variety of rhetorical moves, repressed and inhibited discussion of any writing identity in favor of the (new) monolith of anonymous textuality, or 'transcendental anonymity,' in Michel Foucault's phrase"—a phrase coined in his essay "What Is an Author?"

35. I refer here to the title of Enrique Laguerre's novel *Los amos benévolos*.

Chapter 4. Pedro Pietri's Absurd Scenes of Writing

1. Besides the obvious differences in language usage, what separates the "Spanglish" Nuyorican literature of the 1960s and 1970s from earlier Puerto Rican exile literature is that Nuyorican writers tended to focus more insistently on identity formation in the urban reality that surrounded them and were less concerned with Puerto Rican independence. See Juan Flores's *Divided Borders: Essays on Puerto Rican Identity*, 136–37.

2. "El poeta neorrican al añorar desde lejos la isla donde quiere encontrar sus orígenes se une a esa tradición literaria que surge en los comienzos mismos de nuestras letras. El reencuentro con sus orígenes puede ser traumático. Usualmente lo acompaña el rechazo de sus hermanos insulares que no lo comprenden y hasta lo creen ya norteamericano. Entonces el poeta neoyorrican transforma el viejo mito de Puerto Rico como edén perdido y lo convierte en una utopía interna" (74).

3. "Pietri recoge aquí las coordenadas de grupos migratorios, a quienes la asimilación se hace marcadamente improbable, si no imposible, por su condición económica y racial. De ahí quizá la importancia de ese 'Qué pasa,' no como símbolo de pureza lingüística de una hispanidad intacta e inexistente aún en los países de origen, sino como cultura híbrida de resistencia, como espacio utópico entre lenguajes."

4. "Cuando Pedro Pietri en el ya clásico *Puerto Rican Obituary* termina diciendo 'Aquí negrito y negrita means to be called love, ese 'aquí' funda otro espacio para la literatura puertorriqueña. Ese 'aquí' ensancha el espacio afectivo para darle cabida a un mundo completo de la experiencia puertorriqueña al que se le había negado dignidad poética."

5. Donald A. Crosby, in *The Specter of the Absurd: Sources and Criticisms of Modern Nihilism*, characterizes Camus' notion of the absurd as an "existential nihilism"—that is, a negation of the meaning of life that "need not negate life itself" (35). Crosby also discusses the contributions of Friedrich Nietzsche to the modern notion of nihilism, especially in *The Genealogy of Morals* and *The Will to Power*.

6. Barradas calls these poems surrealist "a falta de mejor nombre" [for lack of a better word] (144). The caveat might refer to the fact that Pietri's poems do not resemble the kind of "automatic writing" practiced by André Breton.

7. "El poeta no es ahora el cantor del obituario de los boricuas explotados sino el ser que destruye el orden intelectual establecido, el que va en contra del tránsito normal dictado por la sociedad, el que viola esa ruta predeterminada."

8. See also Kanellos, *A History of Hispanic Theater*, xiv–xv.

9. ". . . la caricatura vuelve a invertirse, ya que nos traslada, como la puerta giratoria, de un coto cerrado a otro, completando el giro que nos permite percibir la desfiguración del puertorriqueño dentro de su propia colectividad."

10. Marqués also wrote a short story, "La sala" [The living room], in which a father tries to reestablish communication with his family after spending ten years in prison for advocating independentist politics.

11. First performed in 1984 by Miriam Colon's Puerto Rican Traveling Theater, the play was presented in English on Thursday and Friday, and in Spanish on Saturday and Sunday (Trebay 1984, 69). The Spanish version was eventually taken to San Juan, where Pietri was already known for Alfredo Matilla Rivas's translation of "Puerto Rican Obituary" (Matilla Rivas 1992, xi). As the guest of Italian theater critic Mario Maffi, Pietri took *The Masses Are Asses* to Rome in 1988, adding a second act at his host's request since, according to Maffi, the Italian theater public does not like to go home after a single act (Matilla Rivas 1997, viii). The original one-act production in New York received favorable reviews from two *Village Voice* critics, Guy Trebay and Michael Feingold, although Trebay speculates that the Spanish version "may be more stylish" (69) and Feingold assumes that "the performers, like the text, are undoubtedly more at ease, lighter and less stilted, in Spanish than in English" (92). Given Pietri's previous "radical devaluation of language" (recall Dr. Rod/ Dr. Rodríguez), the uneasy and stilted English these critics perceived as a shortcoming is undoubtedly central to the play's antiassimilationist political message. Alberto Sandoval-Sánchez in *José, Can You See?* discusses the tendency for mainstream New York theater critics to misread Latino plays and performances (110–16). Some of Trebay's and Feingold's critiques reveal an underestimation of Pietri's bilingual/ bicultural aesthetics.

12. "La Dama y el Caballero, especialmente éste, quien es más quijotesco, huyen del mundo y crean el suyo propio porque el nuestro es grotesco y absurdo. Pero el que crea el Caballero no es una utopía ni una torre de marfil sino un mundo que refleja la lucha de clases. El mundo del restaurante parisino imaginario es el mundo creado por un proletario que quiere ser burgués y que se burla de su clase."

13. See also Martin Esslin's *Antonin Artaud: The Man and His Work*. Esslin writes: "Artaud's ideas about a new technique and practice of theatre . . . are thus basically an attempt to communicate the fullness of human experience and emotion through by-passing the discursive use of language and by establishing contact between the artist and his audience at a level above—or perhaps below—the merely cerebral appeal of the verbal plane. . . . he was burning to find ways and means of transmitting his experience, his physical suffering, his physical exaltation directly to the minds and bodies of other human beings" (70).

14. ". . . el llamado 'metatexto' de un director escénico podría entorpecer la proposición teórica de Pietri, que intenta aquí una escritura independiente (si ello fuera posible) de la 'interferencia,' o alteración historicista de la mise en scéne."

15. For an analysis of *Glas*'s treatment of autobiography, see Jane Marie Todd's "Autobiography and the Case of the Signature: Reading Derrida's *Glas*."

16. "No sea, mi querido don Miguel . . . que sea usted y no yo el ente de ficción, el que no existe en realidad, ni vivo ni muerto. . . . No sea que usted no pase de ser un pretexto para que mi historia llegue al mundo" (279).

17. A short list of critical approaches that focus on the creator/creation trope in these various works includes: Stephen E. Soud, "Borges the Golem-Maker: Intimations of 'Presence' in 'The Circular Ruins'"; Enrique A. Giordano, "El juego de la creación en Borges"; Frances W. Weber, "Unamuno's *Niebla*: From Novel to Dream"; Iris M. Zavala, "Unamuno: *Niebla*, el sueño y la crisis del sujeto"; Wladimir Krysinski, "La Dislocation des codes, le croisement des récits et la brisure de la représentation dans *Six personnages en quête d'auteur* de L. Pirandello"; and David McDonald, "Derrida and Pirandello: A Post-Structuralist Analysis of *Six Characters in Search of an Author*."

18. The story was published as a bilingual edition by Ediciones Huracán (trans. Alfredo Matilla Rivas). The text appears on both sides of a fold-out sheet, with drawings by José Antonio Peláez framing the text. There are no printed page numbers, so numbers in my citations refer to the successive panels on which the English-language text appears.

19. See Bruce Janoff's "Black Humor, Existentialism, and Absurdity: A Generic Confusion."

20. For definitions of these narratological terms, see Prince, *A Dictionary of Narratology*, 5, 50, 77.

21. ". . . ¿quién se ha perdido en el mundo imaginario del personaje? Sólo hay una respuesta: el narrador. Sólo que si el narrador se 'pierde,' los personajes y los lectores se tienen que 'perder' con él."

Afterword. The Ends of Humor

1. See Manrique Cabrera, *Historia de la literatura puertorriqueña*, 62.

2. See René Marqués's pantomime play *Juan Bobo y la Dama de Occidente: Pantomima puertorriqueña para un ballet occidental*, in which the playwright recasts Juan Bobo as the naïve hero who must navigate through and resist the temptations of the "Occidental" culture of Europe and North America. Also see the recent children's book by Carmen T. Bernier-Grand, *Juan Bobo: Four Folktales from Puerto Rico*, in which the illustrators depict the character as a dark-skinned mulatto rather than as the traditional light-skinned *jíbaro*.

Bibliography

Acevedo, Evaristo. *Teoría e interpretación del humor español*. Madrid: Editora Nacional, 1966.

Alas, Leopoldo. "Mis plagios: Un discurso de Núñez de Arce." 1888. In *Obras completas*, 4:213–314. Madrid: Biblioteca Castro, 1998.

Algarín, Miguel, and Miguel Piñero. *Nuyorican Poetry: An Anthology of Puerto Rican Words and Feelings*. New York: William Morrow, 1975.

Alonso, Manuel. *El jíbaro*. 1849. Introduction by F. Manrique Cabrera and José Antonio Torres Morales. Río Piedras: Colegio Hostos, 1949.

Aparicio, Frances R. "Entre la guaracha y el bolero: Un ciclo de intertextos musicales en la narrativa puertorriqueña." *Revista Iberoamericana* 59.162–3 (1993): 73–89.

———. *Listening to Salsa: Gender, Latin Popular Music, and Puerto Rican Cultures*. Hanover, N.H.: University Press of New England, 1998.

———. "La Vida Es un Spanglish Disparatero: Bilingualism in Nuyorican Poetry." In *European Perspectives on Hispanic Literature of the United States*, edited by Genviève Fabre, 147–60. Houston: Arte Público, 1988.

Aristotle. *Poetics*. Translated by S. H. Butcher. New York: Hill and Wang, 1961.

Artaud, Antonin. *Theater and Its Double*. Vol. 4 of *Collected Works*. Translated by Victor Corti. London: Calder and Boyars, 1974.

Atwood, Margaret. "Bluebeard's Egg." In *Bluebeard's Egg and Other Stories*, 131–64. Boston: Houghton Mifflin, 1986.

———. *The Edible Woman*. Boston: Little, Brown, 1969.

Badenes, José Ignacio. "The Poetic Text as Dandy: Reading the Poetry of Manuel Machado." *Romance Language Annual* 9 (1998): 406–9.

Baker, Edward, trans. *Caliban and Other Essays*, by Roberto Fernández Retamar. Minneapolis: University of Minnesota Press, 1989.

Bakhtin, Mikhail. *The Dialogic Imagination: Four Essays*. Edited by Michael Holquist. Translated by Caryl Emerson and Michael Holquist. Austin: University of Texas Press, 1981.

———. *Rabelais and His World*. 1965. Translated by Hélène Iswolsky. Bloomington: Indiana University Press, 1984.

Baroja, Pío. *La caverna del humorismo*. Madrid: Caro Raggio, 1919.

Barradas, Efraín. *Para leer en puertorriqueño: Acercamiento a la obra de Luis Rafael Sánchez*. Río Piedras: Editorial Cultural, 1981.

———. *Partes de un todo: Ensayos y notas sobre literatura puertorriqueña en los Estados Unidos*. Río Piedras: Editorial de la Universidad de Puerto Rico, 1998.

Barthes, Roland. "The Death of the Author." In *Image, Music, Text*, translated by Stephen Heath, 142–48. New York: Hill and Wang, 1977.

Baudelaire, Charles. "On the Essence of Laughter." In *The Painter of Modern Life, and Other Essays*, edited and translated by Jonathan Mayne, 147–65. London: Phaidon, 1964.

Beckett, Samuel. *Waiting for Godot*. New York: Grove, 1954.

Belaval, Emilio S. *Cuentos para fomentar el turismo*. 1946. Río Piedras: Editorial Cultural, 1985.

Bergson, Henri. *Laughter: An Essay on the Meaning of the Comic*. 1911. Translated by Cloudesley Brereton and Fred Rothwell. Los Angeles: Green Integer, 1999.

Bernier-Grand, Carmen T. *Juan Bobo: Four Folktales from Puerto Rico*. Illustrated by Ernesto Ramos Nieves. New York: HarperCollins, 1994.

Bettelheim, Bruno. *The Uses of Enchantment: The Meaning and Importance of Fairy Tales*. New York: Knopf, 1976.

Boling, Becky. "The Reproduction of Ideology in Ana Lydia Vega's 'Pasión de historia' and 'Caso omiso.'" *Letras Femeninas* 17.1–2 (1991): 89–97.

Bolter, Jay David. *Writing Space: Computers, Hypertext, and the Remediation of Print*. 2nd ed. Mahwah, N.J.: Lawrence Erlbaum Associates, 2001.

Booth, Wayne C. *The Rhetoric of Fiction*. Chicago: University of Chicago Press, 1961.

———. *A Rhetoric of Irony*. Chicago: University of Chicago Press, 1974.

Borges, Jorge Luis. "Las ruinas circulares." In *Ficciones*, 61–69. Buenos Aires: Emecé, 1956.

Bottigheimer, Ruth B. *Grimms' Bad Girls and Bold Boys: The Moral and Social Vision of the Tales*. New Haven: Yale University Press, 1987.

Breton, André. *Anthology of Black Humor*. Translated by Mark Polizzotti. San Francisco: City Lights, 1997.

Butler, Judith. *Gender Trouble: Feminism and the Subversion of Identity*. New York: Routledge, 1990.

Campa, Román de la. "En la utopía redentora del lenguaje: Pedro Pietri y Miguel Algarín." *Americas Review* 16.2 (1988): 46–67.

Camus, Albert. *The Myth of Sisyphus, and Other Essays*. Translated by Justin O'Brien. New York: Knopf, 1955.

Canales, Nemesio R. *Antología de Nemesio R. Canales*. Edited by Servando Montaña Peláez. 2nd ed. Río Piedras: Editorial de la Universidad de Puerto Rico, 2000.

———. *El héroe galopante*. 1921. N.p.: Skuld, 1990.

———. *Obras completas*. Vol. 1, *Meditaciones acres*. Edited by Servando Montaña

Peláez. San Juan: Instituto de Cultura Puertorriqueña; Jayuya: Círculo Cana-liano; San Juan: Ediciones Puerto, 1992.

———. *Paliques*. 1915. Barcelona: Artual, 1993.

Capetillo, Luisa. *Amor y anarquía: Los escritos de Luisa Capetillo*. Edited by Julio Ramos. Río Piedras: Ediciones Huracán, 1992.

Casares, Julio. "Contestación" to Fernández Flórez, *El humor*, 33–62.

Castillo Zapata, Rafael. *Fenomenología del bolero*. Caracas: Monte Avila, 1990.

Certeau, Michel de. *The Practice of Everyday Life*. Translated by Steven Rendall. Berkeley and Los Angeles: University of California Press, 1984.

Cervantes Saavedra, Miguel de. *El ingenioso hidalgo don Quijote de la Mancha*. 1605–15. 2 vols. Edited by Martín de Riquer. 4th ed. Barcelona: Labor, 1973.

Chadwick, Joseph. "'Repito para consumo de los radioyentes': Repetition and Fetish-ism in *La guaracha del Macho Camacho*." *Revista de Estudios Hispánicos* (Río Piedras) 21 (1987): 61–83.

Chiampi, Irlemar. *Barroco y modernidad*. Mexico City: Fondo de Cultura Económica, 2000.

Crosby, Donald A. *The Specter of the Absurd: Sources and Criticisms of Modern Nihilism*. Albany: State University of New York Press, 1988.

Cruz-Malavé, Arnaldo. "Repetition and the Language of the Mass Media in Luis Rafael Sánchez's *La guaracha del Macho Camacho*." *Latin American Literary Review* 13.26 (1985): 35–48.

———. "Para virar al macho: La autobiografía como subversión en la cuentística de Manuel Ramos Otero." *Revista Iberoamericana* 59 (1993): 239–63.

———. "Teaching Puerto Rican Authors: Identity and Modernization in Nuyorican Texts." *ADE Bulletin* 91 (1988): 45–51.

Cuddon, J. A. *A Dictionary of Literary Terms*. 1976. London: Penguin, 1979.

Darío, Rubén. "La canción de los pinos." 1907. In *Rubén Darío esencial*, edited by Arturo Ramoneda, 429–31. Madrid: Taurus, 1991.

Dasenbrock, Reed Way. "Taking It Personally: Reading Derrida's Responses." *College English* 56.3 (1994): 261–79.

Davies, Christie. *Ethnic Humor Around the World: A Comparative Analysis*. Bloomington: Indiana University Press, 1990.

Deleuze, Gilles. *The Logic of Sense*. Edited by Constantin V. Boundas. Translated by Mark Lester and Charles Stivale. New York: Columbia University Press, 1990.

de Man, Paul. "The Rhetoric of Temporality." In *Blindness and Insight: Essays in the Rhetoric of Contemporary Criticism*, 2nd ed., 187–228. Minneapolis: University of Minnesota Press, 1983.

Derrida, Jacques. *Glas*. Translated by John P. Leavey Jr. and Richard Rand. Lincoln: University of Nebraska Press, 1986.

———. *Limited Inc*. Translated by Samuel Weber. Evanston, Ill.: Northwestern University Press, 1988.

———. *Of Grammatology*. Translated by Gayatri Chakravorty Spivak. Rev. ed. Baltimore: Johns Hopkins University Press, 1997.

————. *Writing and Difference*. Translated by Alan Bass. Chicago: University of Chicago Press, 1978.

Descartes, René. *Discours de la méthode/Discourse on the Method*. 1637. Bilingual ed. Translated and edited by George Heffernan. Notre Dame: University of Notre Dame Press, 1994.

Díaz Quiñones, Arcadio. *El arte de bregar: Ensayos*. San Juan: Ediciones Callejón, 2000a.

————. Introduction to *La guaracha del Macho Camacho*, by Luis Rafael Sánchez, 9–95. Madrid: Cátedra, 2000b.

————. *La memoria rota*. 1993. San Juan: Ediciones Huracán, 1996.

Duany, Jorge. *The Puerto Rican Nation on the Move: Identities on the Island and in the United States*. Chapel Hill: University of North Carolina Press, 2002.

Eastman, Max. *The Sense of Humor*. New York: Charles Scribner's Sons, 1921.

Escudero Valentín, Rogelio. *Literatura y periodismo en la obra de Nemesio Canales*. San Juan: Editorial Sin Nombre, 1988.

Esslin, Martin. *Antonin Artaud: The Man and His Work*. London: Calder, 1976.

————. *The Theatre of the Absurd*. 3rd ed., rev. London: Penguin, 1980.

Falcón, Rafael. "Aleluya a la caribeñidad: Los cuentos negristas de Ana Lydia Vega." *Afro-Hispanic Review* 13.2 (1994): 40–44.

Feijóo, Benito Jerónimo. *Teatro crítico universal*. 1728. Edited by Mario J. Valdés. Madrid: Castalia, 1986.

Feingold, Michael. Review of *The Masses Are Asses*, by Pedro Pietri. *Village Voice*, 7 February 1984, 92.

Felman, Shoshana. *The Literary Speech Act: Don Juan with J. L. Austin, or Seduction in Two Languages*. Translated by Catherine Porter. Ithaca: Cornell University Press, 1983.

Fernández Flórez, Wenceslao. *El humor en la literatura española*. Madrid: Buen Suceso, 1945.

Fernández Retamar, Roberto. *Calibán: Apuntes sobre la cultura en nuestra América*. 2nd ed. Mexico: Diógenes, 1972.

Ferré, Rosario. *Los cuentos de Juan Bobo*. Río Piedras: Ediciones Huracán, 1981.

Fish, Stanley. *Is There a Text in This Class? The Authority of Interpretive Communities*. Cambridge, Mass.: Harvard University Press, 1980.

Fite, Warner, trans. *Mist: A Tragicomic Novel*, by Miguel de Unamuno. Urbana: University of Illinois Press, 2000.

Flores, Juan. *Divided Borders: Essays on Puerto Rican Identity*. Houston: Arte Público, 1993.

Fludernik, Monika. "Introduction: Second-Person Narrative and Related Issues." *Style* 28.3 (1994): 281–311.

Foucault, Michel. "What Is an Author?" In *Language, Counter-Memory, Practice: Selected Essays and Interviews*, edited by Donald F. Bouchard, translated by Donald F. Bouchard and Sherry Simon, 113–38. Ithaca: Cornell University Press, 1977.

Freud, Sigmund. "Humour." 1927. In *The Standard Edition of the Complete Psychological Works of Sigmund Freud,* translated and edited by James Strachey, 21:160–66. London: Hogarth, 1961.

———. *Jokes and Their Relation to the Unconscious.* 1905. Translated by James Strachey. New York: Norton, 1960.

Frondizi, Risieri, trans. *Discurso del Método,* by René Descartes. [Río Piedras]: Universidad de Puerto Rico, 1954.

Gaensbauer, Deborah B. *The French Theater of the Absurd.* Boston: Twayne, 1991.

Galván, Delia V. "Sincretismo cultural en estructura policíaca: Ana Lydia Vega y su *Pasión de historia.*" *Americas Review* 21.3–4 (1993): 139–49.

García Calderón, Myrna. *Lecturas desde el fragmento: Escritura contemporánea e imaginario cultural en Puerto Rico.* Lima: LatinoAmericana, 1998.

García Lorca, Federico. *Llanto por Ignacio Sánchez Mejías.* Madrid: Ediciones del Arbol, 1935.

García Passalacqua, Juan M. *Dignidad y jaibería: Temer y ser puertorriqueño.* Puerto Rico: Editorial Cultural, 1993.

———. "The Puerto Ricans: Migrants or Commuters?" In Torre et al., *Commuter Nation,* 103–13.

Gelpí, Juan. "El bolero: Poesía popular urbana." *Revista Casa Silva* 12 (1999): 51–64.

———. *Literatura y paternalismo en Puerto Rico.* San Juan: Editorial de la Universidad de Puerto Rico, 1993.

Genette, Gérard. *Narrative Discourse: An Essay in Method.* Translated by Jane E. Lewin. Ithaca: Cornell University Press, 1980.

———. *Palimpsests: Literature in the Second Degree.* 1982. Translated by Channa Newman and Claude Doubinsky. Lincoln: University of Nebraska Press, 1997.

Gilbert, Sandra M., and Susan Gubar. *The Madwoman in the Attic: The Woman Writer and the Nineteenth-Century Literary Imagination.* 2nd ed. New Haven: Yale University Press, 2000.

Giordano, Enrique A. "El juego de la creación en Borges." *Hispanic Review* 52.3 (1984): 343–66.

Gnutzmann, Rita. "La novela hispanoamericana en segunda persona." *Iberoromania* n.s. 17 (1983): 100–120.

Goldstein, Jeffrey H., and Paul E. McGhee, eds. *The Psychology of Humor: Theoretical Perspectives and Empirical Issues.* New York: Academic Press, 1972.

González Echevarría, Roberto. *La ruta de Severo Sarduy.* Hanover, N.H.: Ediciones del Norte, 1987.

Griffin, Dustin. *Satire: A Critical Reintroduction.* Lexington: University Press of Kentucky, 1994.

Guerra, Lillian. *Popular Expression and National Identity in Puerto Rico: The Struggle for Self, Community, and Nation.* Gainesville: University Press of Florida, 1998.

Guzmán, Pablo. "*La Vida Pura*: A Lord of the Barrio." In Torres and Velázquez, *Puerto Rican Movement,* 155–72.

Hernández, Elizabeth, and Consuelo López Springfield. "Women and Writing in Puerto Rico: An Interview With Ana Lydia Vega." *Callaloo* 17.3 (1994): 816–25.

Hostos, Eugenio María de. *La peregrinación de Bayoán.* 1863. Vol. 1 of *Obras completas.* San Juan: Editorial del Instituto de Cultura Puertorriqueña, 1988.

Huizinga, Johan. *Homo Ludens: A Study of the Play-Element in Culture.* Translated by R. F. C. Hull. London: Routledge and Kegan Paul, 1949.

Hutcheon, Linda. *Irony's Edge: The Theory and Politics of Irony.* London and New York: Routledge, 1995.

———. *Narcissistic Narrative: The Metafictional Paradox.* Waterloo, Ont.: Wilfrid Laurier University Press, 1980.

———. *A Theory of Parody: The Teachings of Twentieth-Century Art Forms.* 1985. Urbana: University of Illinois Press, 2000.

Janoff, Bruce. "Black Humor, Existentialism, and Absurdity: A Generic Confusion." In *Black Humor: Critical Essays,* edited by Alan R. Pratt, 27–39. New York: Garland, 1993.

Kacandes, Irene. *Talk Fiction: Literature and the Talk Explosion.* Lincoln: University of Nebraska Press, 2001.

Kanellos, Nicolás. *A History of Hispanic Theater in the United States: Origins to 1940.* Austin: University of Texas Press, 1990.

Kierkegaard, Søren. *The Concept of Irony, with Continual Reference to Socrates.* Edited and translated by Howard V. Hong and Edna H. Hong. Princeton: Princeton University Press, 1989.

Kirkpatrick, Susan. *Las Románticas: Women Writers and Subjectivity in Spain, 1835–1850.* Berkeley and Los Angeles: University of California Press, 1989. Translated by Amaia Bárcena as *Las Románticas: Escritoras y subjetividad en España, 1835–1850.* Madrid: Cátedra, 1991.

Knox, Norman. *The Word* Irony *and Its Context, 1500–1755.* Durham, N.C.: Duke University Press, 1961.

Krysinski, Wladimir. "La Dislocation des codes, le croisement des récits et la brisure de la représentation dans *Six personnages en quête d'auteur* de L. Pirandello." *Etudes Littéraires* 13.3 (1980): 495–514.

Laguerre, Enrique A. *Benevolent Masters.* 1976. Translated by Gino Parisi. Maplewood, N.J.: Waterfront, 1986.

Laguna-Díaz, Elpidio, trans. "The Flying Bus," by Luis Rafael Sánchez. In *Herencia: The Anthology of Hispanic Literature of the United States,* edited by Nicolás Kanellos, 631–38. Oxford and New York: Oxford University Press, 2002.

Lamarque, Peter. "The Death of the Author: An Analytical Autopsy." *British Journal of Aesthetics* 30.4 (1990): 319–31.

Lang, Candace D. *Irony/Humor: Critical Paradigms.* Baltimore: Johns Hopkins University Press, 1988.

Larra, Mariano José de. *Fígaro: Colección de artículos dramáticos, literarios, políticos y de costumbres.* Barcelona: Crítica, 1997.

Latta, Robert L. *The Basic Humor Process: A Cognitive-Shift Theory and the Case against Incongruity*. Berlin and New York: Mouton de Gruyter, 1999.

Laviera, Tato. *La Carreta Made a U-Turn*. 1979. Houston: Arte Público, 1984.

Leveen, Lois. "Only When I Laugh: Textual Dynamics of Ethnic Humor." *MELUS* 21.4 (1996): 29–55.

López Baralt, Luce. "*La guaracha del Macho Camacho*, saga nacional de la «guachafita» puertorriqueña." *Revista Iberoamericana* 51.130–31 (1985): 103–23.

Lyotard, Jean-François. *The Postmodern Condition: A Report on Knowledge*. 1979. Translated by Geoff Bennington and Brian Massumi. Minneapolis: University of of Minnesota Press, 1984.

Machado, Manuel. *Poesías completas*. Edited by Antonio Fernández Ferrer. Sevilla: Renacimiento, 1993.

Manrique Cabrera, Francisco. *Historia de la literatura puertorriqueña*. New York: Las Américas, 1956.

Mañach, Jorge. *Indagación del choteo*. 1928. In *La crisis de la alta cultura en cuba / Indagación del choteo*, edited by Rosario Rexach, 51–94. Miami: Ediciones Universal, 1991.

Marqués, René. *La carreta*. 1951. Río Piedras: Editorial Cultural, 1983.

———. *Juan Bobo y la Dama de Occidente: Pantomima puertorriqueña para un ballet occidental*. 1955. Río Piedras: Editorial Antillana, 1971.

———. "El puertorriqueño dócil: Literatura y realidad psicológica." In *Ensayos (1953–1971)*, 2nd ed., 173–225. Barcelona: Editorial Antillana, 1972.

———. "La sala." In *En una ciudad llamada San Juan*, 115–25. Havana: Casa de las Américas, 1962.

———. *Los soles truncos*. 1958. In *Teatro*, edited by Francisco M. Vázquez, 1:5–66. Río Piedras: Editorial Antillana, 1986.

Matilla Rivas, Alfredo. "Algunos aspectos del teatro de Pedro Pietri." *Confluencia: Revista Hispánica de Cultura y Literatura* 5.1 (1989): 91–97.

———. Foreword to *Illusions of a Revolving Door*, by Pedro Pietri, xi–xvi.

———. Prologue to *The Masses Are Asses*, by Pedro Pietri, vii–xv.

McDonald, David. "Derrida and Pirandello: A Post-Structuralist Analysis of *Six Characters in Search of an Author*." *Modern Drama* 20 (1977): 421–36.

Méndez-Rodenas, Adriana. *Severo Sarduy: El neobarroco de la trangresión*. Mexico City: Universidad Nacional Autónoma de México, Facultad de Filosofía y Letras, 1983.

Mesonero Romanos, Ramón de. *Escenas y tipos matritenses*. Edited by Enrique Rubio Cremades. Madrid: Cátedra, 1993.

Michelson, Bruce. *Literary Wit*. Amherst: University of Massachusetts Press, 2000.

Miller, Nancy K. "Changing the Subject: Authorship, Writing, and the Reader." In *Feminist Studies, Critical Studies*, edited by Teresa de Lauretis, 102–20. Bloomington: Indiana University Press, 1986.

Mohr, Nicholasa. "Puerto Rican Writers in the United States, Puerto Rican Writers in Puerto Rico: A Separation Beyond Language." *Americas Review* 15.2 (1987): 87–92.

Molina, Tirso de. *El burlador de Sevilla*. 1630. Edited by Alfredo Rodríguez López-Vázquez. Madrid: Cátedra, 1990.

Montaña Peláez, Servando. *Nemesio Canales: Lenguaje y situación*. Río Piedras: Editorial Universitaria, Universidad de Puerto Rico, 1973.

Morales, Iris. "¡PALANTE, SIEMPRE PALANTE! The Young Lords." In Torres and Velázquez, *Puerto Rican Movement*, 210–27.

Morreall, John, ed. *The Philosophy of Laughter and Humor*. Albany: State University of New York Press, 1987.

Müller-Lauter, Wolfgang. *Nietzsche: His Philosophy of Contradictions and the Contradictions of His Philosophy*. 1971. Translated by David J. Parent. Urbana: University of Illinois Press, 1999.

Mulvey, Laura. "Visual Pleasure and Narrative Cinema." In *Visual and Other Pleasures*, 14–36. Bloomington: Indiana University Press, 1989.

Nash, Walter. *The Language of Humour: Style and Technique in Comic Discourse*. London: Longman, 1985.

Navas Ruiz, Ricardo. *El romanticismo español*. 3rd ed. Madrid: Cátedra, 1982.

Negrón de Montilla, Aida. *La americanización de Puerto Rico y el sistema de instrucción pública, 1900–1930*. 1976. Río Piedras: Editorial de la Universidad de Puerto Rico, 1990.

Negrón-Muntaner, Frances, and Ramón Grosfoguel, eds. *Puerto Rican Jam: Rethinking Colonialism and Nationalism*. Minneapolis: University of Minnesota Press, 1997.

Niebylski, Dianna C. *Humoring Resistance: Laughter and the Excessive Body in Latin American Women's Fiction*. Albany: State University of New York Press, 2004.

Nietzsche, Friedrich. *The Birth of Tragedy; and, The Genealogy of Morals*. Translated by Francis Golffing. Garden City, N.Y.: Doubleday, 1956.

Olivera, Otto. *La literatura en periódicos y revistas de Puerto Rico, siglo XIX*. Río Piedras: Editorial de la Universidad de Puerto Rico, 1987.

O'Neill, Patrick. *The Comedy of Entropy: Humour, Narrative, Reading*. Toronto: University of Toronto Press, 1990.

Ortiz, Ricardo. "Revolution's Other Histories: The Sexual, Cultural, and Critical Legacies of Roberto Fernández Retamar's 'Calibán'" *Social Text* 58 (1999): 33–58.

Ortiz Cofer, Judith. *Silent Dancing: A Partial Remembrance of a Puerto Rican Childhood*. Houston: Arte Público, 1990.

Pagán González, Enid. "El humor y la sátira: Segunda mitad del siglo XX." In *22 Conferencias de literatura puertorriqueña*, 212–34. San Juan: Ateneo Puertorriqueño, 1994.

Palés Matos, Luis. *Tuntún de pasa y grifería: Poemas afroantillanos*. San Juan: Biblioteca de Autores Puertorriqueños, 1937.

Paz, Octavio. *Los hijos del limo: Del romanticismo a la vanguardia.* Barcelona: Seix Barral, 1974.

Pedreira, Antonio S. *Insularismo: Ensayos de interpretación puertorriqueña.* 2nd ed. San Juan: Biblioteca de Autores Puertorriqueños, 1942.

———. *El periodismo en Puerto Rico.* Havana: Ucar, García, 1941.

Pérez Firmat, Gustavo. *Literature and Liminality: Festive Readings in the Hispanic Tradition.* Durham, N.C.: Duke University Press, 1986.

Perivolaris, John Dimitri. *Puerto Rican Cultural Identity and the Work of Luis Rafael Sánchez.* Chapel Hill: University of North Carolina Department of Romance Languages, 2000.

Perrault, Charles. *Histoires ou contes du temps passé.* 1697. Paris: Garnier Frères, [1910].

Phillips, Rachel, trans. *Children of the Mire: Modern Poetry from Romanticism to the Avant-Garde,* by Octavio Paz. Enl. ed. Cambridge, Mass.: Harvard University Press, 1991.

Pietri, Pedro. *Illusions of a Revolving Door.* In *Illusions of a Revolving Door: Plays/Teatro,* 35–62.

———. *Illusions of a Revolving Door: Plays/Teatro.* Edited by Alfredo Matilla Rivas. Río Piedras: Editorial de la Universidad de Puerto Rico, 1992.

———. *The Livingroom.* In *Illusions of a Revolving Door: Plays/Teatro,* 63–124.

———. *Lost in the Museum of Natural History.* Illustrated by José Antonio Peláez. Río Piedras: Ediciones Huracán, [1980].

———. *The Masses Are Asses/Las masas son crasas.* Edited and translated by Alfredo Matilla Rivas. San Juan: Instituto de Cultura Puertorriqueña, 1997.

———. *A Play for the Page and Not the Stage.* In *Illusions of a Revolving Door: Plays/Teatro,* 212–14.

———. *Puerto Rican Obituary.* New York: Monthly Review Press, 1973.

———. *Traffic Violations.* Maplewood, N.J.: Waterfront, 1983.

Pirandello, Luigi. *Six Characters in Search of an Author.* In *Pirandello's Major Plays,* translated by Eric Bentley, 65–120. Evanston, Ill.: Northwestern University Press, 1991.

Plato. *Statesman.* Translated by Seth Benardete. Chicago: University of Chicago Press, 1986.

Pollock, Della. "Performing Writing." In *The Ends of Performance,* edited by Peggy Phelan and Jill Lane, 73–103. New York: New York University Press, 1998.

Portilla, Jorge. "Fenomenología del relajo." 1966. In *Fenomenología del relajo y otros ensayos,* 13–95. Mexico City: Fondo de Cultura Económica, 1984.

Prince, Gerald. *A Dictionary of Narratology.* Lincoln: University of Nebraska Press, 1987.

Quevedo, Francisco de. *La hora de todos y la fortuna con seso.* Edited by Jean Bourg, Pierre Dupont, and Pierre Geneste. Madrid: Cátedra, 1987.

Quiroga, José. *Tropics of Desire: Interventions from Queer Latino America.* New York: New York University Press, 2000.

Rabassa, Gregory, trans. *Macho Camacho's Beat*, by Luis Rafael Sánchez. New York: Pantheon, 1980.

Radway, Janice A. *Reading the Romance: Women, Patriarchy, and Popular Literature*. 1984. Chapel Hill: University of North Carolina Press, 1991.

Ramos, Julio. "Cronología mínima de Capetillo." In Capetillo, *Amor y anarquía*, 65–66.

Richardson, Brian. "The Poetics and Politics of Second-Person Narrative." *Genre* 24 (1991): 309–30.

Ríos Avila, Rubén. "El arte de dar lengua en Puerto Rico." In *Polifonía salvaje: Ensayos de cultura y política en la postmodernidad*, edited by Irma Rivera Nieves and Carlos Gil, 328–36. San Juan: Editorial Postdata, 1995.

———. *La raza cómica del sujeto en Puerto Rico*. San Juan: Ediciones Callejón, 2002.

Rivera de Alvarez, Josefina. *Diccionario de literatura puertorriqueña*. Río Piedras: Ediciones de la Torre, 1955.

———. *Literatura puertorriqueña: Su proceso en el tiempo*. Madrid: Ediciones Partenón, 1983.

Roeckelein, Jon E. *The Psychology of Humor: A Reference Guide and Annotated Bibliography*. Westport, Conn.: Greenwood, 2002.

Romeu, José A. *Panorama del periodismo puertorriqueño*. Río Piedras: Editorial de la Universidad de Puerto Rico, 1985.

Rosa, William. "La vision humorística del espacio en la poesía de Pedro Pietri." *Americas Review* 19.1 (1991): 101–10.

Rose, Margaret A. *Parody: Ancient, Modern, and Post-Modern*. Cambridge: Cambridge University Press, 1993.

Russ, Joanna. "Somebody's Trying to Kill Me and I Think It's My Husband: The Modern Gothic." *Journal of Popular Culture* 6 (1973): 666–91.

Sánchez, Luis Rafael. *En cuerpo de camisa*. 1971. Río Piedras: Editorial Antillana, 1975.

———. *La guagua aérea*. 2nd ed. Río Piedras: Editorial Cultural, 1994.

———. *La guaracha del Macho Camacho*. 1976. 18th ed. Buenos Aires: Ediciones de la Flor, 1997.

———. *La importancia de llamarse Daniel Santos: Fabulación*. 1988. Hanover, N.H.: Ediciones del Norte, 1989.

———. "Literatura puertorriqueña y realidad colonial." *Claridad*, 30 November 1974, 14–15.

———. *Quíntuples*. Hanover, N.H.: Ediciones del Norte, 1985.

Sandoval-Sánchez, Alberto. *José, Can You See? Latinos On and Off Broadway*. Madison: University of Wisconsin Press, 1999.

Sarduy, Severo. *Barroco*. Buenos Aires: Sudamericana, 1974.

———. *Cobra*. Buenos Aires: Sudamericana, 1972.

———. *De donde son los cantantes*. 1967. Edited by Roberto González Echevarría. Madrid: Cátedra, 1993.

Sommer, Doris. *Foundational Fictions: The National Romances of Latin America.* Berkeley and Los Angeles: University of California Press, 1991.

———. *Proceed with Caution, When Engaged by Minority Writing in the Americas.* Cambridge, Mass.: Harvard University Press, 1999.

Soud, Stephen E. "Borges the Golem-Maker: Intimations of 'Presence' in 'The Circular Ruins.'" *MLN* 110.4 (1995): 739–54.

Tapia y Rivera, Alejandro. *La cuarterona.* 1867. Vol. 2 of *Obras completas.* San Juan: Insituto de la Cultura Puertorriqueña, 1968.

———. *Póstumo el transmigrado.* 1872–82. Vol. 1 of *Obras completas.*

Tittler, Jonathan. *Narrative Irony in the Contemporary Spanish-American Novel.* Ithaca: Cornell University Press, 1984.

Todd, Jane Marie. "Autobiography and the Case of the Signature: Reading Derrida's *Glas.*" *Comparative Literature* 38.1 (1986): 1–19.

Todorov, Tzvetan. *The Poetics of Prose.* 1971. Translated by Richard Howard. Ithaca: Cornell University Press, 1977.

Tolstoy, Leo. *The Fruits of Culture: A Comedy in Four Acts.* In *Redemption, and Two Other Plays,* 145–245. New York: Boni and Liveright, 1919.

Torre, Carlos Antonio, Hugo Rodríguez Vecchini, and William Burgos, eds. *The Commuter Nation: Perspectives on Puerto Rican Migration.* Río Piedras: Editorial de la Universidad de Puerto Rico, 1994.

Torres, Andrés, and José E. Velázquez, eds. *The Puerto Rican Movement: Voices from the Diaspora.* Philadelphia: Temple University Press, 1998.

Trebay, Guy. Review of *The Masses Are Asses,* by Pedro Pietri. *Village Voice,* 31 January 1984, 69.

Ubersfeld, Anne. *Reading Theatre.* 1977. Translated by Frank Collins. Toronto: University of Toronto Press, 1999.

Unamuno, Miguel de. "Malhumorismo." In *Soliloquios y conversaciones,* 105–15. Madrid: Biblioteca Renacimiento, 1911.

———. *Niebla.* 1914. Edited by Mario J. Valdés. Madrid: Cátedra, 1982.

Urry, John. *The Tourist Gaze: Leisure and Travel in Contemporary Societies.* London: Sage, 1990.

Valdés, Guadalupe. "Code-Switching as a Deliberate Verbal Strategy." In *Latino Language and Communicative Behavior,* edited by Richard P. Durán, 95–108. Norwood, N.J.: Ablex, 1981.

Valle Ferrer, Norma. *Luisa Capetillo: Historia de una mujer proscrita.* [Río Piedras]: Editorial Cultural, 1990.

Vázquez Arce, Carmen. *Por la vereda tropical: Notas sobre la cuentística de Luis Rafael Sánchez.* Buenos Aires: Ediciones de la Flor, 1994.

Vega, Ana Lydia. "De bípeda desplumada a Escritora Puertorriqueña (Con E y P machúsculas)." *Fem* 8.28 (1985): 28–32.

———. *Esperando a Loló y otros delirios generacionales.* San Juan: Editorial de la Universidad de Puerto Rico, 1994.

———. "Pasión de historia." 1987. In *Pasión de historia y otras historias de pasión,* 4th ed., 7–38. Buenos Aires: Ediciones de la Flor, 1994.

Vega, Ana Lydia, and Carmen Lugo Filippi. *Vírgenes y mártires.* 1981. Río Piedras: Editorial Antillana, 1994.

Vega, Bernardo. *Memoirs of Bernardo Vega: A Contribution to the History of the Puerto Rican Community in New York.* Edited by César Andreu Iglesias. Translated by Juan Flores. New York: Monthly Review Press, 1984.

Vélez, Diana L. "Bakhtin and Puerto Rican Narrative: Heteroglossia in Luis Rafael Sánchez's *La importancia de llamarse Daniel Santos.*" *Dispositio* 16.41 (1991): 133–44.

———. "*Pollito Chicken*: Split Subjectivity, National Identity and the Articulation of Female Sexuality in a Narrative by Ana Lydia Vega." *Americas Review* 14.2 (1986): 68–76.

Weber, Frances W. "Unamuno's *Niebla*: From Novel to Dream." *PMLA* 88.2 (1973): 209–18.

Wickberg, Daniel. *The Senses of Humor: Self and Laughter in Modern America.* Ithaca: Cornell University Press, 1998.

Wilde, Oscar. *The Complete Works of Oscar Wilde.* London: Collins, 1966; New York: Perennial Library, 1989.

Williams, Raymond Leslie. *The Postmodern Novel in Latin America: Politics, Culture, and the Crisis of Truth.* New York: St. Martin's, 1995.

Wilson, Sharon Rose. *Margaret Atwood's Fairy-Tale Sexual Politics.* Jackson: University Press of Mississippi, 1993.

Zavala, Iris M. "De heroes y heroínas en lo imaginario social: El discurso amoroso del bolero." *Casa de las Américas* 30.179 (1990): 123–29.

———. Unamuno: *Niebla,* el sueño y la crisis del sujeto." In *Estelas, laberintos, nuevas sendas: Unamuno, Valle-Inclán, García Lorca, la Guerra Civil,* edited by Angel G. Loureiro, 35–50. Barcelona: Anthropos, 1988.

Zeno Gandía, Manuel. *La charca.* 1894. Introduction by Juan Flores. Río Piedras: Ediciones Huracán, 1999.

Zentella, Ana Celia. "Returned Migration, Language, and Identity: Puerto Rican Bilinguals in Dos Worlds/Two Mundos." *International Journal of the Sociology of Language* 84 (1990): 81–100.

Zipes, Jack, trans. *The Complete Fairy Tales of the Brothers Grimm.* Illustrated by John B. Gruelle. 3rd ed. New York: Bantam, 2002.

———, ed. *Don't Bet on the Prince: Contemporary Feminist Fairy Tales in North America.* New York: Methuen, 1986.

Zorrilla, José. *Don Juan Tenorio.* 1844. Edited by David T. Gies. Madrid: Castalia, 1994.

Index

absolute comic, 95

absurd, philosophy of, 123

absurd humor, 112; Freud on, 122; functions of, 125

"absurd" in literature, 122

absurd language, 134, 135

absurd "nowhere," 114

absurd satire, 114

accidental irony, 88, 94

"Adelphos" (Machado), 38–39

affect, 7–8

African heritage, 5; celebration in Sánchez, 64; shared identity across islands, 88–89; tourist/native antagonism, 91, 163n.13; tourist status, 93; women writers on, 17

alazon, 78, 86

Alonso, Manuel A., 3

alter ego, 42, 43

Americanization, 162n.4

anagnorisis, 95

analepses, 145

ángel del hogar, 33

anglicisms, 83

apostrophe, 92

architextual level, 108

Aristotle, 8, 69

Artaud, Antonin, 136, 167n.13

arte de bregar, 1; in diaspora, 133; migration, 49; strategy of, 18, 147

artistic creation, 151n.4

assimilated Puerto Ricans, 79–81, 84, 162n.6; Anglophile façade, 132; marginal status, 119; "Puerto Ricanless scene," 133–34

attitudes to women, condescending tone, 37

authenticity, 91

author, death of, 96–97, 165n.34; death of [female], 96

author-function, 68

authorial agency, functions in Sánchez's world, 74

authorial control, 54

authorial intent: denied, 97; Derrida, 164n.19; irony conveying, 76

authorial status/persona: authenticity and truth, 63; author as comic object, 52, 57; "birth" of persona, 110; exposed, 51; first-person narrator, 102; Puerto Rican women writers, 97–99; reader and, 74; reader's gaze, 52; reading parodies, 107–8; self-deification, 63; self-reflexive humor to unmask, 62–63; Vega, 77

authorship: critiqued, 16; Sánchez's theory of, 67

authorship, claiming, 60–63

avant-garde theater, 136

Bakhtin, Mikhail, 54, 62, 151n.3; centripetal and centrifugal forces in language, 158n.6

baroque, 60

Barrio (New York), 114

bartering episodes, 91, 93–94, 163n.13

Barthes, Roland, 96–97

Being: corrective translation of, 59; performance and, 59

Israel Reyes is associate professor of Spanish and Portuguese at Dartmouth College in Hanover, New Hampshire. His areas of research and teaching include Puerto Rican and Latino literatures and cultures.